CHASING
DREAMTIME

A sea-going hitchhiker's journey
through memory and myth

CHASING
DREAMTIME

A sea-going hitchhiker's journey
through memory and myth

NEVA SULLAWAY

BROOKVIEW PRESS
901 Western Road
Castleton-on-Hudson
New York 12033
www.brookviewpress.com

Published 2005 by Brookview Press, 901 Western Road, Castleton-on-Hudson, New York 12033.

While the names of some people have been changed, the events portrayed in this book are actual occurrences and the places are real.

Manufactured in the United States of America

Cover illustration and book design by Dominic Poon
Map illustrations by Karen Miller Ferguson
Cover photographs from the author's collection

Library of Congress Cataloging-in-Publication Data

Sullaway, Neva, 1952- Chasing dreamtime :
a sea-going hitchhiker's journey through
memory and myth / Neva Sullaway.

　　p. cm.

Includes bibliographical references and index.

ISBN 0-9707649-2-8 (pbk. : alk. paper)

1. Sullaway, Neva, 1952---Travel--Islands of the Pacific.
2. Sullaway, Neva, 1952---Travel--Australia.
3. Seafaring life. I. Title.

G465.S92 2005

910'.9164'8--dc22

2004007774

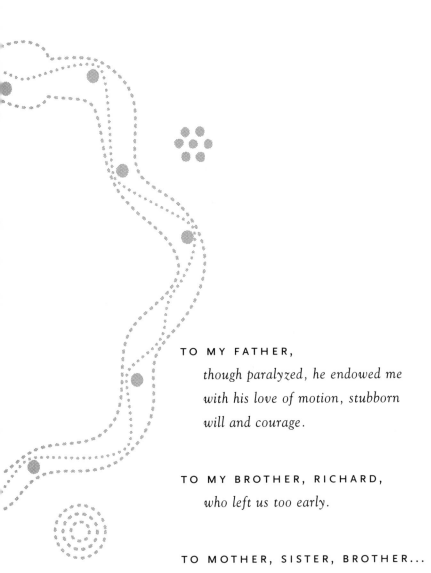

TO MY FATHER,
though paralyzed, he endowed me with his love of motion, stubborn will and courage.

TO MY BROTHER, RICHARD,
who left us too early.

TO MOTHER, SISTER, BROTHER...
love, secrets, wisdom.

Acknowledgements

Thanks to my loving family and friends for listening to these stories all these years. My gratitude to Pam Vose, posthumously, for guiding the early part of my writing journey. To Mike Sirota, writing consultant and editor, whose knowledge of words, understanding of the process and ultimate belief, kept me writing. Thanks to literary agents, Frank Scatoni and Greg Dinkin of Venture Literary, for working long hours on my behalf and going the distance. My deepest gratitude to publisher David Lee Drotar of Brookview Press for taking on *Chasing Dreamtime*, believing in the book, giving it life, and allowing the stories to live on...

Thank you, Neva Sullaway

Author's Note

Throughout the sixteen years that it took to write this book, family, friends, and ultimately editors, always asked, "Is this a true story?" Though there are outlandish events, implausible coincidences, dream images woven throughout and mystical experiences that may be unsettling to the reader, I experienced all these things.

Life is filled with such amazing moments, often lost in the clutter of our frenzied existence. The ocean crystallized those ethereal moments for me and this book is their collective image preserved in words.

I have changed the names of almost everyone involved in the stories. However, in some instances, I couldn't have invented names more suited to the characters. For example, Rodo, King Fred, Tom Neale and Bluey are the names of real people. In the case of the eccentric fishermen of Australia's far north, their own names described them so well that in many cases I let them be: Squids, Branch and India John.

All the scenes in the chapters are based on fact, colored by memory and mixed with imagination. They happened to me and represent the essence of the story as truthfully as possible. At the book's conclusion, several events were compressed into one location.

...Some years ago — never mind how long precisely — having little or no money in my purse, and nothing particular to interest me on shore, I thought I would sail about a little and see the watery part of the world. It is a way I have of driving off the spleen, and regulating the circulation. Whenever I find myself growing grim about the mouth; whenever it is a damp, drizzly November in my soul; whenever I find myself involuntarily pausing before coffin warehouses, and bringing up the rear of every funeral I meet; and especially whenever my hypos get such an upper hand of me, that it requires a strong moral principle to prevent me from deliberately stepping in the street, and methodically knocking people's hats off — then, I account it high time to get to sea as soon as I can...

Moby-Dick by Herman Melville

Preface

It can begin with a smell. Sometimes it happens when I open the door in the morning to pick up the newspaper. A warm, wet blast of South Pacific air sweeps through me and I hear the voices again. It might be Tomai whispering, "I saved you from the shark... You were chosen." I sniff the breeze harder, and harder come the memories. Tom Neale flails the air with his arms, "Don't forget what I told you!"

The air surrounding me is thick and humid; I look to the west. There the Pacific swells bring with them the sound of the drumbeat. The voices get louder, until I remember the fear I felt as the shark cut a path toward me.

The waves crash along the shoreline and with their thundering I remember the hideous thud of the cement boat as it pounded through the mountainous waves of an impending cyclone. The cyclone! Once again I feel the metal barb of Mick's knife prick the soft flesh of my throat. Overwhelmed by memory, I tremble. My fate had wavered between being swallowed by the sea or having my throat slashed by the sailor gone mad.

The sea spills along the shoreline, flooding the sand holes and filling them up. I feel as if the sea is filling me up with the past, the inescapable past. I take a deep, settling breath. Roper Jackson's muffled voice emerges from the chaos of memory. The Aboriginal had led me to the truth. I had touched the didgeridoo and was healed.

Picking up the morning paper, I suddenly remember where I am. I watch the sun dissolve the thick fog of a Southern California morning. The dogs bark, the baby cries. I am alive.

I smile, knowing that somewhere in my soul I will always be chasing Dreamtime.

STRANGE BEGINNINGS

In 1975, after finishing college and a brief marriage, I made a hasty departure from Southern California. I landed in Honolulu, Hawaii, with a dream of sailing around the world alone. To that end, I bought a twenty-six-foot wooden boat.

This dream had its shortcomings — my classic yacht was dilapidated and slowly sinking at dockside. Adding to my woes, I had no money left to outfit her. Nevertheless, I lived and worked on board *Drifter* for over a year before realizing that it was going to take many more years to save enough money to live out my dream. Then, three things happened unexpectedly, altering my course.

While managing a pizza restaurant, I was robbed at gunpoint. The shaky gunman told me to hand over all the money or he'd shoot me. While I loaded up a "To Go" pizza box with $400, a female customer leapt out of her chair screaming hysterically, "He's got a gun! He's going to shoot!" Strangely, a line from an old Clint Eastwood shoot'em-up ran through my mind and I handed over the box with a smile and asked him if he wanted a Coke with it. This confluence of emotion rattled the gunman even more; he disappeared out the door. The next day, I was fired from my job for giving the guy the money and not knowing the make of his gun, even though I'd given a full description of the robber to the police.

Soon after losing my job, a young man from Alaska saw me at work on my boat. He admired my fine little yacht so much that he offered me three times the amount of money I had paid for her. I accepted his offer and greedily took the $4,500 in cash and stuffed it into the back pocket of my tattered shorts.

Stepping off *Drifter*, I realized that not only had I lost my home, but I had nowhere to go. I had a backpack and a terrible restlessness gnawing at me. Combing the docks of the Ala Wai Harbor, I looked for a ride to anywhere. It didn't take long before I found a beautiful wooden cutter headed for the South Pacific.

Unfortunately, we didn't get very far. En route to the "Big Island" of Hawaii, a nasty midnight squall knocked the boat over in the middle of the Alenuihāhā channel. With her mast buried in the water, she started sinking. Then, somewhat miraculously, a wave came alongside and lifted her upright. Though bruised and bloodied, the skipper and I managed to bail our way to the Big Island. There, the yacht was hauled out for extensive repairs for an indeterminate amount of time and money. My crewing skills were no longer needed.

With my dreams nearly scuttled, I flew to Papeete, Tahiti, in July of 1976. I arrived just in time to celebrate the French Bastille Week festivities and my twenty-fourth birthday.

PART ONE

CHASING

WHERE DO WE COME FROM?

WHAT ARE WE?

WHERE ARE WE GOING?

Title of Paul Gauguin painting, 1897, oil on canvas
Museum of Fine Arts, Boston, Tompkins Collection

Chapter One

PRISON!

The imposing gendarme stabbed his heels into the creaking floorboards as he circled me. His words spun overhead, slashed and mangled by the knife-edge of the fan blades. I watched the blades go around and around. With his voice on the rise, the French policeman shook the wooden backrest of my chair.

"*Vous allez en Prison!*" he shouted, as if there were more than two of us in that desolate room.

I knew that word "*Prison.*" It was the only word he had spoken that I did know. But what was my offense?

Squinting to see past the epaulet on the policeman's right shoulder, I caught a glimpse of the yachts bobbing at their turbulent moorings. Why hadn't I sailed off to American Samoa with Taylor that morning? Why had I insisted on staying in Papeete for the Fête?

The black-eyed gendarme caught me there, as I stared longingly out of the open-air window. He clicked his heels once more and railed against my inattentiveness. "*Mademoiselle!*"

His tirade was suddenly interrupted by the arrival of his trenchcoated assistant. He was the very same gendarme who had apprehended me in the morning, requesting to see my passport and return ticket. But I had just cashed in my return ticket. After all, I had come to the South Pacific to stay forever.

I hadn't been in Papeete for more than a week. I'd hung about as innocently as the rest of the young travelers lugging their heavy, overstuffed backpacks, buying cheap Algerian red wine and baguettes of sweet-smelling French bread with creamy white cheese.

Meandering along the quay, I was always pleasantly interrupted by a friendly "hello" tossed in on the tropic breeze.

"I'll give you a lift to Samoa. We can wait out the season there," my friend Taylor had called over from his thirty-foot yacht.

I had declined Taylor's offer and said goodbye to him the same morning of my arrest. It was no time to be leaving. Bastille week celebrations were well underway. The copra boats were still bringing in Tahitians from the outer islands. Each night the air, wrapped in its sweet succulence, carried with it the melodies of the Islands. One could wander along the quay, saunter through the open-air markets, or settle into a rickety chair at Quinn's Bar and still hear the constant, rhythmic sound of the drumbeat.

The loud click of the gendarme's heels crushed my reveries. He paced around me again, looking furious. Suddenly a third man, with a slight build and a thinning crop of reddish-blond hair, entered the room. He didn't look like a policeman; he wore a pair of burgundy swim trunks and a loose-fitting floral shirt. His eyes were soft blue, discreet and cautious. He spoke French fluently, graciously, while shaking hands with the perplexed gendarme. Their voices became subdued.

The gendarme suddenly snatched the papers from his assistant's hand and gave them to the fair-haired man, who scanned and signed them. They all shook hands. The Frenchman then grabbed the papers and fanning the air with them, flew into his final rage: "*Partez, PARTEZ!*"

"Come on then," the gaunt fellow said to me. "Let's get out of here before he changes his bloody frog mind."

The cool breeze of English freshened my ears. I followed my savior out the door of the Commissariat de Police and back onto the familiar boulevard that swept the edge of the harbor.

"Thanks," I said, relieved to be out of the clutches of the gendarme. "I'm afraid my high school French isn't doing too well. How did you—"

"Walk on," the Englishman interrupted sharply, "and don't look back." We walked halfway down the boulevard in silence before my savior spoke again. "I suppose you know who I am."

"No, I have no idea. I thought—"

"William sent for me," the frail man continued, as if I knew who he was referring to. "He'd heard you'd been taken in by the gendarmes. Of course, you can get into some awful strife with those fellows. I don't know if you understood, my dear, that you were off to prison." The fellow looked askance at me. "You'd put them in a rather embarrassing position. You see, they haven't any facilities to accommodate a female prisoner."

"Prisoner! But I haven't done anything wrong."

"Of course you have, my dear. You cashed in your return ticket to the United States. The travel agency reports all such transactions to the Police."

The man took a deep breath. "You were close enough to prison all right. And they have a nasty habit of throwing away the key in matters like this."

The stranger continued to admonish me as if he were a father come to fetch his itinerant daughter from the clink. "From this moment forward you're bonded to me, which is a bit of a bloody nuisance. They want you out of here. It means we'll have to get underway as soon as possible." Clearing his throat irritably, he added, "I'm sorry, my name's Edward."

"Mine's Neva," I said, realizing he must have already known it. "I'm from California. I turned in my ticket because my bank didn't transfer my money and—"

"You needn't bother explaining it to me, my dear. You're bonded now and that's the end of it."

I bumped along next to Edward with my left arm swinging and tangling in his. It was as if I instinctively took the word "bonded" to mean handcuffed. "I'm afraid I don't quite understand what bonded means."

Edward sucked in a despairing breath between his thin, freckled lips. "It means that I guaranteed your passage out of the Society Islands as swiftly as possible. And that means," he continued, "that you must sail with us, checking in and out of each port as we go."

Edward also mentioned that my bag had already been deposited on board Patience, and that I should be prepared to contribute one hundred dollars for stores, which would cover about six months' sailing. It seemed a fair enough bargain to me.

William was at the landing to greet us.

"William!" I laughed with surprise, recognizing the young Englishman to whom I had been introduced on board Taylor's yacht. Taylor had warned me about William's reputation as a "ladies' man," chasing the local Tahitian girls and seducing them with his British charm.

William didn't look at all surprised to see me at the landing. Turning to Edward he applauded my arrival. "I say, good job, Skipper, you managed to rescue her from the froggies, eh."

Edward looked at me with a hint of suspicion. "Rather distasteful, the whole incident, if you ask me."

"Off we go then." William smiled as he welcomed me aboard the rubber dinghy. He rowed us toward a thirty-eight-foot ketch. The yacht rested idle and alone in the wide expanse of Maeva Bay, graced only by the massive volcanic domes of Moorea.

"We'll be getting underway tomorrow then," Edward announced with an anxious glance toward William, as we nudged up against the hull of Patience.

I boarded her awkwardly, missing my handhold on the lifelines. Falling forward, the edge of my nose skimmed the toes of our fourth crew member, Clarissa. I followed the hairy pathway from her ankles up toward the crease of her wrinkled knees. There hung the frayed edges of a faded print dress. I lay helplessly underneath the shadow of her nose, a most promontory point. Of Clarissa's pronounced features, her square jowls were the most severe, etched harshly against a fixed matronly stare.

"Blast!" she scolded William. "You didn't forget to buy me that material, did you?"

"Clari, this is Neva." He ignored her question. "American she is, got caught up with the froggies. They were going to march her off to the guillotine. Can you imagine, the old wankers!

"I should think it's going to be a bit crowded with a fourth." Clari glared at me as I crawled on board. That was to be the extent of our introduction.

Clari and I were at odds from the start. She made no attempt to hide the fact that she hailed from a prominent, upper-crust British family. William was quick to point out that her father was a Lord and had considerable political clout back in England. And so, I was now a part of her ruling domain. She let me know immediately that I was a great inconvenience to her, yet I had to depend on her for the smallest of services. She introduced me to the shipboard routine: how everything was stowed, where I would sleep (in the aft cabin with her), how to cook on board, how to do laundry... on down to the most trivial details. In short, she was my caretaker. I guessed she found my company mildly amusing at first, but soon enough Clari made it clear that she would rather see me eaten by sharks.

Throughout my first evening on board the British yacht, I felt an awkward mix of gratitude and discomfort. William, Edward and Clari talked among themselves. It was plain conversation, much of which concerned our getting underway. I broke in only once to offer to buy fresh vegetables before we embarked in the morning, to which Clari quickly put me in my place.

"We don't eat fresh vegetables at sea. Everything in Tahiti is much too expensive and we have our own stores."

"You wouldn't mind if I just bought some things with my own money?" I asked meekly, going to the galley sink to help with the dishes.

"I've told you, we don't eat them." Clari slammed her dishes into the sink. "That's the fresh water spigot. Use the salt water pump for washing."

Edward waited for Clari to push by him. Reaching around me, he grabbed the tea towel and said, "Right then, let's finish up these dishes."

After finishing tea and the dishes I followed William to the afterdeck, hoping to find an ally. We could hear Clari below, shifting her cans of peaches, tuna, sardines and soup into a new rank and file in the lazaret under Edward's bunk. Edward sat at the navigation table, reviewing the local chart of the Society Islands while smoking his pipe.

The sun had spilled its palette of shocking red over the darkening silhouette of Moorea. On shore, the day's celebrations were drawing to a close in preparation for the evening's festivities. The faint timbre of drums could be heard, coming from land. From where we sat offshore, it seemed as if the island itself breathed with the drumbeat, as if the beat came up through the alluvial soil and moved the bodies of the islanders in their dance.

William leaned against the rail with the slowly descending sun beaming in over his shoulders, filtering through the scorched spirals of his hair. His face was young, boyish and deceptive. Somewhere about the shoulders, he grew into a broad man. Life at sea had given him well-developed muscles, tanning his pale English skin, making it coarser, giving him a more rugged look than his homeland would normally allow.

I couldn't help but watch the dance and play of his whimsical blue eyes against mine and against the sea. He draped his arms over the lifelines, teasing me with his broad grin. "So, how do you think you'll get on?"

I assumed William spoke quietly for privacy. But that was not the real reason for my silence. He laughed at my reserve. "I see, it all must look a bit muddled right now. Well, not to worry, we'll get you out of here."

"That's just it." I tried to keep my confusion contained. "I don't know how all this happened and I don't even know where we're going."

"Bloody hell, who does? But the point is, you're not in jail." He leaned closer to me and whispered, "If you can put up with Clari's twittering about, we'll have a good time of it. Edward's a good chap, honestly; he just has his ways. You won't find a better skipper. It will all come clear in time."

William patted my shoulder and then headed toward the companionway. He glanced back and added, "Not to worry."

The sun slipped into the shadows. The drumbeat pounded harder, as if to pull my attention through the dusk into the burgeoning night. It was an immediate, demanding sound. Somewhere in the darkness of the island dream, the Tahitians were telling their story through the dance. I could hear the rhythms in the distance and remember how the dance aroused me. How the man moved his thighs against the woman, pursuing her, wanting her, while she drew him seductively to her. Once their energies were entwined, nothing could break their trance. The drumbeat pounded harder, their bodies in unison.

Soon the darkness enveloped me. With it came a somberness I wasn't prepared for. Pulling my knees up to my chin, I wrapped my arms around them. I was now bonded crew on a yacht heading west. Those thoughts lingered as the horizon fused the sea and sky into one unbound territory.

Looking toward the darkening peaks of Moorea, I had a momentary glimpse of my father sitting unevenly in his cushioned chair, the paralyzed right side of his body slumped over. He had always looked as if he carried a burden too heavy for him. Perhaps he did. He'd been stricken with polio in his prime, twenty-seven years old. He was young, athletic and handsome.

I shivered, though there was nothing about the balmy tropical evening that warranted it. It was a strange thing to live in fear of paralysis. Constant motion seemed the only antidote.

My thoughts were suddenly interrupted by a slight rocking of the boat. I turned to find my three shipmates preparing to row to shore for their last night's celebration. William, my closest ally, was the oarsman.

I pulled my arms tighter about me, wondering why I hadn't been asked to go with them. Avoiding the answer, I went into the aft cabin and rummaged through my backpack for some paper and a pen. Returning topside, I began a letter to my parents. It would be lighthearted, I decided, no mention of prison or being bonded. "It's so beautiful here," I scribbled under the half-extinguished light of the moon, "you can't imagine..."

On I went, writing how lucky I was to be *invited* to go sailing with three "experienced British sailors." I assured them all was well; I was embarking on a grand adventure, "...not exactly sure how long..."

I could still hear the Tahitian drums as I wrote. The primal rhythms surrounded me; they came from nowhere and everywhere.

Chapter Two

THE ARTIST'S ISLAND

It was a short day sail to the island of Moorea, our first port of call after being ousted from Papeete.

I had the most curious sensation of not being able to grasp where I was in the world. There was the smattering of islands strewn across the mercurial desert of blue sea. Clouds drifted in carelessly from other worlds, condensing into one another. They shrouded the grand vaulting peaks. Those peaks then pierced the clouds, sending down torrents of rain, washing the islands in rich, verdant colors. The islands steamed with moisture, sending off plumes of delicious floral mists.

That is how the island of Tahiti appeared to me as we sailed away from the crush of tourists at the market stalls, away from the cacophony of island women and children and chickens in the open-air buses, away from the screech of Renaults going to and from the small spider web of civilization.

We passed through the coral-fringed entrance to Moorea with the sea boiling and frothing over the threatening reef, then flowing into the placid bay. We cast anchor in shallow water, under the shadow of the stark geometric peak of Roto Nui.

Our world was still. Nothing existed beyond the sound of the South Pacific lapping against our hull. A mild ripple now and again cracked the perfect mirror of lush greens imposed over the tourmaline sea.

The four of us were momentarily held together by the delicate silence. I attempted a casual conversation with Clari, but she turned away from me and took up her sketchpad. I watched as her hand moved quickly and expertly over the heavy art paper.

"That's very nice," I said timidly.

Clari huffed and looked annoyed at my comment. She moved farther along the coach roof.

Edward was equally aloof. He took up his pipe with the methodical gentleness that was peculiar to his nature, and settled into his chart work. Grieg's *Peer Gynt Suite No. 1* drifted up the companionway, wrapped inside a balmy breeze of smoke.

William moved restlessly about the deck, straightening the anchor chain forward, then going aft to check the stern line, then forward again. I caught him scowling at us, as if we were his captors, unwilling to set him free.

Thirty-eight feet of fiberglass contained the four of us, unlikely mates, pressed together in the small confinement. The Brits must have been quite impatient with me. They had negotiated their course halfway around the world to reach this paradisiacal refuge, only to find themselves suddenly expelled through their own act of goodwill. Edward's gallantry and fluent French had saved me from prison, yet we were all now under the same sentence. The French government had allowed us the extravagance of two days in each island port as we exited the Society Island chain.

As yet I had no way of knowing the intricacies of the relationships on board. I knew William was aching to be ashore. We could easily run off and explore the hidden clefts of mountains winding so mysteriously through the jungle. His enticing glances told me so.

As far as Clari's watchfulness over me was concerned, it seemed wiser to assume it was motherly instinct rather than pure, unfiltered jealousy.

Edward kept well apart from us. He was different from William. He had somehow managed to retain his British pallor even after six months' sailing. He was genteel, delicate and covetous of his privacy. He busied himself with the odd jobs on board, making it clear that he preferred music and his pipe to our company and had no desire to go ashore.

As everyone fell into their preoccupations, I took up my pen and paper. William leaned over my shoulder as I scribbled away.

"You aren't upset with me, are you?" he asked.

"Why should I be?"

"Well, you've been awfully quiet." He prodded me. "I suppose you miss Taylor."

"Tay— Taylor was just a good friend. I always knew he was going to sail away."

William slid down from the coach roof next to me.

"Yes, but he did want you to go with him. He told me so himself."

"Did he?" I raised my head and stared directly into William's coquettish eyes. "What else did he tell you?"

"Well..." William crossed his feet, rubbing them together. "Actually, he said that you were lovers."

"Oh." I choked on his words. "How considerate of him."

After a moment's pause, William pushed a little closer.

"I told him I'd look after you. He had seen the gendarme take you in, so he sailed by *Patience* to let us know."

He must have felt me pull away slightly because he added quickly, "Oh, don't be starchy. We'll pass by American Samoa. You'll see him again."

I looked at William quizzically, still wondering what he was getting at.

"What I'm trying to say is that I'm glad you're here. We've been getting a bit edgy lately. It's a nice change, you know, having another crew on board."

I asked about Clari's reaction to my arrival, hoping to pry something of the truth from him.

"Don't worry about her," William said. "She's just had it all to herself for too long, loves to rule the roost."

Just then, Clari poked her head up from below deck, asking William to fetch some stores from underneath his forward bunk. Turning to me, she said harshly, "We'll be going ashore early tomorrow, as our time here is so *awfully* short."

William winked at me as if to say, *Don't pay any attention to her.*

Clari turned back down the companionway, glaring at me with disapproval. "You'd do well to clean up your bunk," she added sternly, before disappearing below deck. I bristled at her choice of words, although I knew that Clari meant I should roll up my sleeping bag so the humid air and flies wouldn't fill it up in my absence. Everything else I owned was in my backpack, which doubled as my lumpy pillow at night. The "cleaning" could wait.

I went back to my scribbling, retreating inside the delicate melody of *Peer Gynt's* suite. Each precious note seemed to carry with it something of an exquisite, suffering beauty. I tried to write about the abounding beauty of Moorea and found I couldn't. There were no words that could adequately describe the indelible colors of the sea or the feeling of resting on the yacht in the shadow of the enormous volcanic peaks. They reached toward the heavens, forming hollow, crescent-shaped thrones for the ancient gods to rest upon. And there the gods sat looking down on us, wondering perhaps, as I did, about the fragility of our existence.

We rowed ashore early the next morning. I could hardly restrain myself from running down the path toward the mountains. Instead, I waited patiently for William and Clari to tie up the dinghy and finish haggling about which direction we should walk.

"Lovely, of course—" I overhead William say. "Look there, why don't we follow that path up to the top of Roto Nui?"

"No!" Clari snapped. "I'm going on to the gallery. It's not far and it should be interesting."

She came over to me and in a commanding voice said, "We're going on to the gallery. You can come if you like. Do you know anything about art?"

She brushed by me, uninterested in my answer. Instead, she strode off like a sergeant on a potentially fatal reconnaissance mission.

We soon came upon a small wood-framed building, nestled in a palm-covered valley. The sign posted at the entrance read *Musée Gauguin*. Clari walked toward the open-air gallery announcing haughtily, "I've seen his originals in Europe." She turned to me. "Do you know Gauguin?"

I stumbled ignorantly behind her. "Sure, yeah, I know him."

A tall swarthy man appeared at the gallery door to welcome us. "Come, come, you can look around." He invited us in. Pulling me in through the doorway, his hand clasped over mine, he crushed my fingers with his grip. Each time I tried to withdraw my crimped fingers, he pressed his gold ring more severely into my flesh. His accent was not French, even to my untrained ears. His voice was too loud, too obstreperous for the small gallery. I could not wriggle free from him as he guided me along the brilliantly canvassed walls. He dragged me to every corner of the room.

"Look, masterpieces, every one of them. Originals to be sure. Gauguin! Pure genius!"

I nodded enthusiastically. "The colors are amazing."

"You *are* American, aren't you?"

My knuckles gave out a crack. The curator smiled and finally retreated. I blushed in confusion and looked around helplessly for William. Clari sidled over to me, her arms folded, and scolded me in schoolmarm fashion.

"Originals indeed! This fellow's having you on, my dear. They are as fake as the ring on his finger. You silly twit. What do they teach in those American schools?"

She railed relentlessly as she swept me out of her way, still mumbling. "Of course that letch grabs the Americans, they wouldn't know the difference."

"Oh come now, Clari." William had joined us. "Don't be so hard on her. Not everyone was schooled in Paris."

"Originals, indeed!" she repeated.

Still, I will always think of Moorea as Gauguin's Moorea (even though, in truth, he never lived there). If Gauguin colored the water coral, if he washed the sky in light wisps of mauve and tinted the women with golden floods of light, then I must consider it a pleasure having seen his prints at the *Musée*.

After our visit to the impostor's gallery, I fell into a rather dank mood. All of the morning's lightness had faded from my step. I hunched my shoulders in defeat, cowering under Clari's derisive remarks. In fact, she soured the delicacies around us. The sweet-scented plumaria, seductive gardenias and wild orchids laced the thicket of damp green — a luscious bed of flowery dreams I wanted to run headlong into and bury myself.

I was preparing a mental list of grievances, one of which pertained to hunger. Clari maintained that we shouldn't eat our stores on the boat. I became preoccupied with what we should eat. It occurred to me that we might pluck one of those juicy, overripe pawpaws or some mangos from the trees and thereby satisfy the need directly. Stalks of bananas hung about like so many rows in a grocery store, but there seemed something offensive to the Brits in eating food not yet tainted by human hands.

Unable to resist the urge any longer, I reached up and plucked an overripe pawpaw from a tree. I lost my grip momentarily and the delicate fruit rolled onto the ground. The fall had cleanly split it in two, so I picked it up and started sucking the sweet meat out of one half. This set Clari off on another tirade. "Gawd, look at her. Disgusting! She's not only completely ignorant, she's got manners suited to a cockney as well."

William's mouth fell open as he turned to watch my reaction.

I threw the pawpaw into the bush and walked by Clari with my eyes downcast. I wasn't sure why she had a certain power over me and I couldn't imagine why Edward and William would put up with her.

Scuffing my sandals on the dirt road, I walked dejectedly, thinking about Clari and how intimidated I was by her. Instead of looking up at the magnificence surrounding me and gaining some strength from it, I wallowed in my gutlessness. I hated being a coward.

I let Clari's words paralyze me. Why? I had been brought up not to talk back to people. That *was* impolite. It was also a nice way of avoiding confrontations. Or maybe it was the fact that Clari had used the same words the Catholic nuns had used, "ignorant, stupid..." and I had just learned to accept them. After all, wasn't I used to being humiliated in front of my peers?

Walking along the dirt road on Moorea, surrounded by its exquisite beauty, I remembered how torturous grade school had been. I could still feel the hot, soldering barb of pain as Sister Mary Bernadette twisted my ear and forced me to stick my tongue to the dry, dusty blackboard. "See this Ignorant Child…" she exclaimed to my second grade class, after I had stumbled over words, unable to read. She wrenched my ear a notch tighter. "God's punishing her."

I was a near perfect object for torture. Tall and lanky with an unassailable belief in God's wrath and my wickedness, I stood out from the other children in my class. I held my tongue to the chalkboard as long as I was told, never flinching.

"Ignorant, stupid…" The words had lodged themselves inside me like a cancerous tumor. I couldn't rid myself of the wretched labels even after my "lazy eye" had been discovered and I wore an eye patch and glasses. I soon found that I could see clearly and read easily, but my inward vision was forever distorted.

As I walked along that road, I wanted to defend myself against Clari's criticisms, but I remained as compliant as I had been in grade school. More than standing up to Clari, I needed to grab my own fears by the throat and choke the life out of them. I wanted to stop being afraid, if only I could clearly see what it was I was afraid of.

Chapter Three

THE KING OF PENRHYN

Bora Bora. I expected my first glimpse of her to be untouched, unspoiled, with only a fading glimmer of frail light cast over the fisherman's net. I expected to glimpse her as the first Europeans had thousands of miles from their own shores, having never known such places existed. I strained to see the thatched roof huts half hidden under the veil of palms with barely a whisper of movement as the islanders prepared for the arrival of dusk.

But our yacht followed the wake of thousands of others. What was to our eyes an intoxicating beauty had been discovered long before us — had been penned, inked, painted, etched, wooed, sung about, seduced and made love to under its gracious palms. We were only distant admirers, pressed to get on with our voyage by the nagging bureaucracy.

In the course of a few weeks, my supposed lifetime in the Society Islands had been spent. (Remember, I had intended to live there forever.) We had to leave those alluring shores soon after our arrival. I'm not exaggerating when I say that I have no clue how King Fred secured his passage on board *Patience*. All I know is that one afternoon William, Clari and I had set off on an excursion scouring the motus, the small islands that ring Bora Bora.

There, I passed simple hours dipping into the calm and tepid waters, not even blue, but translucent. The sea's clarity was startling, unreal, a trick of the eye. The world became inverted, with the winsome sky wiggling at my toes. A drifting cloud became the white pillow I sat upon to watch the color play. The delicately painted miniatures: the angelfish, butterflies, tangs and moorish idols, went scudding by. I spent many hours just so, sitting cross-legged, waist deep, staring at the sea-sky, mesmerized by the fluttering, silver-braided fins.

Every once in a while I felt pressed to look up, not really knowing why. There, across the glittering lagoon, fell the broad shadows of Pahia and Temanu. The sunlight projected the towering peaks of two fierce warriors, casting them with a god-like presence over the protected lagoon. I knew them as Spirits, defending an island against intruders like us.

Curiously, Clari, William and I didn't frolic in the water together as friends might. As soon as we touched land of any sort we broke apart, pursuing our own pleasures. Clari went in search of seashells for her artwork. I noticed she had little practice with them, picking up the freshest ones, still brightly colored and quivering with some fleshy snail-like creature. She'd snatch one up and tuck it away in her pocket — the pocket of her finest frock, which she always wore on such outings. Didn't she know that in a day or two all the life would drain out of her treasure, leaving a cracked, brittle shell and a handsome stink in her best dress?

William went off exploring. Neither lack of expanse nor flora discouraged his adventurous nature. He was a boy in his heart — a funny, capricious well-heeled kid.

In relatively high spirits after our outing, we straggled back to the yacht to find the ketch lower on her lines by inches. Apparently, we had taken on several hundred pounds of rice, sugar, flour and

King Fred. His arrival appeared to be coincidental; however, he in no small way changed all our lives.

The King was amazingly short, considering his stature in the Islands. But he made up for his lack of longitude with an impressive latitude. He had an enormous belly sagging over his khaki shorts, which despaired of keeping the mounds of rippling brown flesh confined therein. It was apparent from the start that he swung a great deal of weight about the islands. After all, he was the King of the Penrhyn atoll.

None of us had ever heard of the place before; nevertheless we set off on a covert mission with the most abbreviated of explanations. We were to transport Fred to Penrhyn with the supplies, for which we would be amply rewarded. Exactly what that reward might be was not told to us. The only tangible clue as to where we were headed was a compass course setting us north by northwest, toward a small atoll.

We sailed for six days and nights in relatively tight quarters. William, with his British sense of royal propriety, surrendered the forward, v-berth bunk to His Highness. This arrangement created a domino effect of problems. The King preferred to lie in his bunk and rest the majority of our time at sea. When I went forward to use the head, I was then seated on the toilet within an arm's length of the King's head. Though a thin wooden bulkhead separated us, it was not a comfortable position to be in.

William had to sleep on the salon floorboards, the salon being a small communal area next to the galley, where one could sit on the settee berths and eat or read. This new arrangement didn't please

Edward at all. The salon was generally his domain. He slept on the settee bunk butted up against the navigation station. The galley was opposite the nav. station, allowing Edward the luxury of making tea while smoking his pipe and studying the charts.

Further aft was the covered cockpit, where each of us in turn, by day and lonely night, manned the wheel and compass. (Except King Fred, who had no shipboard duties.)

Clari and I shared the aft cabin. It had two quarter berths wedged together under the sloping cabin top, leaving us with a space akin to a six-foot coffin. In good weather it invited a comforting breeze through the companionway, drying the soak of sweat from our bodies, leaving only the faintest imprint of salt crystals to bed down with. In rough weather it was a moldy cellar, a breeder of dampened nightmares, a slow rocking womb that sheltered us from the shuddering thuds of the sea battering the hull.

I came to know every sound on board: the lilting roll of the bow slightly off-balanced, the clink and rattle of the anchor chain sliding in its locker, the bow lifting over the rushing sea swell, then the final thundering roll as it slid underneath us.

For those six days, we sailed on a fairly calm and constant sea. There were no storms to threaten our load; nothing unusual interrupted our passage. Yet there was something about this part of the journey that rose up out of the depths of a starry night to frighten me.

Usually, I welcomed those intimate midnight watches, away from Clari's blow-torch snoring, when I could clear my mind of the daily chatter and wait for the free flow of untethered thoughts. Mystified by the night play in the mythical sky, I often watched the graceful swan Cygnus wing its way along the Milky Way, marked by Deneb at its tail. Not far behind the swan flies Aquila, the eagle, both of them (depending on the legend) curious disguises for Jupiter.

I was always drawn to Scorpius and Sagittarius, prominent characters in the equatorial night sky. There stands the archer, Sagittarius, half-man, half-horse poised in the heavens, aiming his arrow at the threatening Scorpius. Bright red Antares lies at the heart of the scorpion — a heavenly stoplight perhaps, or a pulsing heartbeat.

Hercules, my hero, defends against the night dramas, against the snakes, which slither malevolently across the sky. Yet the serpent holder, Ophiuchus, is an illustrious physician, known throughout the celestial heavens as a great healer. He dutifully holds the Rainbow Serpent by the neck, waiting for the snake to shed his skin and emerge healthy and refreshed for his new life.

But look, don't be fooled by all this genteel myth-making. There, slithering low across the southern sky is Hydra, the evil water-serpent. It is not a comforting sight. With my own skin beginning to crawl, I remember the celestial lore of how Hercules tried to slay the nine-headed serpent and how each time he lopped off one of its heads, the snake grew two heads in its place — multiplying, growing larger, taking over the whole night sky perhaps.

Here comes fear again. I hate snakes. I was surrounded by snakes as a kid, either real or imagined. They were all over the stained-glass windows of our church and somehow they managed to crawl into my dreams as well. From a young age, I slept with a knife hidden in a box next to my bed to fend off those demons of the night. Now Hydra lay coiled in the heavens above. And so I blamed the celestial *theatre noir* for causing my nocturnal aberrations.

One particularly drowsy night I stood at the helm and while looking down at the compass, the seesawing numbers hypnotized me. Those numbers became long thin fingers that reached out and grabbed me by the throat. The farther I slipped into my trance, the more profoundly I was overcome by a sound of some large animal's heavy breathing. My heart quickened as I peered through the night's blackness and saw the enormous wrinkled, gray chest of an elephant as it lay dying. The sound of heavy breathing went on and on. My own breathing began to heave in my chest as I whispered into the cobalt night, "Grandpa, is that you?"

I heard a muffled laugh, like his — like Gran's.

Suddenly, his spirit seized me. I could see all too clearly Gran's safari pictures decorating our walls at home. He'd been around the world at least thirteen times. Traveling in the same circles as Hemingway, Gran had earned the title "Senior Big Game Hunter of the World" for all his trophies — dead animal skins. I grew up with those bloody images on the walls of my favorite playroom. There was the rifle, the blood, Gran's huge belly and the dead elephant staring at me.

By inheriting his wife's name, Neva, I have always felt myself struggling with an intangible link to him. What little time I had spent with him as a child, he always loomed over me with such an intimidating presence that I couldn't wait to be free of him. I never saw him as anyone related to our family, and yet he was our patriarch. Though I feared my grandfather's enormous sense of power and strength, I did share his love of travel and adventure. While he shot animals with hunting rifles, I preferred to shoot them with a 35mm camera.

My grandmother died somewhere around the time I was born. I once saw her paintings and admired her for them. They mirrored the soul of a beautiful woman. The only other odd detail I knew about her was that she always wore stylish hats. I have felt her loss in my dreams where she has visited me, but I have no real recollection of her. I've never worn hats and can't draw beyond the level of a four-year-old, so I've always wondered what strange amalgam of traits I did inherit from her.

My father had an adventurous spirit, but polio had left him paralyzed. It was one of the nightmares I carried with me. I dreamt over and over again of going to bed, only to awaken completely paralyzed, as he did.

My mother married my father not long after he got out of the hospital. Though his initial prognosis, after being completely paralyzed by polio, was that he would never walk again, he did. He married a beautiful young woman and had four children. Since mother had to look after father as well, the four of us battled fiercely for her affection.

Along with Mother's sheer physical beauty, she exuded an inviolable strength, which was no doubt formed at an early age. Facing the loss of her mother at age seven, she looked after her father, until he died when she was a teenager. She then lost both brothers. Her sister, fourteen years her senior, took on the role of mother and father.

Mother attributed her inner strength to her unshakable belief in God and the Catholic Church. My father so loved my mother and respected her views that he followed the Catholic dictum and never talked to us about his beliefs or his God. In fact, I never knew he was Episcopalian until I was in my teens and already scarred by Catholicism.

I always loved coming home to father after Sunday church. He welcomed me back with a warm hug, calming my shaken spirit. The house, warmed by the sound of the blues, was filled with the delicious smells of simmering sausage and pancakes. Father flipped pancakes with the blues. He couldn't stand or kneel in church, so the blues were his conduit to God.

Still standing at the wheel, my trance was suddenly broken. A great behemoth rose from the underworld, rising with a bitter flame scorching the somnolent mask of night. There rises Fred, the King of Penrhyn, trying to squeeze through the forward hatch, while sucking on raw onions and coconut.

As yet I hadn't spoken a word to the King. I didn't even know what language he spoke. Standing with my hands frozen to the wheel, I heard a sound like "Aaahhhuuunnnggghhhaaa" resounding from Fred's enormous chest.

"Are you all right?" I leaned over, trying to see if the weighty King was going to make it through the square opening.

"Aaahhhuuunnnggghhhaaa," came his answer.

What I didn't know was that the sound I was trying to decipher was really more like a native burp than a word. King Fred spoke English perfectly.

"You following the necklace?" he asked, rather oddly, I thought.

"What?" I turned to the King, now standing next to me. Fred raised his arm, pointing to the dim stars just above the horizon. "You see our island has the pearls and it's sending up the pearls from the sea. Soon it will be a beautiful necklace." Fred swept his arm in a shallow arc from the horizon skyward. "When it is full, I am home."

I must have looked confused. Fred added, "You feel the wind and waves pushing us?"

Realizing I was a slow learner, he pointed to the horizon again. I was stuck in the thought that Edward was teaching me to navigate at night by using the pointer stars. He reminded me that stars were of no use if they were too low on the horizon, with little angle to create a celestial triangle. But here was Fred pointing at the horizon, trying to trick me into believing I could find a set of stars to steer by.

This time I followed the line of Fred's massive arm, trying to pick out a few stars that I might consider "pearls" from all the millions I could see. He laughed at my ineptness. "You need your numbers to see."

As if looking down the sighting range of a gun, I followed the direction of Fred's finger more closely. Closing my left eye, I found his shimmering stars. I checked the compass and realized the star pattern matched our compass course to Penrhyn. I smiled as Fred's stomach rolled in rounded waves of laughter. "There," he said, "now you can rest your eyes and follow the path laid out before you." It was the first real bit of wisdom I'd heard in a long time.

On our seventh day out of French Polynesia, Edward called the crew on deck in preparation for landfall. William climbed up the rigging so he could be the first to sight land. Edward took on a peculiar demeanor as he lurched against the lifelines at the bow, straining like a hound smelling its prey. The liquid blue of his eyes were frozen in concentration.

He called aloft to William, "Should be five minutes past the hour, two points off the starboard bow."

I watched from my steadier perch on the coach roof, glancing at my watch, then to the blistering glaze of sea... three minutes... four minutes... five minutes. William's voice rang through the humid air like a pistol shot, "Land ho! Two points off the starboard bow!"

We were momentarily stunned by the instant of perfection. Edward's expression did not change a tick. His celestial navigation had proven flawless. At that moment, I realized how much I admired his skill as a seaman, yet I still wondered about him. He didn't seem to experience our elation at sighting the low-lying atoll, or any emotion as we did. My attention shifted toward land.

Once having spotted the atoll, those last few miles to shore conjured up the most exotic expectations of what land would offer us. My sea-going preoccupation with childhood memories was quickly replaced by anticipation. Secretly, I imagined a royal welcome by the islanders of Penrhyn. After all, we were not only loaded down with essential supplies for them, we were bringing home their King.

Chapter Four

TOMAI

We slipped inside the narrow passage guarding Omoka village by following the thick callus on Fred's index finger. Had his finger wavered in any direction, our journey might have ended there, scuttled on the craggy, coral-spiked reef. As it was, we crept into the shallow lagoon and the waters fell silent. Our small yacht surrendered quietly to the motionless sea like a tired soldier.

His Majesty announced that we would be boarded. We had to secure permission from two Cook Island government officials if we wished to stay in the lagoon. King Fred suggested that we offer our inspectors some magazines, cigarettes, tobacco, canned food or anything that might predispose the officials to leniency. Fred emphasized that few outsiders had ever been allowed to anchor in the lagoon, and even fewer non-islanders had ever negotiated their way to shore. But King Fred made it clear that, luckily, he was there to save us. That is, Fred and the flour, sugar, rice and lollies.

In the middle of this exchange, I began to tremble. Inexplicably weak and feverish, I steadied myself against the lifelines. I felt hot. The burning intensified. My forehead was on fire and my throat raged with a desperate thirst. I thought only of cooling waters... cooling waters.

On impulse, I dove over the side of the yacht into the blissfully cool sea. Somewhere in the darkness there was a terrible thrashing in the water. Normally I was a strong swimmer, but I was struggling just to keep my head above the surface. My lungs were weak; I couldn't catch my breath. All was darkness surrounding me. I didn't see — didn't see the shark circling; I only felt something brush past my legs.

Suddenly, a strong, well-muscled male body crushed me hard against the hull of the boat. The man clasped his arms around me and handed me up to two stocky islanders. They in turn hoisted me over the gunwales. Edward stepped forward and grabbed my shoulders, shaking me. "What in the bloody hell, woman, do you think you are doing?"

William interjected, "I say, she does look ghastly pale."

Then, Clari, "...should have left her to the shark, silly Yank."

I didn't have the strength to respond. Standing there, shivering in the tropical heat, I was consumed by a raging fever. I must have sunk to my knees. From then on, my link to the land of the living was severed and my journey to Hades began.

Hades is hot. It is the home of all the voices. It is peopled by the past, the present, and to some degree, the future. When I say I journeyed there, I mean that my delirium, which lasted for several days and nights, took me to the murkiest corners of memory. Never a joyous alchemy, it made me all the more feverish, all the more thirsty. It sent me calling for people I didn't know. They were mere shadows against a faltering candlelight. I couldn't see past the flame's dancing reflection on the wall — weird shapes and shadows, first moving toward me, then disappearing back into the wall again. I heard melodious chanting, coming from somewhere.

Soaked in sweat, I bolted upright once and tried to grab the mysterious shadow, but it vanished just as my hands reached for it. I thought I was dying and that the angels and the devil were fighting over my soul.

After three days of delirium, I slowly drifted back into consciousness. It was then that I began to think my journey to Hades was at an end.

I lay on a cot in a small room, under a thatched roof. Its open-air windows faced the sea, offering one of the most splendid views I would ever hope to live or die by. Staring out, I wasn't completely sure whether I was alive, dreaming or dead; they were clearly one and the same.

I slowly became aware of the weary visage of Edward as he sat at the edge of my bed. He looked quite haggard from his days and nights of trying to nurse me back to health.

"I say," he began, "do you think you could manage a cup'a tea? You've been out for bloody days. We've been terribly worried. A lightening case of glandular fever, I suspect."

As he administered the hot sweet tea, Edward explained how he had caught me as I sank to my knees. When he realized that I was suffering from a raging fever, he pleaded with the "officials" to take me ashore.

"I took your temperature... don't suppose you remember much, right over the top it was, just above 104 degrees. I didn't think you would last."

Then he explained how lucky it was that I had become sick.

"If you hadn't fallen ill," he mused, "those officials from Rarotonga would have sent us back to sea directly. As it was, they were furious that Fred had managed to off-load the supplies. They want to starve these people for some absurd political reason. Our King Fred sneaks about the Society Islands trying to bargain food and supplies for the hats and fans they make…"

While Edward had spent endless hours at my bedside, William found little time to visit. When he finally did come, he paced around my hospital bed, begging me to remain ill.

"Yes, of course, lovely you're getting on, but for goodness sake, can't you just lie there for an extra day or two? You can't imagine what it's like; we're absolutely raking in the fish, one hundred at a time. I'll tell you about our King Freddie, all right. Our Freddie can dive to forty feet and pull up a gold mine in pearls, and he's got some brew of gin that will knock your knickers off. It's great sport, honestly."

William was adamant that I should stay in bed, but I soon found out that Clari was not so disposed to island living. She arrived at my bed, red-faced and huffing from heat exhaustion. Fanning herself with her new palm-frond woven hat, she tapped her foot impatiently, as if on the count of three I should bound out of bed, miraculously cured.

"I can't endure much more of this," she pouted. "I've learned how to weave a hat and all that sort of rubbish, but the bloody gnats are insufferable. It's all getting to be a bit of a bore. You will be better soon, won't you?"

I was barely lucid through those conversations and merely shook my head with indifference.

The nights were altogether different. I fell back into the strange hallucinatory state, watching fantastic images creep along the thin walls of my room. I continued to hear voices and chants of some sort. When I had been feverish, I had found it all very frightening and threatening, but after the fever had passed, the gentle humming became soothing. It gave me strength. Each morning I awoke stronger, more contented — a contentment I hadn't experienced on the boat.

It was during my fifth night in the "hospital" that the obscure shadows on the wall took on the form of a young man. I didn't recognize him until he drew closer to me, coming within range of the flickering candlelight. Those powerful eyes had held me captive every night. The wiry shadow crawling along the walls in the early hours of the morning, those thin fingers cooling my burning forehead with a light mist of water, belonged to him.

"Are you awake?" the young man whispered in a low, secretive voice.

He bent his thin physique into the glow of candlelight. It illuminated his warm features: the gentle curve of his high cheekbones, his perfect row of gleaming white teeth. His skin appeared much lighter than the dark-skinned, ruddy-complected islanders I'd glimpsed passing by my open-air window. He said his name was Tomai. I wondered why he had come to my bed every night; what was he looking for? Had he never seen a white-skinned girl before? But his skin was hardly darker than mine. I guessed he was in his late teens.

Tomai spoke softly, trying to enunciate each word of his broken English very carefully. He told me that his mother was American and his father was an islander. He'd had the opportunity to go to school in Rarotonga and he had even visited New Zealand. He was different, he said, from the full-blooded islanders. Tomai wanted a different life.

He spoke at first with grave seriousness, but soon his face was illuminated by a wide smile. Leaning close to my ear he said, "The schoolmaster thinks I'm very smart. My English gets better if I practice."

He turned abruptly toward the doorway. I watched amazed as his shadow slipped back into the distorted shapes on the wall. So, the shadow on the wall had been Tomai. His brown hand had dropped the cooling water onto my forehead. It was Tomai, not Edward, who had stepped soundlessly into the hut, circling my bed like some primitive spirit.

As he returned to my bedside, I noticed that Tomai was rather tall for an islander. His face had no real harshness, not like the shadows on the wall, and in my dreams... in my dreams.

Tomai interrupted my thoughts by proudly displaying what appeared to be an ancient, rusty radio. He turned the knobs anxiously as he sat on my bed, leaning against the curve of my body. "I find this from the boat that goes down on the reef. I fix it and fix everything."

I had as yet not spoken a word to the young man. He continued on as if it was quite unnecessary that I should. His whole body quaked with excitement as he turned the knobs, searching for the one miraculous moment when the sound might come on, and so it did. A terrible fibrillation shook the single side-band radio as it choked on some garbled static. Then it wheezed out the most ear-piercing pitches, cutting through the gentle night like a jagged buzz saw.

This extravagant racket, however, seemed the very essence of Tomai's delight. He laughed and rocked with the strange distortions. It occurred to me that perhaps he took those horrific noises to be the music of the western world. I matched his smile with mine, and so he seemed pleased that he had made me feel more at home. After a short while, the radio gave out its final high-pitched trill and died. Tomai laughed even more gleefully. "No more, no more, I fix it again."

Tomai stood up and looked at me, this time his expression was serious, his eyes absorbing. "I sing you back to the island. The sharks were fighting for your spirit."

I had no idea what he meant. I only understood that he had stayed near me every night since the illness had begun and in some way he had helped me back to the land of the living.

"Tomorrow you go to church with us," he said firmly, "and we give thanks for you." He smiled again, adding, "You see life here is good, and you stay."

Tomai left me with the unsettling knowledge of our secret friendship. It was not like a heady infatuation; it was a quiet, tender affection. I kept seeing him throughout the long night, moving in and out of the flickering shadows. His words, "you stay with us," seemed to circle around me, echoing and rebounding off the naked walls. His words, his eyes, his touch; Tomai stayed with me in my dreams.

Sunday was our last day on the island. Clari loaned me one of her dowdy frocks for church. It was stiff as a board from all the saltwater washings, so it hung drab and lifeless from my broad shoulders. In sharp contrast, the island women gathered in simple but brilliantly colored pareus, which swayed sensuously with their bodies as they walked.

The church was probably only one hundred paces from the "hospital," yet I hadn't seen it before. It had a tall, white, steeple, with slender, elongated windows framing a seaward aspect. It was a small, simple enough building, but the craftsmanship was superb considering the lack of wood and resources on the island. I suspected that earlier Christians might have shipped it in and rebuilt it on the site where it rested.

As we gathered at the entrance, I felt my old trepidation on the rise. I was not much of a churchgoer anymore. A stringent regimen of daily mass while in Catholic grade school had dampened my religious fervor. As a result, I developed some peculiar behaviors during those rituals. My spells often came in the middle of the Gospel, no doubt encouraged by the tight buttons on my uniform collar, derailing the flow of oxygen to my brain. Just as my world became a purplish hue, the Monsignor exposed our communal guilt and shame as sinners. In a violent storm of words, the priest flew into such uncontrollable rages against our heinous crimes that I would, as a rule, collapse under the heaviness of my own guilt. I usually suffered the shortness of breath first and then, as the shame of my sins slowly snaked its way through my body, eventually bumping into my spirit, my knees buckled under the sublime pressure. I gradually, gracefully dropped to the floor, where the smell of polished leather fought off the putrid odors of mortal sin. I suppose my habit of fainting was the only way I had of giving my flagging spirit a rest.

The religious gatherings in the islands, however, never provoked such demons; on the contrary, they took me closer to the heavens than I ever thought possible. Having doubted God's beneficence after the treacheries of grade school, I thought perhaps I had innocently stumbled upon His better half in Penrhyn.

As we entered the church, we followed local custom and peeled off in genders — male to the left, female to the right. Hardly seated, the congregation filled the air with song, each voice knowing precisely which octave to assume in order to achieve perfect harmony. I could not fathom how, out of such complexity, they could reach such simplicity of tone. How the sound of one voice, combined with forty others, could transform song into something more than music, more than harmony. It became the purest of all sounds. Their communal voice resounded off the vaulted roof, vibrating just above our heads, then it receded like a thunderous wave having pummeled the shoreline.

After the sound had floated out with the Pacific breeze, I felt a cold chill run along my spine, a residue of the fever perhaps. I shivered uncontrollably, bowing my head with the others. Clari shifted about uncomfortably in our stiff wooden pew, waiting for the next movement. A young man stepped up to the pulpit and prepared to read from the Bible. There he was again, my shadow and rescuer, Tomai.

I suppose, by then, I had begun to take his appearances a bit too seriously. While he gave thanks for our arrival on the island and my return to health, I could not have known (as everyone else on the island did), that Tomai had interpreted his saving me from the sharks as a definitive sign that I was to be his wife.

After Tomai's short entreaty, the congregation resumed its song as we left the church. By the end, I felt quite invigorated by their powerful invocation. They had echoed the healing chants that I had heard from my sick bed.

And that was it. No one rose above us to denounce our existence; we simply celebrated it.

After the church service, King Fred directed us to rest through the noonday heat. A gathering of his clan, which included almost everyone on the island, was to take place in the late afternoon. The fishermen took their spears to the reef and waited for the sun to lower in the sky. Nearing dusk the fish began their feeding frenzy, and their evening meal became ours.

At the end of the day we gathered at Fred's house, which, despite his stature and royal lineage, didn't look any different from the other spartan, thatched-roof huts on the island. But as William had told me, King Fred did have a secure place for the food supplies, which included his cache of gin. That fact alone described the source of Fred's power on the island.

According to the custom in the islands, the women ate separately from the men. Guests were treated differently, however, and we ate with our host. Edward, William, Clari and I sat cross-legged on the earthen floor, while Fred guided us through the sumptuous feast. Though the islanders were so extremely short on supplies (we might have been the last "supply boat" for twelve months), they offered us every delicacy possible. They took their catch-of-the-day and by smothering it in a variety of sauces (whose origin was not always evident), they could cleverly disguise the same dish used over and over again. Thus a variety of exotic aromas and unfamiliar tastes tempted us. I recognized the coconut mixtures and the sweetness of the banana flavor all melded together with bits of fish parts, with a huge dollop of heavy taro on the side.

Clari and William tore into the feast at once, while Edward conversed with Fred in an intense and serious manner. Fred's presence partially eclipsed my view of Tomai, who sat at a respectful distance behind the King. I could feel the press of his watchful eyes following my every move. It would have been improper for me to meet his gaze, so I sat nibbling my crayfish, while dripping coconut milk into my soggy lap.

When we were full to bursting, Fred announced that everyone should join in the music and dancing. I was still too weak to stand for any length of time, so I excused myself and retired to the boat. I knew it would be the last time I would see any of them, so I went timidly up to King Fred to thank him. He seemed to enjoy my reticence. Fred let out a big snorting laugh and announced to everyone in the room, "Yes, rest, get stronger. Stay with us. You stay with us now."

I misinterpreted his words, assuming they reflected the islander's endless generosity, so I thanked King Fred and said goodbye.

Tomai followed me to the skiff. "You must not go," he said with finality as we stood at the water's edge.

Tomai's intense black eyes jarred a disturbing memory. Scanning the horizon, I remembered the ache in my shoulders as I was pressed hard against the hull of the boat. Was it Tomai who had lifted me toward safety? Is that why he had kept watch over me throughout those delirious nights? The young man was quick to answer my unspoken questions.

"When I saved you from the shark," he said, "I knew you were chosen for me. King Fred is my uncle, he said it is so."

To my surprise he added, "One day, the island will be ours. Sleep with my love tonight; give me your sign tomorrow... never to leave here." Tomai reached over and, taking my hand, pressed a saltwater pearl into my palm.

His powerful eyes held me transfixed. Though I had thought I wanted to live in the South Pacific forever, I hadn't really considered it in concrete terms. I immediately thought of my family and how I would communicate with them — two letters a year at best. Books, what would I do without books? I couldn't imagine a world without Hesse, Nabokov, Flaubert, D.H. Lawrence, Melville and others at my beck and call. Though we had a small supply of books on the yacht, we always had fresh circulation when we joined up with other yachties. The shared booty was usually awful romances, really awful romances, but they passed the time.

I couldn't tell Tomai that I wouldn't marry him because of books, so I said, "I have a place, my own place, I'm trying to get to..."

Though I didn't actually understand what I meant, Tomai seemed to. The memory of our intimate nights of song and conversation came back to me. As much as I wanted to preserve those tender moments, I knew I wouldn't stay. I thanked Tomai for his gift, leaving his desires unanswered.

I saw Tomai for the last time the next morning as we weighed anchor. He paddled his canoe ahead of us, guiding us through the narrow reef passage. Our sails filled as we glided by him. He dug his paddle deeper into open sea. I waved goodbye. Tomai's paddle stroke did not stop until his small craft was at the very edge of our horizon.

Once underway, William sidled over to me with his usual levity. "Well, good job, we're on our way, eh. Another day there and you mightn't have gotten away at all. Look, you've got to be a little more careful with these island blokes, you know. You can't just go gadding about, breaking everyone's heart."

Clari stepped into the conversation uninvited. "Look at those silly-goose tears in her eyes. Yes, imagine it, you could have stayed there forever, on that horrible little island... with all those ignorant people."

We continued sailing west. One year later, my parents received a letter from Penrhyn Island with a carefully written message from Tomai asking for permission to marry me.

Chapter Five

MYTHS & MEMORIES

If I was feeling a flush of melancholy at our departure from Penrhyn, Clari and William were more like jubilant pirates. Clari sported her collection of hand-woven hats and fans embedded with cats-eye, while William hoarded his bounty of saltwater pearls. Edward, of course, had none of it; he busied himself with the job of skippering the boat.

Tensions were rising on board and could only be defused by the promise of land. Our prudent skipper set us on a course farther west, with a landfall within four days — four days, a millennium when the moods of four people turn sour.

Magnifying our discontent, our whole world seemed to conspire against us. The constant breeze that had been so loyally coaxing us onward suddenly abated, leaving us breathless in mid-stream. The sea unfolded into a perfectly mirrored sky spread in every direction. There was no above or below, only a universe of eternal reflections and the hollow sound of water lapping against our hull. Along with the sense of floating weightless, there was also an oppressive vacuity in the silent sea breeze.

In sailing terms, we drifted backward more than three miles a day. Our skipper, who excelled at mathematical calculations, labored over the grim facts for some hours before emerging from the cabin, nearly embalmed in his own sweat. As Edward announced our negative progress, our grumblings increased. Although I couldn't pinpoint the crux of our annoyance, it kept resurfacing in the most peculiar fashion.

Our breakfast, for instance, was beginning to lose its enjoyment. It might have been the fact that we were low on supplies; the jam and butter were gone. This might seem a small matter to landlubbers who can run to the store for supplies, but it might be weeks before we had anything to entice the heavy bricks of saltwater bread down our throats. It was only a short time after the butter ran out that I learned to enjoy the British concoction of "fry bread" — bread fried in oil. This cooking method didn't do much to lighten the overall poundage of the bread, but it did slip more easily down the alimentary canal.

In any case, it was about the same time that the small hoardings began. Clari was quick to point out the diminishing level in the sugar jar, knowing I was the only one to use sugar in my tea. She habitually reminded us that if "we" hadn't taken on the extra crew, "we" wouldn't be so low on supplies. In fact, as the supplies diminished, Clari's dislike of me seemed to increase disproportionately. In answer to her derisive behavior I retreated further into my own world, which was inhabited by books and daydreams.

Though I was never low on daydreams, I was definitely running low on books. I had finished Michener's *Hawaii*, which was probably what prompted my jumping into the sea to cure my fever in the first place. Just like in his book, when the first missionaries arrived with all their catchy European diseases, the islanders jumped into the sea to soothe their fevers, and died. Offering the book to Clari, she announced that she wasn't in the least interested in reading "one of your banal Yank authors."

I had already read the three small novellas by Hermann Hesse. He was a good solid read with lots of philosophic meanderings to mull over, perfect for lost romantics like myself.

Jung's *Unconscious Mind* was at the bottom of my backpack, rightfully stuck below all my "stuff." So I thumbed through Edward's collection of sailing books, medical handbooks, navigation guides and the Hiscocks' cruising books, which Edward coveted. Reading sailing stories when at sea, though, was not my idea of enlightenment.

I passed the balance of the daytime as one does at sea: repairing sails, washing crusty clothes in saltwater and thinking about the next meal, but only after my daily navigation lesson with Edward had been completed.

I followed Edward about, as I had my father, intent on learning all the magic of his wisdom. As I crawled gingerly over the coach roof with the stopwatch, Edward carried the sextant in his hand so dexterously. He carried it elevated and braced away from his body as if it were a crystal ball, and indeed it was; without it we would have nothing but a compass and the stars to guide us. That would have been sufficient for the Polynesians like King Fred, who had generations of celestial folklore to guide their navigators, but we were virtually blind men in comparison to their knowledge.

I thought of Rodo, the Tahitian navigator I had met in Hawaii. I had been invited to dine on a beautiful cruising yacht, just returned from Tahiti, and moored near my sinking wooden sloop in the Ala Wai Harbor. Rodo had been invited by the State of Hawaii to be the navigator on board the *Hokule'a*, a replica of a Polynesian double-hulled sailing canoe. He had previously met the sailing couple in Tahiti and was invited to the yacht upon his arrival on Oahu. Exactly why I had been included in this celebrated mix of people, I can't recall.

Though my recollection of the evening is slightly blurred due, in part, to the amount of warm beer and wine consumed, I do remember sitting next to the slightly-built, bronzed-skinned, silver-haired Tahitian, laughing until my cheeks hurt. He was charming and gracious, and told delightful stories using his English, French and Tahitian when needed for the story, all without ever changing his smile.

When we had finished our mahi mahi, I sat rolling the fish's eyeball around my plate not really knowing what to do next. Rodo picked up his fish eye and, holding it like an olive, popped the slimy, discolored ball into his mouth. It looked a lot bigger than my throat would dare accommodate and so I just sat pushing it about with my fork, afraid to stab it, touch it, or engage it in any way. Rodo insisted that I eat the eyeball, saying, "How will you ever see, if you don't eat the eyeball? It helps me read the waves and see the wind. I must find the correct star over Tahiti or we will all be lost. What if it is cloudy? I must see through the cloud. How will I see any of this, if I don't eat the eyeball?"

It was a convincing argument, though I was not really convinced. I took a stab at the fish eye, thinking I should at least be polite about this. I thought if I pulverized it like caviar, it might be more palatable.

"No, no, no," the navigator admonished me with a smile. "Like this." Rodo picked up the eye and demonstrated how I should drop it down my throat whole. The acid started to churn in my stomach. Rodo pushed the graying eye in my direction, its large black center staring at me.

"For your sight, eat it."

I grabbed the slippery eyeball, popped it into my mouth with no intention of chewing it. I swallowed it whole. It seemed to compress nicely in my throat, then re-inflate when it hit my stomach. There it sat, undisturbed, for two days. Whether or not my congenital farsightedness was gratified or not, I can't be sure. I did see a lot of stars in the South Pacific clearly, and there the story lies.

I awaited the nights like a lonely lover. I was sure that if I waited long enough and looked hard enough, I would understand something about the night sky. I wanted to know the stars the way the Polynesians knew them. I wanted to hear their stories as spoken through the whisper of a night's secret breeze. I wanted to board my own canoe and paddle down Eridanus, the River of stars. There, I could leave behind all the malignant memories of Earth that plagued me and escape my petty fears and anger. More than that, I wanted to escape the world of senseless wars, of gruesome injustice, of anger, hatred, brutality — all I had witnessed back on land. I desperately wanted to escape it all, but memory obfuscated the celestial brilliance and all the possibilities that lay beyond my understanding.

One night, in the middle of the graveyard shift, William joined me at my post. "I couldn't sleep," he whispered in my ear, lingering a moment longer than necessary. "Do you mind if I sit with you awhile?"

I shrugged my shoulders with a slight indifference, wanting the night all to myself.

"I get so bloody fed up with Clari sometimes, I can't stand it," William went on. "We mustn't wake them. You've got to understand, Clari's always had this — I don't know where she got it from, she has a bloody crush on me. She follows me about all the time, you know, drives me mad. Ever since you came on board, she's only been getting worse, unbearable, in fact."

I kept my eyes on our course, feeling relieved to have my ally back again.

William continued, "I've had a bit of a chat with Edward about dumping her off in Fiji, but he won't have any of it. She's his cousin, you see, so he can't just throw her off the boat. Besides, her father's a Lord, and it might cause a terrible row amongst our families."

The pieces of the puzzle were slowly falling together. I'd had clues, of course, concerning my shipmates' status. They spoke of the old boys' club, fox hunting, their estates and dinner with members of the Royal Family as if they were universally common occurrences.

William's careful whisperings were suddenly interrupted by a sonorous snore, which sounded like a whale breaching the surface. It came again, but what direction did it come from? Clari's cabin! Even in her sleep she pursued us.

William snuggled in closer, ready to recount the whole Penrhyn story: "I suppose it was the fever that sent you over, then that damn Tomai went in to fetch you and before you know it, you belonged to him or some such damn thing. He wouldn't let anybody near you for days. Of course, I'm glad you weren't all torn to bits by the sharks, but what bloody business was it of his?" William shook his head with an air of disdain.

"Of all the silly nonsense, the islanders took it as a sign that you were to be his wife."

William stopped his bantering for a moment, searching for my reaction. I remained expressionless, not wanting him to know how naive I'd been about the whole situation.

He continued, "They even had the poor manners to suggest to Edward that we'd have a curse of some sort placed on us for taking you away."

"A curse!" I exclaimed, loud enough to wake up everyone. "I had no idea."

"That's not the least of it." William relished the lurid details. "They said nothing short of death would end it."

We pulled our heads back for a moment and stared into the overhanging dome of sparkling lights. The surrounding coal blackness reminded me of Tomai's consuming eyes. The island dream had stolen me for a time. William was slowly bringing me back to the familiar world we shared. I felt relieved and less lonely.

My hand somehow found its way into William's. We were both suddenly aware of the pressure he was exerting on my hand. He turned to me apologetically. "I'm sorry, but I've gotten quite fond of you these past few weeks and I'd just had it with that island bloke. I knew I couldn't pursue anything — in such tight quarters." He smiled mischievously. "It gets so messy with Clari and all, but there will be a time when we'll be on land and I'll have you all to myself, no mother hens or island curses, eh."

Until that moment, I hadn't a clue as to William's feelings about me. Either Clari or Edward had mediated all our exchanges, and I had been sightseeing, swimming, sailing or sick. I had William neatly categorized as a charming teaser. I thought him attractive, intelligent, sharp-witted and vastly more sophisticated than me, and I agreed with his assessment of the situation. I could well imagine how Clari would respond to an overt display of affection, or even the slightest sign that William might lean toward my friendship.

Since it was necessary to conduct our conversation with the utmost discretion, I quietly moved closer to William and kissed him on the cheek, after which he stared at me for some time. My gesture was meant to confirm our friendship, not to put him in shock. After a time, he leaned over and kissed me very seriously on the lips.

"Good night," he whispered, "perhaps I shall sleep a bit better now."

As William turned toward the forward hatch, I could feel the light touch of trade winds begin to fill the sails again. It was hopeful. Perhaps the gentle breezes would coax us onward, away from the stagnating tension on board.

Chapter Six

TOM NEALE'S ISLAND

"I chose to live in the Pacific Islands because life there moves at the sort of pace which you feel God must have had in mind originally when He made the sun to keep us warm and provided the fruits of the earth for the taking... I sometimes wonder what it was in my blood that had brought me to live among them..."

Tom Neale, *An Island to Oneself*

We finally made progress toward our destination, the Suvarov atoll. The chart showed a loose chain of sand spits tethered together by spiky reef shelves. Though it seemed a desolate landfall, Edward was insistent on stopping at the atoll. He desperately wanted to meet Tom Neale.

I have my own reasons for remembering this place well. There was an ominous warning at the entrance of the lagoon. A steel gray skeleton of a ship lay profoundly dead upon its coral grave. She writhed upon her burial ground, grinding against her fate, twisting her ossified metal bones, creaking and moaning with a thousand ghostly voices of sailors echoing throughout her sunken tomb. I heard the sailors cry, saw their wriggling, fleshless hands rise up through the battered portholes, waving with the sea-green grass like prisoners' hands pressed up against their bars. We glided solemnly past the sunken ship, heeding the sailors' warning, rising up from the sailors' grave.

Edward had heard of Tom Neale, a New Zealander, who lived on one of Suvarov's small islets for some twenty years. Though Edward never said it directly, I knew that he had secretly looked forward to meeting Tom for a long time. We dropped anchor in the sandy-bottomed lagoon off Anchorage Island, where Tom supposedly lived. It was the first time I had seen Edward so full of anticipation. He stepped into the rubber dinghy shaky and off-balance. I was afraid he was going to have another one of his epileptic seizures, which he was prone to onshore.

After securing the yacht, we rowed in on a small sea swell, which cast us up on the beach. We rolled into each other laughing at the unexpected lurch landward. Our chaotic noise sounded awful, echoing off the solid trunks of coconut trees. Dropping into a stiff silence, we could hear the ever so slight footfall of our host as he crept through the thicket.

Tom Neale was so emaciated from exposure to the sea and sun, he reminded me of the inhabitants of that unlucky vessel trapped on the reef. His weathered skin was stretched from rib to rib like cowhide staked out for tanning. The notches on his belt were pulled to their extreme in an effort to hold his ragged shorts above the narrow gauntlet of his hips. This scrawny New Zealander hardly seemed the figure of the man who had reached near mythic proportion as far afield as England.

Edward was the first to step forward and speak to the wiry man leaning on a stick. "Mr. Neale, my name is Edward Lowen, shipped out of Portsmouth, England. I have, of course, heard of you and have so looked forward to this meeting. But I want to assure you, we don't want to disturb you in any way."

We waited breathlessly for the legend to speak. Tom's eyes held a mystery under languid lids, never betraying an emotion or the truth of what he saw. He was silent, summing us up quickly. Then, tipping his stick toward the thicket of creepers, pandanus and gardenias, he directed us to follow him, saying almost inaudibly, "Ah, you wouldn't be the first—"

We went down a path, which was narrow and pebbled by crushed seashells with remnants of coral reef. Being the last in line, I kept straining around Clari's broad head to catch a glimpse of what lie ahead. It appeared to me a small civilized jungle where the vegetation served to wall in his domicile. I was not sure what to expect of Tom's "home." I wondered if it would reflect one man's castle, or the shelter of a recluse, half-eaten alive by solitude and too much sun.

Much to my relief, the small hut looked in every way like home. It was simple, though abounding with small comforts (so it seemed in comparison to our thirty-eight-foot boat).

His small garden supported a lively population of roosters and hens. Whether they held any clues as to why Tom's vegetable patch looked a bit spare can only be guessed at. I wondered how he had survived all those years.

As the others trekked around behind the simple hut to view his cook-house, I fell out of line, pulled inside the meager shelter by an overwhelming curiosity. There before me, in the inner sanctum of the small open-air hut, lay an amazing collection of literature. Books were stacked in every corner of his otherwise unadorned homestead; in fact, they made up the entire decor and appeared to be the sole entertainment in his life. Among the stacks of worn and moldering editions, I picked up Conrad's *Lord Jim*. I loved Conrad's writings and was thrilled to happen upon this beloved book. Its jacket was frayed and partially torn. I hadn't completed the first sentence before the book disintegrated in my hands. What had been a book a moment before was now a pile of mildewed scraps, which I nervously pushed back into their original square shape.

Before rejoining the others, I caught a fleeting glimpse of Tom's sleeping room where a solitary wood-framed bed stood, clothed in remarkably clean linen. Everything was swept clean and extremely tidy. With a sturdy wooden table and two chairs, the place looked remarkably comfortable.

Tom appeared to be quite the consummate handyman and capable housewife. He, in fact, reminded me a lot of Edward, who could fix anything on the boat, and always insisted that everything "live in its place." Judging from the laundry drying outside, Tom and Edward also shared the same nervous obsession for washing tea towels.

As I tiptoed around the corner, I overheard Tom explaining, with the greatest attention to detail, how he had managed to secure the roof of his thatched hut by a series of stayed wires fixed to the ground. It saved him the effort of having to rebuild his hut after every hurricane season. There stood his simple cookhouse, two water tanks and, farther on, a shed and bathhouse.

Edward listened intently while the three of us, the restless crew, waited impatiently to roam about the rest of the island. William was the first to prepare his exit by questioning Tom about where he might best locate our dinner. Tom was quiet for a moment, as he crossed his arms and whisked his index finger across his lips.

"You'll find," he said with a calculated hesitancy, "all you need on the reef ledge — crays, cod, parrotfish. As I get older, I go for what's easiest to catch."

Then he added with a stern warning, "Mind the tide, eh, it rises quickly."

In the next moment William was off, motioning me with a furtive wink. Clari bounded after us like a foxhound. We left the Skipper and Tom to enjoy their own company, or whatever company solitary people enjoy.

As we followed the path back through the jungly tangle of clapping palms and coconut trees, Clari's voice throttled William at the back of his sunburnt neck.

"William, what are you going to do?"

"I'm going spearfishing on the reef," he yelled over his shoulder. "I should think it better to go alone as we've only got one spear."

William turned to me just as Clari stumbled through the last bit of thicket.

"Look, you go the long way around the island and I'll meet you on the reef," he whispered. "I'm sick of that bloody cow following us about."

"Oh William," Clari whined, "I want to go fishing with you. Pleeeeeeeez…"

William was quite the tactician. His departure on board the dinghy was accomplished with such panache that Clari wasn't even aware she had been abandoned. She hugged the shoreline and waited for his return.

I retreated into the grove of palms and retraced the path once again. Foraging through the thicket, I covered my tracks as I went, hoping to free myself from Clari.

At first I chose the path that circled the island, but it kept casting me back onto the exposed beach, so I decided to climb the small hill behind Tom's hut. I thought the initial incline might be off-putting to Clari. She was sporting her best frock, which rose to many occasions, but never to climbing hills.

It was barely a hill, so I reached the top quickly. From my solitary perch I inhaled a deep, liberating breath of resplendent South Pacific air and thought of absolutely nothing but the sweetness of my victory, having eluded Clari, at least for a time.

I felt like a conqueror, an adventurer, alone at last and happily so. I trembled with the taste of solitude. To celebrate, I decided to try climbing a tall, sturdy palm. I had some difficulty scaling the first twelve feet. Following the custom of the islanders, I cast out my arms like grappling hooks and my legs like a monkey's.

Suddenly I felt dizzy and breathless, and not at all sure that my quest was worth the queasier broader view. At eighteen feet above ground, my fear of heights overpowered me. I clung tenuously to the gnarly bark, which had carved ancient etchings into my thighs. The blood from the cuts ran cool and thick, trickling down the inside of my legs.

Then my universe suddenly kaleidoscoped shut. All the colors of the universe streamed through the dark center of my pupils in long, thin strings of starlight. My fear had sucked all the strength out of my arms. I fell out of the tree and hit the ground with a heavy thud. Terrible breaking and snapping sounds trailed me as I somersaulted down the backside of the hill. The string of starlights collapsed into a black hole of darkness, while the cracking and breaking sounds receded into a gentle humming.

"Bloody hell, what have you done to yourself this time? Gave me a fright! I thought you were some bloody great animal or something." The familiar sound of Clari's commanding voice startled me back into consciousness.

I opened my eyes with the wide-eyed frenzy of a prisoner before the guillotine. I was stretched out rather miserably at the bottom of the hill. Every inch of me was either soiled, scratched, or embedded with some prickly sliver of reed, weed or thorn. While Clari looked on, annoyed at my intrusion, I wondered if I had broken anything.

As it turned out I was quite a rubbery character. The gods had hurled me out of the heavens and tossed me back to earth, unharmed. I picked myself up, pulled the thorns from my skin, and fell into a doomed stagger behind Clari. She was so riddled with disgust at my unlady-like tumble, she spoke without turning to look at me.

"He's playing you for a fool, you know. William and I have been together since leaving England. He's just playing with you to get my attention. You know that, don't you?"

Once again I was having trouble forming the words that would humiliate her, as deeply as I felt humiliated. At the very moment I began to stutter, a coconut flew out of the sky like a bulbous meteor and landed between Clari and me.

"Goodness," Clari jumped out of the way, surprised by the sneak attack. "I daresay coconut would go well with the fish. Why don't you have a go at it."

Of course, I should be the one to open it with no tools, rip it open with my bare hands like Tarzan and Jane. Giving Clari a meager grimace, I picked up the coconut, weighing it in, trying to figure out how to approach the task of opening it. I had watched the islanders crack open the beast using a sharply pointed stick fixed firmly in the ground. After peeling away the outer husk and holding the coconut just at the right angle over the spearhead stick, I'd seen the natives split it cleanly in one go. That, however, was not to be my fortune. I found a sharp stick, buried it in the ground, husked the coconut, steadied myself, aimed, heaved all my weight into the trajectory and struck the first blow as cleanly as I thought possible. The coconut did nothing but roll out of my hands and plop on the ground, accusing me of being a fraud. I tried again and again, much to Clari's enjoyment. She began to giggle — a silly, sadistic kind of giggle — which in turn threw an uncanny amount of energy through my veins. I fell into a rhythmic sledge-hammering of the nut, pressing all my complaints into the axing. Finally, with the image of Clari's head replacing the nut, I skewered the softer membrane perfectly with the spearhead stick, poking a respectable drinking spout into its center. Glorious victory loomed as I drank the sweet milk, savoring each blessed drop. Handing it over to Clari, I inadvertently dropped the slippery nut on her foot, her favorite tapping, "I'm so impatient," foot. Her eyes exploded with anger as she set her mongrel jaw like a lioness about to pounce.

"Why you stupid... You are a fool! He's toying with you and you don't even see it. You're hopeless, absolutely hopeless..."

Still smarting, Clari limped off. Puffing and mumbling to herself, she raged on against me.

But I had opened the coconut.

William was waiting somewhere on the reef shelf. I set off toward the reef, across the black bed of coral heads. It was a mysterious wasteland of harbored life, until the tide rose, bringing in a rush of water and sea life. I stepped from one coral ridge to the next in a rather fatiguing exercise to avoid any further punctures.

Finally, I spotted William leaning over a crevice, his spear locked and ready to harpoon a colorful parrotfish.

"Good job, you're here." He glanced over his shoulder to see if Clari was closing in on us. "I think we've got her off the scent for the time being. This is bloody good sport. We'll have tea in no time."

William's face beamed with enthusiasm; raw energy seemed to flow through his veins, continually radiating from him. He did look a bit like a young warrior with his spear in hand, bare-chested and tanned, with those wild locks of sun-bleached curls. He went on breathlessly, "You take the sack and I'll take the spear. You actually don't need the spear, you only have to run after the poor little buggas until their gills start puffing and they have to stop for a rest. Then, you pick them up and heave 'em into the ol' sack while they're still flapping."

"Bloody hell," he yelled, excitedly, "here comes tea now!"

I spun around. There was a long scar in the reef, forming a wild rivulet when the tide started rising. The waves funneled in through this narrow channel, bringing with them schools of unwary fish. Flopped onto the exposed coral heads by the sea swell, the fish were left to find their own way to safety.

We pounced after an unlucky school of blue parrotfish. They immediately began puffing with nervous exhaustion while trapped inside blind coral caverns. William stepped over the tide pools and grabbed the slippery silver blue fish by their inflated bellies while calling for the sack. I held the gunnysack as he piled in at least twelve flapping fins. Their brilliant colors slowly faded as we captured them in that gauzy cell. I thought I heard a common cry go up from somewhere, the sunken ship, perhaps, still surging on the reef.

I was weighed down by our load and felt a sudden disappointment that the "hunt" had been so easy. It really wasn't much of a sport after all. But William still had that gleam of sweaty anticipation about him. He crossed over the water-filled gully and stationed himself farther upriver for the next rush. We were separated by the incoming tide and another fifty feet of coral footsteps. I stood there awkwardly trying to control the snapping tails inside the slimy sack. Then I heard an ominous warning from William.

"Bloody hell, *watch out!*

I followed the tip of his spear, which pointed toward the opening of the narrow channel. Large ocean swells thundered over the reef, forcing a ton of water into the coral alleyway. The tide was rising so fast that I was already knee-deep and unable to move against the incoming rush of water. I remembered Tom's warning too late.

As I desperately tried to maintain my balance against the undertow, I saw the unmistakable fin. I had already seen it too many times in my nightmares to mistake it — the devil incarnate and the most primordially beautiful creature of the deep. He was a six-foot reef shark in search of a delicacy. I watched him glide toward me. His motion was smooth and elegant as he made a menacing circle. I stood frozen with the bag of bait in my hand. Then the gray-brown fin cut a silver trail toward me in a deadly invitation. His jaw opened.

As the sea rushed in around my hips, I was paralyzed, trapped in the reef's scar. I heard the hammering of my heart echoing in my head and screamed, "*You sonofabitch!*"

Just as the shark's jaw was leveled at my waist, I raised the sack and swung it at his snout. The startling blow closed that demon jaw. With a flick of his tail he spun around and fled seaward.

No sooner had I caught my breath than a fleet of reinforcements arrived. Five to six more sharks swiftly funneled toward me. I had no more nerve to stand still for an assault, so I chased them with my sack, trying to step over the waves as they flooded in. In the next moment, a small surge swept me onto the reef shelf, just as it had the parrotfish, which I still clung to, as if they were my sole protection.

I teetered on the coral shelf as all the adrenaline suddenly drained out of my system. I must have been weaving a bit when William finally arrived at my side. His face was blanched a sickly pale gray.

"I say, I thought you were done for," he puffed, breathless. "I've never... well, it's just that... I tried you see, getting over, but really, it happened so quickly, and they just... the buggas... bloody hell... you hit them!"

As William grabbed my elbow, I could feel him shaking just as severely as I was. We took our trembling and turned it into convulsive laughter.

"Bloody good thing you hung onto our tea," he said. "I only wish it had been Clari. She would have made the fellows happy."

"Sharks seem more attracted to me!" I exclaimed.

William took the sack from my locked grip as we helped each other over the spiked reef, which was quickly disappearing into the sea. When we reached the sandy shoreline he turned to me.

"Look, I can't go back there yet," he said. "Let's sit awhile. Clari will be steaming that we've gone off for so long. Might as well make the best of it, eh."

"Yeah, I bumped into Clari on my way to find you. She was already steaming. Quite sure of your feelings—"

William sharply interrupted my light-hearted approach.

"Oh, please! You won't be drawn in by her nonsense, will you! Good God, if she shipped off tomorrow, I'd be overjoyed."

William abandoned his catch and took my hand. We crept stealthily out of view, around the gentle rise of hill, the very same one I had fallen from earlier. We settled into the tide line, close enough to the gentle wash of blue to be cooled, close enough to see the bellies of sharks through the gossamer window of breaking waves.

Watching the sharks glide through the waves so close offshore was an eerie sight. Once again I thought of those sailors impaled on the reef for eternity. I thought of Tom Neale and how he'd lived on the island for twenty years. I couldn't imagine what would drive a man to live in such isolation under such stark conditions, yet I was in awe of his ability to do it. Then my thoughts turned to the curse the Penrhyn islanders had placed on us.

"I'm not sure if it's me or this island," I said, "but there's something so — you don't suppose there *is* some sort of curse on us — maybe just on me, for leaving Tomai."

"Oh really," William laughed, "you don't believe in that sort of rubbish, do you? You've just had a bit of bad luck that's all. And besides, you're still alive."

Through all his humoring, I couldn't shake my apprehension. I wanted to have a serious conversation to allay my fears, but I found William always liked decoys.

"Why do you suppose Tom would live here all these years, by himself?" I asked him. "It seems so — strange to me and yet, in some way, I envy him."

William drew small hieroglyphics in the sand. "I can't say as I would know. I suppose he got fed up with things and chucked it all in, just as we have."

"Don't you suppose he's terribly lonely?"

"Some people don't seem to mind being alone. They need it in fact. Look at Edward, he never wants to go ashore, always wants to stay on board and busy himself with the yacht. The yacht is his mistress, just like the island is Tom's."

"Do you know where you're going, William? I mean, do you know why you are out here?"

I stumbled awkwardly through my thoughts, remembering Tomai and the shark, and nearly losing my life to the sharks on the reef. I had the recurring feeling of something dreadful following me, something I couldn't escape.

"Gawd, you ask an awful lot of questions." William fell back on his decoy. "You shouldn't think so much, my dear, that's your downfall, you think too much for your own good." His eyes suddenly reverted to their luminous brashness. "Of course, I know where I'm going! I'm off to New Zealand to make my fortune."

"I wish I knew," I said forlornly. "I just keep moving, hoping to find something — and, I don't know even know what it is."

William laughed again. "Let me assure you, we are on a beautiful island in the middle of the glorious South Pacific."

He scrutinized me closely. "I do wonder about you," he said, brushing the sunbleached strands of hair out of my eyes. "All that sadness in those beautiful eyes."

Just as William said this, a wave rose up in a tumult of white water. It looked ready to break over us with immense force. The sun splintered into a fine mist of filtered light as the wall of water collapsed over our heads. The light, the land, the sea, the sand, became one. I felt the pulling force of all the magnified energies. I had nothing to resist with, no energy left, no breath in reserve to carry me through the undertow. There was nothing to anchor me. I slipped helplessly into the streaming tide. Dragged swiftly out to sea, I expected to find my shark again. This time, he would escort me into the afterlife.

The sea, however, retreated as unexpectedly as it had attacked. Cast back onshore, I was left exposed and panting in fright, just like my parrotfish. When I looked up, William's shadow was cast full length over me. He contemplated my corpse cheerfully.

"I say, I'm beginning to believe that rubbish about a curse on us. Almost lost you again. I shall have to keep a better hold on you."

His shadow lowered over me as we slipped into the gentle wash of sea. The sea drenched us in laughter. We moved inside it, letting the sea play with us, making love to it and to each other.

On our last evening at anchor, we invited Tom to dine with us on board *Patience*. I never did know what to make of him, the thin sparrow of a man, flighty, delicate and so reserved. He spoke rather wistfully of his years on the island as he recalled the yachts that had called in to meet him. They had left behind the precious food of his existence, the stacks of books and tinned food, which he kept in storage for the rainy season. Since he had written his book, *An Island to Oneself*, Tom complained that too many yachties had stopped in to gawk at him, ending his solitary existence.

I listened closely to everything Tom said. I desperately wanted to ask him why he remained on the island. As if reading my thoughts, he mentioned that he had left the island several times to go back to Rarotonga. As he grew older, he had realized the possibility of dying alone on the island. He said he was afraid of not going quickly enough, of having some illness that might make dying a long, torturous affair. Tom was very matter-of-fact. He seemed tired and I wondered if he was trying to tell us something, if at seventy-four years old he felt an impending change. Surely a man who could translate the slightest change of sea breeze could sense his own passage.

I tried not to feel sorry for Tom. I knew he had achieved everything he wanted in life, managing what most people never would — he had lived in a true Paradise. I knocked back a hard hit of King Fred's numbing gin in a quiet toast to him.

I was bewildered by Tom's farewell gesture the next morning. Perhaps it held a clue to his past. He stood at the water's edge as we hauled up the anchor and set our sails. The man suddenly shook and trembled as if taken by a memory or fit of remorse. I thought maybe he wanted to go with us, perhaps his time had come and he wanted to leave the island forever. His arms swung and flailed the air, as if warning us of an imminent danger — the reef, perhaps? He called out to Edward, to Edward alone.

"Edward, don't forget what I told you. *Don't forget.*"

Edward looked intently at the quaking old man, now waving quite madly at us. Our anchor broke the surface and the yacht began to sail toward open sea.

"Don't forget..." The last of Tom's voice trailed off like a whispering talisman, skipping from wavetop to wavetop.

"Edward, whatever you do, *Never Get Married!*"

The fragile old man repeated this twice before his words were swallowed by the sound of rushing seawater pounding the coral reef.

I found this curious advice from a man on an island of his own.

Chapter Seven

ATMOSPHERIC PRESSURE

We were nearing the most easterly islands in the Fijian chain. There were more than three hundred islands and we were hoping to find one — the main island of Viti Levu.

Edward was anxious. He said we had to press on. "Mind your course and sail trim, we need to get on with it." I wasn't sure what he meant or what the urgency was until the weather changed.

The wind died away. The seas flattened as we drifted along aimlessly in the currents. Only the steely gray clouds spoke to us, told us unsettling rumors of high winds and severe seas, but we saw nothing — nothing but steel and iron caste grays washed from the sky to the horizon, then into the sea.

Something in the atmosphere was changing. It was hard to tell whether our nerves caused the tense atmosphere, or if the falling barometric pressure created our volatile state. Something was changing. It was November and the beginning of summer in the Southern Hemisphere. We had casually slipped inside the cyclone belt, where everything changes.

As I would soon find out, cyclones are devilish creatures. They play with you as if you are an insignificant amusement of the Fates. They gather up all their wind-power and come steaming toward you only to veer away at the last possible moment, leaving you to contemplate the deadly, immeasurable silence. And so we shared the feeling of being surrounded by something malevolent, of knowing there was no way out, no exit signs, no off-ramps, no escape.

Bad omens had been with us since leaving Suvarov. William, who was our laughter, our smile, our liaison with the skipper, had become an invalid within a week. What started out as a small scratch on his shin grew into a pustule, then a boil, which grew daily, swelling his leg into one throbbing red vein about to burst. His misery marked the end of his spear fishing days and our stolen moments together.

It became apparent that some primitive surgery had to be performed to save his leg. The skipper acted as the surgeon and Clari was the nurse. The main thrust of her job was to keep the valuable drops of golden whiskey from dribbling too freely down William's tilted chin. I steered the boat and thus avoided any glimpse of the crude bisectioning of my friend's leg.

The operation was a success. Edward was able to incise the wound, drain it and stem the flood of infection, but there was still a good deal of post-operative nursing left to do. Each day Edward dutifully changed the pus-filled gauze and cleaned the wound with hydrogen peroxide, before replacing a fresh gauze drenched in drawing ointment. Our great fear, the constant threat in the tropics, was that the infection might spread. Gangrene could set in and William would lose his leg.

As it was, William was left with a gaping pit in his leg, which gave us a clear view of the underlying bone. The wound gradually dried, leaving a mass of weak, mottled tissue to knit back together. William's humor congealed as well, leaving him irritable and out of sorts. When he was able to hobble painfully around the boat, the odd wave came through, throwing him off-balance against a bulkhead; his curses filled the forbidding atmosphere. No one escaped his petulant moods.

The atmosphere finally erupted one afternoon as William and I sat in the cockpit, while Clari went through the lazarettes, announcing the status of each food item. The flour and sugar were gone. That should have been good news — no more bricks of saltwater bread for breakfast. Clari discovered that weevils had burrowed into the long grain rice and were busy procreating at an astonishing rate. I had no hand in that, but she stepped up the companionway ladder and fumed at me anyway.

We had plenty of English Breakfast Tea left, but no cooking fuel to boil water. The untreated water in our tanks had gone brackish, "the color of the Thames," Clari said, while pumping our precious fresh water down the sink to show us.

We had plenty of tinned peaches, so I suggested we put our heads together for a game of *Peaches and What for Dinner?* Clari nearly strangled my attempt at humor. Lunging topside, clutching the last of the chocolate cookies to her breast, she unleashed her anger at me. "You, you wretched bitch, you ate them, didn't you?"

I pulled back from her accusation. She wagged the bag at my face, declaring I wouldn't be allowed to have one more "bickie" because I was the cause of *all* the distress on board the boat. I heard Edward chewing on his pipe and mumbling from the nav. station, "Oh for goodness sake, woman, have your bickies and be done with it."

Clari continued to threaten me with the last of the cookies. It was hard to imagine how a little wafer covered in a thin glaze of chocolate could drive someone mad, but the bickie had obviously become a symbol of everything she hated about me. Clari was reaching breaking point.

William's face was twisted in pain and anger. He yelled at her, "That's it!" He threw himself at Clari, one arm outstretched, as if he meant to push her overboard. Clari lurched back against the cockpit coaming and the bag flew into the air scattering the bickies, like pirated doubloons, into the sea. Our treasure and sweet pleasure, gone.

"*Il n'y en a plus!*" William announced, waving his magic wand. "All gone."

Clari was beside herself with rage. She went below whimpering and sulking.

I repressed a laugh that was trying to burst through my cheeks, but then William turned on me.

"I'll be glad to get off this bloody boat, especially with you and Clari at each other all the time… drive us all mad."

I had certainly misjudged the value of the British bickie.

Clari went straight to Edward with her sniffling and tears. Pressing my ear against the dorade, which sits above deck admitting air for below-deck circulation and also serves as a microphone for conversations, I listened anxiously as she tried her case before the magistrate. Clari admitted to Edward that she was not quite sure what had gone wrong, or why she had become so irritable of late, but things had gone so much more smoothly before I had floundered on board. She added that she could not tolerate me any longer.

I listened to her litany of complaints. She said that I was in her way. "Neva panders to William's needs and she has no idea how to cook our meals properly." Clari continued down a long list of offenses, "…and she's wasteful, typical American."

Clari thought it best that I should be put ashore in Fiji. I pressed my ear harder against the dorade, hoping to hear Edward come to my defense. Instead, all I could make out was the sucking sound of his lips on his pipe. After a long prelude of puffing Edward said, "I see, yes, there has been a problem for some time, though I do think you could be a bit more civil to her, my dear."

Clari's constant sniffling disguised some of her words. She finally blurted what was really bothering her, which I distinctly understood. "You and William treat her as if she can do no wrong, yet we know nothing of her background; her education is sorely lacking."

"My dear," Edward interrupted, "I don't think social status is really at issue here. Do you? Neva does her chores. I don't think she sets out to deliberately antagonize you?"

Clari's response was drowned out by a rush of tears. There were more tears and sniffles and puffing, but no final decree. I went over to William, who was dozing on the cockpit cushion with his leg propped up over the deck coaming.

"William," I whispered as loud as I dare, "I've just heard Clari say she wants me to leave the boat. Has Edward said anything? Would he throw me off the boat, leave me ashore?"

"Edward? No." William hesitated. "I shouldn't think so. No, don't worry. She's only having another whinge, trying for a bit of attention."

William's quick dismissal of the matter only heightened my fears. There was no pursuing the matter as Clari climbed up the companionway, brushed by me and descended down into our dank catacomb aft.

I waited for Clari to settle into her novelette before going forward to Edward to plead my own case. He had come up on deck and gone forward to the bow, as if expecting my company. He gazed out to sea in the saddest of meditations. I sat down beside him quietly and waited for him to break the silence. The spirals of smoke curled out from between the edges of Edward's lips for an uncomfortable amount of time before he spoke.

"You know, a man can dream a lifetime about the things he wants to do... and never do them. I left England to sail the South Pacific, to get away from all the constraints, the petty nonsense, the superficial rubbish."

Edward drew in a draft and crossed his legs carefully. "I had my reasons. Damned if I'm going to let this squabbling ruin it. Life's too short."

Edward and I had never really spoken on a personal level. Usually, our conversations related to sailing. Now, I was listening to him intently, hoping to find a clue concerning his feelings about my presence on board. It was an awkward moment. After all, it was Edward who had managed my release from prison and subsequent "bonding" to the boat. Curiously, Edward had also presented me with a beautiful piece of hand-painted Tahitian cloth as a gift before we left Bora Bora. He had laid the material across my lap saying, "I thought this might suit you," and then quickly disappeared up the companionway. I hadn't known what to make of his gesture. He had left me in stunned silence and we never mentioned it again.

I had spent many hours with Edward, learning navigation, studying the stars, painstakingly going through the mathematical calculations. Whenever my charted position proved correct, he patted me enthusiastically on the shoulder, saying, "Well done, my dear, well done."

Though I knew so little about him, I trusted Edward instinctively. I even imagined that he was one of the few stalwart individuals who might still be considered "honorable." This trust, coupled with our friendship, momentarily allayed my fears.

After a long silence, Edward withdrew his pipe slowly, as if he were a man carrying a great burden.

"What made you leave America?" he asked.

Surprised by the personal question, I was quiet for a moment. Then I launched in, answering as evasively as I could.

"Leave? Things just happened... it was more like an accident."

I had no intention of telling Edward that after barely one year of marriage at age twenty-two, I had loaded up my bicycle with a spare change of clothes and ridden away from an abusive husband, and that I suffered from constant nightmares as a result. Day and night, I was pursued by the shadow of a man following me. It had become imperative to keep moving. I still carried with me not only a constant fear, but an unrelenting feeling of guilt and shame. I changed my story slightly for Edward, but it was still moderately factual.

"I remember the actual moment I decided to leave. I was riding my bicycle along a busy street and a car forced me off the road and I hit some stones, fell off the bike and hit my head. When I opened my eyes, I was staring through the branches of a tree and the sun hit me in the eyes. I heard a voice say, 'Get up, get up, get away from here.' So I did."

Edward chuckled to himself. "Oh my dear, you're not serious?"

"Well, yes. There were other reasons. I just felt... so... completely lost. My brothers were in Vietnam while my sister marched for peace in Washington. There was the war, drugs, all the feminist stuff, sort of all mixed up together. I was scared... confused... I wanted to get on the outside of it all."

I considered that a partial truth. There were other reasons, but they were buried so deep it would take years to pry them loose. At the time, I considered myself an escapee of sorts, running from something, to something, neither of which I was sure of. That there was no escape was beyond my grasp.

Edward continued his line of questioning. "And your family, aren't they wondering where you are?"

"Yes, I suppose they are, but I write everything down and send it to them. My father, he's... paralyzed. The only way I have of helping him is to keep moving."

"I'm so sorry, I had no idea," Edward said sincerely. "But surely you don't plan to keep moving indefinitely... for his sake?"

Edward paused, then added sympathetically, "I know, it's a terrible thing to watch someone you love wither away... Mother... she..." He struggled with each word. "She died of cancer, slowly... painfully. I will never love anyone more."

Edward's voice broke off and his eyes misted over. He stared intently toward the bleak horizon and then whispered, "I'll tell you this, I envied Tom on his island. He's somehow managed to escape all this... all the pain of..."

Edward's voice broke off again. I sat there gazing out to sea, listening to the boat rock. It sounded like a kind of weeping all of its own. We rocked back and forth together, finding some comfort in our shared grief. It was the unspoken link to our friendship.

I had envied Tom, too, and agreed with him that getting married was a big mistake. Everything would be different, if only I had spoken up and not let an angry man overpower me. If only I had kept running on the morning of my wedding, instead of returning home to face that spurious ceremony. I remember staring out of the front window of our family home where the small ceremony was held and hearing the words "'til death do you part." I stood absolutely frozen by those words; the priest might as well have been a black-hooded executioner leading me off to the guillotine.

"I'm sorry about Clari," I said, finally interrupting my somber thoughts. "I'm sorry I can't seem to do anything to make things OK between us."

Edward turned his head away from me with the same air of unrelieved sorrow.

"Not to worry. We'll get to Suva and make a fresh start."

I wanted to press Edward further, to make sure he had no intention of leaving me on shore. But his sadness at that moment was so consuming, I chose to leave him alone with his memories.

The night air was still, thick and moist; it was suffocating. Soaked in sweat, I tossed fitfully in my damp bunk, listening to every condemning sound on the boat. The anchor chain slid from side to side in the forward locker, while above deck all the halyards were snapping against the mast in endless disharmony. The sails slapped back and forth, empty and lifeless. The boat's unsettling yawing was a harbinger of distress — the cyclone was pressing in on us. I could smell its nearness.

Clari held the first evening watch. As she steered our course through the impenetrable blackness, I heard her begin to whimper. It was like a half-whisper trying to scream. I listened intently from my bunk near the wheelhouse. I could have easily sat up and asked her what the trouble was; instead, I coiled up like a cat and kept to myself.

Her whimpering got louder, as if her lips were going to break open at any moment with an enormous howling cry. Then I heard her scream. It was the terrifying scream of someone gone mad. I lunged from my bunk and went topside with only one reflex guiding me. Grabbing Clari's shoulders, I shook her violently. "Shut up! For Christsake, stop it!" I yelled at her. I almost slapped her across the face. My arm was raised, suspended in mid-air, when I saw Edward standing next to me in the wheelhouse. His presence seemed to calm Clari a bit, though she kept on whimpering and shivering.

"We're going in circles, I can't make it stop... I can't stop it... we're going in circles," she repeated blindly.

Edward leaned over the wheel to check the compass. Then he explained in a soft voice, "Yes, you're quite right, we are going in circles. It's just the wind, my dear... just the wind."

He motioned me to lead her to her bunk. I guided her into the cabin, where she collapsed, still trembling. There she lay, staring blankly at the cabin top, until sleep relieved her of the nightmare.

I returned to the wheelhouse where Edward watched the compass turn through 360 degrees, as the wind eddied around us.

"What happened to her? Was it my fault? I didn't want to hurt her. I just wanted her to snap out of it." I waited anxiously for Edward's response. His eyes were fixed on the compass.

"Your fault? I shouldn't think so. We've been at the edge of this bloody cyclone... rattles the nerves, that's all." Edward readjusted his pipe as if preparing himself for the worst. With his teeth clenched, holding his pipe steady he mused, "Some people shouldn't go to sea. She doesn't belong out here and that's the end of it." Edward looked askance at me and in a gentle voice he added, "You should get some rest, my dear. We'll be in for some bad weather soon."

Once again I lay restlessly in my bunk, waiting for Armageddon. I thought of Edward's despondency over the loss of his mother and all the gloom that threatened to envelop us. I thought about being paralyzed... paralyzed by fear, by love or loss of love. In the face of the cyclone, I thought if I lived with fear long enough, maybe I would find the real source of my fear. Then, maybe, I wouldn't fear it anymore.

We eddied with the wind all that night. Uncharted lights flickered about us like fireflies. The sails slapped mercilessly. We yawed back and forth, rising and falling against the fragile stillness.

The gray morning light splayed over the hidden shapes that had followed us through our night's vigil. We had drifted into a minefield of small odd-shaped islands, which were scattered hazardously along our passageway to Viti Levu. Miraculously, Edward had been able to identify our position on the chart by spotting a lighthouse on a high bluff overlooking one of the small islands.

Everyone's mood lightened at the news that we were within a day's sail of Suva. Clari rose from her bunk and William opened up the last can of sardines. We found wind as I steered our proper course toward the mountain of clouds, layered to the heavens in distinct hues of gray-purple-blue.

I have only one compressed and dimmed impression of our approach to the main harbor of Suva, Fiji. It was the moment when the defined shapes emerged from the sooty cloud cover. Thick columns of burning copra smoke were mixed with the leaden sky and through this dense cover a working city gradually emerged. For the first time in many months, we were confronted with a teeming city. The wilderness of South Pacific was behind us and the bustling city of Suva lay before us.

We were quickly released from the customs dock and directed urgently to our anchorage at the Royal Suva Yacht Club. Once there, we immediately laid out our heaviest anchors made fast with the stoutest chain and rope. No sooner had we snugged them into the mud and rock bottom securing us to earth, than the red cyclone flags were launched from the Yacht Club poles. By the time our dinghy was lashed upside down on top of the pier, the trees were already bending over the rooftops. The sound of breaking and tearing had begun and the crack of branches whipped over our heads. We ran to the Club, trying to dodge the flying debris swirling in the air.

The Club was elbow-to-elbow with noisy, anxious sailors, all seeking refuge from the ominous storm. I nudged my way in between two crusty old salts and heard the one sailor say, "She'll be ninety knots in the hour, mate."

...and that was the bloody truth.

Chapter Eight

BETRAYAL

I was set ashore in Suva. Not long after our arrival, Edward delivered the dictum. I knew by the way he carried his pipe close to his lips that there was something serious brewing. The pipe was a civilized weapon. It allowed one the luxury of choosing words carefully, while delivering the bad news with a kind of rhythmic justice.

"Could we have a word?" Edward inhaled slowly.

I pushed aside the huge dacron sail I was stitching and sat down next to him on the coach roof. William and Clari were ashore, buying supplies for our departure.

"It seems things are not quite what I had hoped." Edward exhaled a draft of smoke. "Clari will not let this matter of you rest. As you know, she is quite capable of making life unbearable for all of us." Edward ground his teeth on the pipe stem. "Besides, I've just had a letter from my uncle, Lord Hadridge. He reiterated, in no uncertain terms, that I am responsible for getting Clari safely to New Zealand. You see, I had promised—"

I cut off Edward's soliloquy in mid-sentence. "I have to leave the boat, don't I?"

"I was hoping you might consider flying to Auckland to join us there, after she's gone." Edward momentarily withdrew the pipe-stem. "You're an excellent crew and I've enjoyed your company."

What a strange invitation, I thought. Edward had rescued me from prison, now I must leave, and when all is well again, I can return! I am an "excellent crew" but no better than Clari! I sat quietly, mulling over the inequity of the situation, while Edward puffed nervously on his pipe. The rising smoke momentarily blurred my vision of him.

"I think I should get my things together. I'd like to leave before they come back to the boat."

My life fitted easily into one backpack. Nevertheless, there was the small matter of my speedy departure, which I had neglected to consider. I had to wait for William and Clari to return with the dinghy. I sat on the coach roof with my bag propped up against my leg, waiting... waiting and remembering.

All the memories of the past six months hovered around me like vultures trying to pick apart my heart and soul. Tomai's memory was still close by, circling me, just as the mysterious voices in the night had surrounded me. The steely gray fin of the shark speeding toward me, a wave crashing over my head, making love to William, our laughter, the hard press of the sun rubbing against our shoulders... somehow, it had all gone wrong.

I had no idea what to do next, except look for another crewing position, though the prospects looked grim. The cyclone season was well upon us and most of the boats had already headed south toward safety.

Finally, I saw William and Clari untie the dinghy from the dock and make their way out toward *Patience*.

"I say, the markets are splendid. You can talk the Indians down to nothing." Clari flung her sacks full of fresh bread, flour and sugar over the rails. "I daresay, I think we got the best of them. Don't you, William?"

William was busy securing the dinghy and didn't seem to hear Clari's question. Instead he caught sight of my bag and stood in the dinghy staring at me.

"What's all this?" William pointed to my bag.

"I'm moving ashore. Would you mind rowing me back to the Club?"

"Don't be silly, there's no cause for this. Hang on, let's have a chat with Edward."

Clari was in high spirits. "I should think it's for the best, don't you, William? My goodness, we could use the extra storage space."

I stood between William and the companionway explaining that I had already said goodbye to Edward. I asked him again, in a very controlled and quiet manner, if he would please take me ashore. He understood then that something irrevocable had transpired.

We both got in the dinghy and headed toward land. I thought for a moment that Clari was turning to bid me a polite farewell. Instead, she called out to William, "I shouldn't be too long if I were you, we've got storing to do."

And so the shackles were broken open and I was freed from Clari, forever.

As we rowed ashore, I explained the circumstances of my leaving to William. He listened, displaying neither surprise nor regret at the outcome of the voyage.

"Never mind, at least you're free of her now. You can fly to Auckland and we'll meet up there, eh? Get a flat, away from that ol' cow. Gawd, it's going to be a miserable trip without you, bloody twenty days if we're lucky."

For a moment, I felt a faint glimmer of hope. I thought I'd caught a glimpse of the old William, before his leg had festered and before the tensions between Clari and me had become unbearable. I was tempted to believe him. Perhaps I could fly to Auckland where we would take up our journey again, without Clari.

After landing ashore, we sat dangling our feet over the muddy bay-water. Shaken by the constant buffeting of another tropical disturbance, I felt that engulfing wave of loneliness wash over me again. William offered little comfort.

"Look, the weather's turning, we'll be off soon." Avoiding my gaze, William looked back at the boat. "Write down my sister's number in Auckland, she'll look after you 'til we get there."

While I rummaged through my pack for a pen, burying my head, I asked if "soon" meant today.

William continued talking cheerfully. "Oh, I daresay, there's no good sense in waiting."

"Did you know — did you know Edward wanted me off the boat?"

"Blast, it's all dismal. Absolutely dismal. But I'll see you in Auckland shortly, eh." William kissed me quickly on the cheek.

"Well, I must be off." He started untying the dinghy. "Clari will get after me if I don't get back. See you in Auckland." He waved from the dinghy.

I watched forlornly as William shoved off and rowed hurriedly back toward *Patience*.

From the sea wall, I could see my former shipmates move about the deck, storing the dinghy, readying the sails. At any moment, I thought William might make a gesture that I could return — there was a change of heart, all the ill will was mended. But after an hour's preparation, William hauled in the anchor and *Patience* turned her bow toward open sea. No one looked landward. They had their gaze fixed on their new destination, New Zealand.

I spent several weeks on Viti Levu trying to find some direction. Through a series of outlandish coincidences, I was invited to stay at the American Peace Corps house perched atop a hill overlooking the harbor. It seemed a stroke of good luck to find a bed out of the rain, under the auspices of such well-intentioned young men — all seven of them.

They were an interesting lot. Mostly Americans, unremarkable in looks, they all wore heavy spectacles which seemed to define their dispositions. Their mission was completely dedicated to the capture and study of the tsetse fly. From what I observed, by day, their task was to lay on their backs with their shirts rolled up and wait for a tsetse fly to land on them. One corpsman was to lure the fly in for a landing, while the other was to capture the itinerant fly in a glass vial. It seemed all research was done mostly on one's backside from the comfortable environs atop the hill.

While the insect vials remained mostly vacant from one day to the next, empty beer cans were successfully piled high throughout the tepid evenings, as the motley crew debated the day's lack of success. With arms and legs flung over the edges of stained couches, the young researchers strained to hear the buzz of their next victim, and failing that, they continued their tsetse discussions ad nauseam. Unfortunately, I had little to offer to their discussions. I began to understand how the dreaded fly could induce sleeping sickness; the mere mention of it made me drowsy.

It was during one of those late night discussions that talk of our new President-elect caught my attention. While the researchers were excitedly debating his foreign policy, I hedged around trying to find out his name!

"So you guys think he's a pretty good guy?" Somebody made a joke about peanut farming and I realized I couldn't piece together the inside joke. I hadn't seen a newspaper since leaving Tahiti. We often tried to get international news on our radio on board *Patience*, but the BBC broadcasts were too garbled with static.

I waited. I waited for nearly an hour before someone said, "I hear Carter is a big supporter of the Peace Corps, so we should be fine over here..."

I didn't find out much more until I read a scathing letter from my father, fuming about having a Democrat back in office. I didn't have much of an opinion either way. The first time I was old enough to vote, I had voted for Nixon and that didn't turn out too well. Politics and religion were high on my list of topics to avoid.

Aside from my meager political and tsetse observations, I spent most days roaming around the stifling city of Suva, never quite feeling comfortable. The sickeningly sweet smell of burning copra permeated every street and grimy alleyway. It was ironic to think that the end result of all the burning and soot might be a coconut oil perfume of the finest scent.

I enjoyed the Fijians. They are a welcoming and physically stunning group of people. A smile always seemed poised at the edge of their dark, thick lips and their eyes — their luminous, coal-fired eyes reflected an unbound spirit. For the most part, the Fijians were farmers or rural workers, preferring country life to the city. I admired the Fijian women I saw in town, who happily went about their work as nannies and maids for the wealthier homeowners — many of them British expats. The Fijian nannies played with the children, like children, and so spent the day laughing and giggling through their chores.

As Clari so smartly observed, the Indians were very shrewd merchants. Small and wiry with slicked-back hair, they maintained a constant stream of chatter at their market stalls, always bargaining, always trying to foist their wares on tourists like myself. It seemed to me the two nationalities were a discordant mix, not unlike the French and Tahitians in Polynesia.

As each day passed, I grew more anxious to be away, to be at sea, to hear the rush of water instead of the ceaseless prattle of bargaining. I wanted to head in any direction, other than be land bound. After a week at the Peace Corps enclave, I left my entomologist countrymen to their research and boarded a rickety open-air bus headed for Nandi. The terrain changed almost immediately, as we moved away from the sooty city toward the less populated mountain regions. The air cooled appreciably as the wooden-sided crate rumbled and rattled its way up the deeply scarred inclines, each turn looking more impossible than the last. The ancient bus with its hard-chined cabin and stiff wooden benches tossed us mercilessly about, reminding me of a raging storm at sea. I was coming up bruised at every turn. As we reached the rain sheds of the foothills, we were all but awash in our own muddy sea. With my backside, elbows and knees equally bruised, we came to a merciful halt in front of a small wooden structure — a lean-to of sorts. One by one, the handful of Fijians and Indians filed out and I soon realized we had arrived at a primitive rest stop. It was within the confines of this stench-ridden temple that I decided on another change of course.

The bus driver was happy to dispose of me, assuring me that at some point in the day the Suva bus would be by. Having a solid grasp of Pacific time, I doubted that and prepared to hike and camp my way back to Suva.

After a few days of beachcombing, I drifted aimlessly back to the Royal Suva Yacht Club. It was my only point of reference in all of Fiji.

I could blame the friendly Fijian barman, I suppose, for my next deviation in course. He welcomed me back to the bar with a wide smile and listened to my revised travel plans. Laughing, always laughing, he pointed toward a rattan chair with someone slouched deep inside it. The Fijian "topped up" my glass of beer saying, "That sailor thar, Ma'am, he been waitin' and waitin'."

"Waitin' for what?"

"A sailor, Ma'am. He need another sailor to get going... away from the storms."

I wanted to get going too. Gathering up my beer and a rum chaser for the camouflaged sailor, I headed toward him.

It was a mistake that nearly cost me my life.

Chapter Nine

THE WAR ZONE

"So, what took ya so long, I've been waitin' fer bloody hours?" slurred the Irishman, as he glanced up at me.

I told the surly sailor my name and my hope of catching a ride to New Zealand.

"Well, I've been sittin' here for bloody hours. You don't look Kiwi. Awh, never mind, chip in for supplies and we're away. M'name's Mick," he grumbled. I shrugged my shoulders, apparently confirming my new crewing position. Mick raised his arm in a toast and launched in on his sailing adventures, single-handing across the Pacific.

Had I been more cautious or less desperate (or had more money), I would have turned away from the prickly drunk. I should have taken the line-up of empty pint glasses as a warning sign and gone looking for the Nandi bus again. But instead, I made up excuses for him: he probably drinks too much because he's Irish; he drinks a little more because he's a sailor; maybe he has one more because he's a loner. I told myself that away from the seduction of land he'd sober up; if he'd already sailed 6,000 miles by himself, surely he could sail a few more downwind to New Zealand. Once again, I was dead wrong.

Rearranging my chair in several positions, I thought I could easily back away from the situation, no harm done. But the desire to get back to sea and away from the cyclone belt kept prodding me along.

From a distance, Mick had looked like a scruffy school kid thrown out of class and put in detention, but up close he was more complex. Ringlets of russet hair fell over his face in every direction, leaving no clear path toward his eyes. Had I gotten a decent view of his eyes, I would have left him there, slouched in his chair and on the brink of despair. I was also swayed by the decoy of freckles peppering his skin with tinctures of red and oranges, like the blazing sunset over Moorea. It cast him with a touch of boyish innocence, something I must have accidentally superimposed over his character, because he never showed a trace of it from that moment on. I was wrong again.

Mick had been waiting for a sailor to meet him at the bar and I had inadvertently filled the position. I looked over at the barman scrubbing the bar-top, still chuckling to himself. He was used to shuffling the deck for the hands of Fate.

And my Fate was sealed that simply.

The day we set off from Suva was remarkable solely for the brutal stare of that hideously violent sky. I took it to be a bad omen and I was not wrong on that account.

Our sea was benign. It lay like an enormous quagmire below our keel, slowing our own recklessly plotted destiny. From our first day at sea and for all the days thereafter, our conversation was minimal. Therefore I neglected to gather much more than the barest essentials about the sketchy past of my skipper Mick. I guessed the Irishman was thirty-ish by the mention of his military duty in Vietnam. In a feeble attempt to ease my fears about sailing with him, I asked him where his boat had been built. Unfortunately the answer did not ease my fears in the least. He had built the thirty-two-foot cement boat in his aunt's backyard in Santa Barbara, California, with the hope of sailing alone around the world. He had decided to take on crew only to help him through the shipping lanes, which passed between Fiji and New Zealand.

Sobering up did not have the impact I had hoped for. In fact, Mick was even more sullen. Given to long sulky silences, he rarely spoke and I mistakenly attributed this to a placid nature, or perhaps, an introspective bent. At first, I didn't mind this idiosyncrasy in the least. I fell into it myself without ever divulging any of my own personal details beyond my name and where my family lived. It was as if we were ghosts, set upon that sea for all eternity.

We floated along on a mild sea of delusions; gray, desultory, moody gray. We kept on until the wind died away altogether, bringing our cement hull to a halt. I contemplated the whole idea of sailing on a cement boat at great length and found it rather mystifying. How did that bit of powder and water manage to float anyway? What if we were holed by a whale? I had heard many accounts of whales tossing boats about and much more recently than Melville's great white. The curvy, bumpy gray of our hull made for a perfect match for some love-lorn whale in mating season.

We floated. We drifted. We rocked. It could have been an agreeable state, but it wasn't. With the boat upright cooking should be easier, sails could be mended and all the routine chores accomplished. There should even be some spare time to read, sleep and daydream. However, that was not the case. While there was not a breath of wind, the still-life reflections were cracked and broken by a huge sea slapping against our inanimate hull. This added an eerie cacophony of noises to our dispirited vessel. The halyards clanged against the mast with a nervous ping... ping... ping. They had all gone slack as the sails collapsed into stale folds, which hung lifeless on the mast. The shrouds snapped irritatingly as the boat yawed and rolled on the huge sea swell. With no canvas left to steady her, she pitched uncontrollably, floundered, wallowed. It was like being caught in the grip of a terrible death-throe with no chance of commuting the sentence. We sat in silent despair as the sea sent strong warnings of another threatening cyclone.

Hour after hour through the night, through the vigilance of day, we waited, but there was only the sounds of clinking, clanging, chinking, clacking, pinging — a nervous spasming of our entire being in that still, innocent sea.

We were well into the foul mood of our fourth trapped day when my captain chose to unsettle the gods, decry the seas and threaten me. Mick had come on deck wearing a blazing red robe, which swirled about him like a matador's cape. This robe, which I didn't see either before or after the incident, had no belt and hid nothing of the man's bare, slender body. I could see the muscles on his lean legs strung as tightly as the stay wires he clung to. As he moved about the boat, the cape swirled around his frenzied body, his chest heaving. He gasped for air as if the stillness was bereft of oxygen. His jaws were clenched so severely that the edges of the bones seemed ready to pierce through the flesh of his cheeks. His eyes were as wild as an unbroken stallion at tether.

It was my watch. Before Mick's sudden appearance, I had been aft at the tiller, checking the steering vane and compass. At first, I thought he was playing at something, perhaps going to enact a bit of Shakespeare to pass the time, but I soon realized Mick was trapped in his own tragedy.

He stood at the mast, madly yelling a litany of curses aimed first at the heavens: "Goddamn you, goddamn you to hell. I hate you, bloody Jesus. I goddamn hate you..." He swore on and on into that soundless void of barren, bleak sky.

Then Mick raged toward me. With his red cape swirling behind him, he grabbed the gutting knife from inside the companionway and just as quickly leapt into the cockpit next to me. Shoving the cold, metal knife blade up against my throat, Mick slowly, tormentingly, stroked the flesh of my neck with its razor-sharp metal edge. I sat stunned and motionless.

"You... you goddamn Americans. I'm Irish, don't you see... Irish!" Mick ranted on. "I didn't belong in your bloody dirty war. Do you understand? Ireland is my home. I don't need your bloody country..." Mick moved the knife up along the ridge of my nose. My eyes locked onto its flickering metallic edge.

I was not listening closely to what he said, I didn't need to. The knife, rocking from my left ear to my right, sent out a clear enough message. It played like the ticktock of a grandfather clock, counting off the diminishing seconds of my life.

"Go below." Mick pricked my neck with the weapon. "I can't stand that bloody racket. Do you hear me? Goddamnit, it's too damn noisy."

I tried pleading with him. "I'll stop it Mick. I'll tie off the halyards and they won't make so much noise."

"Shut up and go below!" Mick grabbed me by the shoulder with one hand, while prodding me in the back with the tip of the blade. He shoved me roughly into my bunk and stood over me with the knife's deadly serration brushing my skin like the jaws of my demon shark. The cabin was dank and breathless. An involuntary shiver began in my arms and slowly overtook me. I repressed a desire to gasp for air, desperate to hold in my fear. I tried to distract his rage, but I only fueled it.

"I know what you mean," I stuttered helplessly. "My brothers went—"

"*Fuck you, Fuck you.* You don't know anything. Do you know anything about war? Tell me, do you know a fuckin' thing about war? Christ, all the bodies, all the blood. I don't know how many I shot. BANG!" Mick dug the knife into my temple. Brandishing it like a pistol he shouted, "*BANG, BANG, BANG,*" each time digging the knife a notch deeper.

I finally realized Mick was no longer on a boat in the middle of the ocean; he was back in Vietnam. The ocean swells were now bunkers where the enemy hid, and the sharp pinging of the shrouds was gunfire. Most terrifying of all, I was the enemy.

I could feel a stream of blood flowing down my cheek like heavy red tears. I was so locked in fear, I couldn't have moved in any direction had I the will to.

Mick "shot" me with the knife over and over again. After each BANG he rambled on, trying to string together his gruesome war images. Through each scenario, I was the enemy. He had to shoot me first. That much was clear to him. He had to shoot me first.

Suddenly Mick was hit by a stray bullet, not from any weapon I had, but from his own memory. He doubled over, clutching his chest, screaming in pain, "Christ, help me! Somebody help me."

The knife slipped from his grip. Slumping onto the bunk, he cried. His body contorted in pain, convulsing with each breath. The assault had crippled him.

Each heave and awful sigh of the boat seared straight through me. I feared it might jostle him into another dangerous reverie. I lay in wait while the sea held us both captive. The stale air reeked of violence.

Chapter Ten

THE CYCLONE

The edge of the cyclone was upon us in moments, the waves white-tipped and furious. The wind reached a blinding rage, frothing the tips of waves, shrouding us in salt spray. My eyes stung from the constant battering of saltwater.

Mick was back on deck. Foul weather pants had replaced his red robe. He seemed to have no memory of what had transpired between us. He ignored me completely and went forward to unwind the tangled jib halyard from the headstay.

Without any warning, Mick was thrown forward by the force of a wave lifting our stern. He missed grabbing the lifelines altogether and only managed to catch the edge of the storm jib as he went over the side.

As Mick was pulled underwater by the force of the boat sliding down the face of a wave, his eyes widened with terror. He was flogged mercilessly against the side of the boat, bashing into it as the sea swell rolled under us, momentarily lifting him out of the water. The heavy hull then crashed down into the next wave, diving into it with a tremendous surging power. The froth of sea exploded around us, the boat driving on, rushing, as the sea rushed. Mick never yelled for my help, but struggled senselessly to find his own way back on board. He couldn't hold on much longer.

I stood motionless, held back by an inclination to let the sea take him. I could handle the boat well enough myself. I could sail her safely to shore with no more knife-wielding threats from my deranged skipper. It was only the slightest hesitation, a quick flashing thought. Yet I watched calmly as his hands slipped slowly along the sail's edge. It was his last handhold on existence.

I imagined a cold wave curling over him, sucking him toward eternity, crushing his anger, destroying his burdened soul. Then instinct overtook me. I lay flush on the deck and offered my arm as a lifeline. This gave Mick just enough leverage to pull himself back on deck to safety. No words spoken.

I crawled back to the cockpit. The waves had grown into small mountains, overtaking us from astern, driving us harder into the sunken belly of doom.

We slowly lashed down the sails, which were flailing and tearing in the tempest. Each move was so laborious and calculated, I felt like a mountain climber assailing the heights without oxygen. A heavy exhaustion blurred every movement.

My body and mind suddenly met a blank numbness. It was like vertigo, a feeling of falling without being able to stop oneself. Blindly, I felt my way below deck to my bunk. Every time I opened my eyes the cabin started spinning around me. I could barely make out the numbers on the anemometer above my head. The needle had risen from forty to sixty-five knots of wind. All the sounds of fury had merged into one hideous howling. As I lay there, I was enveloped by a consummate fear. My world became a tunnel of seesawing objects fading in and out of view. Terrifying images besieged me. I could still feel the razor-sharp edge of Mick's knife jabbing my skin and the demonic look of pure hatred in his eyes. Thrown in every direction by the chaotic swell, I covered my head, protecting myself from the constant assault.

At the height of the storm's fury, Mick descended the companionway. He was soaked to the bone and looked amazingly refreshed by the brutal terror of it all. Leaning over the navigation table with a flashlight, he stared at our *unmarked* path on the soiled, wet chart. The fact that we did not exist at any point on the entire chart of the South Pacific did not seem to disturb him in the least.

The skipper, my captain in command, had neglected to log any information concerning our location. Making matters worse, he had forbidden me access to the chart table and the navigation tools.

Mick turned his glazed stare toward me. "You scared?" he asked with a half-cocked smile.

Tears welled in the corners of my eyes and streamed down my cheeks. I hesitated, then wailed, "Yes, I'm scared. We don't even know where we are. Of course I'm scared."

His mood swung back toward murderous. He slammed the dividers down on the navigation table. "Goddamnit, I know where we are," he yelled, incensed by my accusation. "Don't you ever say I don't know where we are."

The truth was he couldn't possibly have known where we were. We'd had no sun since the beginning of our journey, so Mick hadn't taken any sunsights. He hadn't kept a shred of information concerning our progress: our compass course, speed, time, distance — nothing at all. Our chart was blank, proof of his sheer insanity.

For safety's sake, I retreated into myself. I knew that above all else, I must steer clear of his anger. It was far too dangerous for both of us. I chose instead the well-padded security of my bunk and the obscurity of a desperate sleep. It was not really a sleep, but more a closing down of all my senses. I pulled myself inward, where the beat of my heart and the pumping of blood and oxygen through my veins were the only reassuring sounds I could hear.

That night I had no comforting visions, no consoling thoughts. God seemed too distant and harsh to pray to. How could He possibly hear me above the tumult anyway? There was nothing left but to keep battling despair.

Violently rocked in the catacomb of darkness, I feared the sea as much as I feared Mick. One of those enormous walls of whitewater could easily rise over the stern quarter and cascade into our cockpit in a fatal ambush. I feared drowning in that dark inescapable coffin.

I won't say then that I slept, but rather that I waited in some altered form of consciousness for the light to chase the demons away.

Mick's footsteps overhead were my first welcome to the day. I rubbed my eyes and pulled myself up the companionway to find a chaos of lines, halyards and shredded sailcloth collapsed in defeat over the deck. The wind had proved to be a bitter enemy, cutting the sails free from their lashings. The mainsail had two long horizontal gashes, which meant hours of stitching. Looking over our battlefield of disarray, I knew all the halyards would have to be retrieved and rerun.

I suddenly recognized hope in the middle of the fray. Mick went aloft to untangle the mess of wires and lines at the top of the mast. As he swung at forty-five-degree angles over the undulating swell, I saw a bit of luck in our disaster. Creeping below deck, I went straight to the navigation table with the anxious hope of plotting our dead-reckoning position before his return to deck. I had carefully stored all the pertinent information in my memory for safekeeping: our course before the storm, our speed, the current, drift and direction. Bending over the chart, I reconstructed our journey as quickly as I could.

I swore at Mick as I tried to steady the dividers in my hand. Why hadn't he kept a dead-reckoning position? It was suicidal not to. Those thoughts got tangled in the simplest calculations. The time it took me to plot one single line of position seemed excruciatingly long.

Finally, I plotted a point on the chart that seemed to make sense. I guessed that the cyclone had pushed us north of our intended track to Auckland. Considering the force of the storm and our previous course, I placed us just off the northern tip of New Zealand.

I heard Mick back on deck. My heart raced at the sound of his footfall. Hurriedly, I tried to jam all the tools in the navigation table, but a wave caught me off-guard and the tools went crashing in every direction. In another moment, he was peering down the companionway.

"What're ya doin' down there?" he yelled at me from above. You're supposed to be stitchin' that main."

I jerked back from the chart table, trying to distance myself from the evidence. Seeing the parallel ruler, divider and plotter scattered on the cabinsole threw Mick into a renewed frenzy. He grabbed the hatchcover and swung down over the steps. Landing next to me, he stared savagely. "Keep your goddamn chicken-scratch off my charts. You hear me?" Raising his forearm, he swiped me across the chin with his fist.

That was the moment of reckoning. The force of his fist on my chin knocked the horrid memory loose. I felt it again, a second time. It was the memory, the other time in my life I had known physical violence; the only other time I had been hit across the face.

> *The man whose ugly visage chases me across oceans, who holds me prisoner against my will, who tries to suffocate me, camouflaging his anger in sadistic lovemaking rituals. Husband. Murderer of Innocence. I run. I keep running. But I cannot outrun memory.*

I felt an ugly hate sear me, an anger so consuming that I suddenly felt capable of anything. The gutting knife was not far from my grip, but I held myself steady. That was Mick's weapon. I had to depend on mine. His mind was confused; mine was clear — I wanted to survive.

"Don't you ever go near— I'll take care of that right now." Mick scowled as he flew toward the sextant box. "I'll make damn sure — damn fucking sure — you don't get near it."

Mick shook the sextant box as if it was full of cheap silverware instead of the delicately calibrated instrument upon which our lives depended. He tucked the key to the box somewhere underneath his bunk.

The last and cruelest blow was yet to come. Mick turned to me with a cocky smile slowly unraveling from the left side of his mouth toward the right. I didn't know what to expect. He picked up a pencil and holding it in front of my nose, he laughed. "You think you're so damn bloody smart, don't you?" With his newly found weapon, Mick erased all my computations: the point, the plotted line, our position... everything. Our existence in the South Pacific was gone in an instant. Satisfied with his final act of madness, he returned topside.

I stared blankly at the chart. *It doesn't matter. I can reconstruct it again... and again, if I have to.* I clenched my fist and pounded the top of the navigation table. *Damn you. You idiot. You idiot! Idiot for sailing with a madman. Damn fool for not heeding the cyclone warnings... Idiot for ever thinking of following William to New Zealand... Fool... Damn stupid fool of a woman...*

On and on I went, berating myself, hating Mick, brutalized by memory and cursing that damnable sea.

Chapter Eleven

LAND HO!

I moved around the boat under a dark spell — mournful, dispirited. There was nothing hopeful to grab onto. I felt powerless against Mick's unpredictable rages and powerless against the sea. I could see no answer to it all, except sighting land, and there was no land in sight.

Leaning forlornly over the lifelines, I searched the horizon in vain for any hint of land. Fatigue had numbed my senses so severely that my fear had become a dull ache. My strength was so diminished by the constant vigilance, I felt stripped of all my defenses. There was nothing left to fight with.

My dreary thoughts were suddenly interrupted by the sight of a strange streak of light in the distance. I stared into the graveyard sea with the stare of a fool, not knowing what it was I was staring at. A flutter, a flap, the soaring wing tip of a bird skipping over the wave tops? No, not a bird, not gliding, not dancing off waves; it was a boat pounding over the whitewater! My eyes strained through the coarse-grained gray. The sails rose, disappeared and rose again. With a soothing pleasure I watched the small yacht approach us. It was our first sight of anything not water or sky in twenty days.

"Look, Jesus, look! What fuckin' good luck. What damn fuckin' good luck." Mick's voice rang through my ears like clashing cymbals.

"We'll get a position from them and be on our way. Damn, I knew we were just off Auckland." Mick continued irrationally, "They're probably just heading out, eh, just out of the harbor."

Against all my better instincts, I began to believe we were saved and would find our way.

"Ahoy," hailed my demonic skipper, as if our guests would not notice a mad Irishman leaping up and down on the deck of a canoe-shaped craft.

"Ahoy there," a deep voice floated back through the misty gray. There were two people on board, both suited up in their foul weather gear and indistinguishable from each other, except for the shaggy black beard of one sailor.

It was a rocky beginning as they disappeared at the count of five in between the troughs of waves, taking their words with them. Nevertheless, we waved on and on as if we were all blood brothers and sisters reunited after a long separation.

"Hello, hello," came their call to us. "Terrible storm," the bearded sailor shouted.

Mick echoed back to them, "Aye, terrible."

Their craft, a solid little yacht just bigger than our own thirty-two footer, rose and fell over the waves with the most uncomfortable motion. Our neighbor steadied himself against the shrouds and yelled over, "Can you give us your position? The storm... we need to check our course... no sunsight for days."

I chuckled to myself, "Twenty degrees off the rhumbline to hell, and welcome to it!"

I could feel the energy whir about Mick. He needed an answer, a guess, a vague supposition.

Mick launched back absurdly, "Say again. Can't hear you. Just out of Auckland, eh?"

He'd heard the sailor all right, but Mick would never admit that he hadn't kept a dead-reckoning position since leaving Fiji.

They were heading into a twenty-foot sea and we were running off it. As they were knocked back from making headway, we barreled along, sliding down the wave faces. Then they disappeared. I suppose it was better than admitting that nobody knew where we were.

We stood our watches, fixing our eyes on the compass, then to the horizon, expectant of that first glimpse of land. Mick was convinced it would be Auckland. I prayed we'd see North Cape, the northern tip of New Zealand, soon. I knew it was the only bit of land between us and the Roaring Forties.

I came to my morning watch, bumped out of my bunk by the knock of a wave. It felt all wrong. Waves have a consistency like a heartbeat, pulsing strong and rhythmic. So when the wave threw me in a new direction, I took it as a warning. I put on every bit of damp clothing I had left, threw on my foulies, and struggled up the companionway. The vessel lurched again, running the gunwales underwater.

I came on deck to find Mick pinned between the twin stays at the stern. My skipper's stare was so vacant that I assumed all reason had left him. There was no hint of land. I was quite alone on that forsaken sea; my skipper had finally abandoned himself. There was nothing I could do but wait for his physical collapse. I knew his sleeplessness was my final weapon. I knew by his mumblings that he was delirious from lack of sleep and sleep would soon overtake him.

On our twenty-second morning at sea a streak of blinding white light struck through the porthole, piercing my eyes. The light was so brilliant that I could not get my eyes to focus beyond it. I dragged myself topside, groping for the rails and rubbing my eyes as I went. The light hit me again, harder this time. There... the sun... blazing through the hard cleft in the severed mountain chain... LAND HO! But no, I thought, I must not speak a word. Mick had finally succumbed to sleep that night. He was deeply asleep. All my efforts turned toward taking a sunsight and finding our location. During the night, I had found the key to the sextant box, which Mick had hid from me. I had only to carefully lift the sextant from the box he kept on the shelf above his head. I held my breath, which made my hands tremble as I raised the sextant over his head. He didn't stir. Quickly I took the time of day and the sunsight, and finished the calculations. I plotted our position, putting us just off North Cape and the northern tip of New Zealand. We had missed Mick's destination by hundreds of miles.

"We've spotted land," I announced carefully in plural form, while tucking the calculations into the inner lining of my woolen underwear.

"Land, land?" Mick dashed up the companionway, shoving me aside with the burning glaze of a madman. He looked landward with a blank expression for a long time. I knew he was doubting what he saw. Long fingers of light split the sharply carved cliffs. The rolling hills swept back from the sea in wavelike formations as far as our vision could see. It was decidedly not a city, not civilization, but a point of land I knew from my calculations to be the very edge of our existence. Had we sailed farther on, had we gone another night, we would have gone past the northern tip of New Zealand, sailing into the Roaring Forties and on toward Antarctica. My charted position put us at "Three Kings, the one spot on earth to steer clear of..." as I'd overheard a gritty sailor say one afternoon back at the Royal Suva Yacht Club. Hard of hearing, the old weather-scared sailor had yelled at me:

"Tis a mean bit of ocean, and meaner still, just there, where three oceans meet... just there, Three Kings." The sailor had pressed his stubby forefinger over a stained spot on his chart, shaking the map of the ocean as if he was cursing it and me at the same time. "And worst of all," he had said even louder, "the shallows build the steepest mountains of sea I've ever seen."

Mick and I had sailed right into the deadly triangle of oceans. And, by God, it was a mean bit of sea.

A fine white-winged albatross dipped over our bow, soaring around us as if guardian of our Fate. I sat feasting my eyes on every rise and fall of land, on every shade of purple, blue, gray, brown and green, that was not in liquid form, but rather a solid, still, immovable land mass, which I would soon be standing on.

By day's end we had reached a sea-worn pass leading into a bay strewn with small lush islands. The Bay of Islands expanded before my eyes. Small pockets of homes were nestled in coves. Farmhouses were scattered over soft undulating hills, so lavishly carpeted. Fat cows grazed down the gentle slopes of hills to the water's edge.

This was a land I had never known before, but it seemed so familiar to me. From a distance at sea, I recognized the rural pastures of my youth; the sweet smell of rich green grass washed over me. The freshness of the air brought an intensification of every smell and earthen color. After the suffocating closeness of the boat, my senses tingled with life again. I gulped in the air like someone rising to the surface after nearly drowning. I was safe. Mick could no longer assail me. The sea fell into a gentle pattern as the wind followed us from astern. My body trembled with renewed strength. Tears streamed down my cheeks.

"Land, land ho!" I yelled triumphantly.

Chapter Twelve

THE MAGPIE

I was ready to go ashore as soon as our lines hit the dock, but I was bound to the boat, waiting for the arrival of the New Zealand customs officials. Mick sat opposite me at the settee, hanging his head like a sorry pup.

"I know yer upset with me. I don't really... I can't really... remember exactly." Mick struggled pathetically for an explanation. "Look, we'll go ashore and I'll buy ya a beer."

Shaking furiously, I yelled, "Buy me a beer. BUY ME A BEER! Are you crazy? We could have been lost out there, gone, dead. BUY ME A BEER!"

I was about to launch into an abusive tirade when I heard the two officials clamber on board. Still shaking, I begged them to be quick about their business. Watching me with concern the tallest of the two men turned and asked, "What's gone on here, luv? Are you right?"

I drew in a deep breath, wavering between two inclinations — silence, or shouting, "HE'S PSYCHO!" I took the middle road.

"I've got to get off this boat. NOW!"

I tried to calm myself so as not to arouse their suspicions and be detained longer. The concerned official watched my every move closely. "Look, luv, if you have something to tell us, better do it now, eh?"

I tried repressing my anger. "We don't get along, that's all. I can't stand being near him another minute."

The officials both looked relieved. The stubby fellow gave out a hearty laugh. "Awh yeah, seen this one a hundred times. Well, give us a look at your passport, luv, and you're off."

Weaving on legs unused to land, I set off along a dirt road. To where? Other than the geographic location of the Bay of Islands on a nautical chart, I didn't really know where I was, or where I was going.

The very first place I came to was a campground laid out before me like an invitation to heaven. It was as if it had been created expressly for my visit. There was not a soul in sight. No one to collect the camping fee I didn't have, and no one to disrupt a sinfully long, hot shower. I needed a fair bit of water to rinse the twenty-two days of sea grit off my leathered skin. While surreptitiously washing and rinsing my hair three times, I half-sang the chorus to a Bob Dylan song within the echoing brick walls of the shower stall:

> "*How does it feel*
> *How does it feel*
> *To be on your own*
> *With no direction home*
> *Like a complete unknown*
> *Like a rolling stone?*"

After an infinitely refreshing shower, I placed a collect call to Auckland, hoping to find William at his sister's house.

"William," I whispered to the sky, "be there, please, be there."

A woman answered the phone. I assumed, without questioning her, that she was William's sister. Her voice sounded distant and confused. "Who?" she queried me twice before a hesitant recognition changed her tone. "Awh, the American girl. Righto, luv, I'm sorry. I'm holding a gaggle of mail for you. William's got himself a flat with his girlfriend... hasn't given me the number yet."

"Girlfriend? Are you sure? I was supposed to meet him in Auckland. I'm the one... we were going to get an apartment together, you see..."

There was a long pause, followed by a clearing of her throat. "Well, I am sorry, luv, but William's with a New Zealander now. Met her at the pub as soon as he stepped ashore. You're welcome to stop by for your mail, of course, but I must ring off now. Sorry luv, ta da." The phone clicked.

My voice trailed behind hers, "But— I was— the one."

I never saw William again.

After picking up my mail and cashing the check my parents had sent me as a Christmas gift, I put one foot after another and walked. I hiked over the North Island, took the ferry to Picton on the South Island and headed farther south. Hoping to forget William? No, I understood by then that we were not of the sea any longer. It was the sea that had brought us together; on land we were a different sort.

I searched in vain for something to fill my soul. Why was I so empty? Why did I have to keep moving so incessantly? Why did I have to journey so far away from my family, following some undefined path to nowhere?

Exploring the southern shoreline, I wandered along the sharply pebbled coast. Mesmerized by the brilliant, ferocious sea that surrounds those arcadian islands, I listened joyfully to the bark and snore of enormous sea lions basking in the chilly summer sun. I followed the marching sea gulls lining the shoreline, awaiting a gust of wind to lift them skyward. I waited too, hoping the wind would take my flagging spirit soaring with them. Time passed unnoticed — days, weeks, perhaps months.

One day I left the coastal route altogether. Cutting through droves of comical sheep and lazy fat cows, I crossed directly over enormous, unfenced grasslands. The open pastures gradually turned into unkempt fields of low thicket. Gazing at the map, I became intent on finding a secluded lake before nightfall. Indifferent to the changing terrain, I ignored the increasingly heavy slosh of mud, reaching above my boot-tops.

The cool evening mist began to settle into the marshy lowlands, fenced in all directions by harshly nettled brush. I slowly became aware that I could no longer follow my watch's compass direction and that the ground underneath me was thick, deepening mud. I knew by the sound of lapping water that the lake was not far off, yet every step forward brought me deeper into a quagmire. At first only my ankles were submerged. Then, with the next step, I sank into the muck up to my knees. Looking back to retrace my steps, every evidence of my path had been sucked into the devouring brown mud. I remembered with a sudden horror the quicksand I had once experienced as a child. Like some giant ghoul, the mud had swallowed my canoe paddle, leaving me to drift helplessly among the reeds of a narrow estuary.

Just as the thick mud threatened to pull me down, I stretched flat on top of it and dragged myself from reed to reed through the muck. I finally found firmer ground. Rolling onto my back, gasping for breath under the claw-like branches of a ghostly pale tree, I was nearly paralyzed by an eerie feeling. Looking up at the tree, I saw a carved wooden sign hanging from a rusty nail. The large letters carved into the sign read: *TABOO*. In smaller print below was etched: *Maori burial ground. No Passing.*

As the heavy mist shrouded the marsh-eaten stumps, I felt a deathly cold chill seep into me. Shivering in the cold, I clasped my knees and rocked back and forth trying to control the surging fear. A black-beaked magpie landed overhead on a branch of the ancient tree. The bird aimed his sharp, menacing beak at me and, letting out a malicious shriek, he dove at me. He came so close I could feel the up-draft from his wing-tips sweep over my head. I stayed in my huddle, cowering like a defenseless animal. Just as swiftly, the black and white avenger flew away, leaving me to ponder his assault.

The bird, like the sea, like Mick, made me feel so vulnerable. I rocked back and forth for a long time with tears streaming down my cheeks, reliving the nightmare of being on that damnable boat with Mick. It occurred to me that the bird was warning me. More than my trespassing on sacred burial grounds, I felt an ominous warning about my future — that something even more malevolent awaited me.

Perhaps I had fallen asleep, but somewhere in the night I heard a chanting — the same indecipherable sounds that had surrounded my bed in Penrhyn. The shark circled me once again. There was a terrible thrashing in the water. As I clawed my way to the surface, instead of safety, I saw the magpie preparing to dive at me again.

The morning light brought with it a sense of serenity and beauty. All the threatening nuances of night had evaporated under the gentle touch of morning sun. I had ended up near the lakeshore after all. Its waters shimmered in the morning light like a sacred jewel. Out of curiosity, I retraced my steps from the night before to see how I had made my way through the muck to the shoreline. I never did find any hint of my trail. I didn't find a ghostly pale tree, nor did I see any evidence of the muck-like quagmire that had so entrapped me.

Though the lake had appeared so inviting, I felt anxious to get away from it. I headed toward the mountains of the South Island and began a steady ascent toward a summit, which promised a grand view of the hidden valleys. The Routeburn track out of Queenstown was well-trodden, requiring no special equipment or skills other than strong legs and a willing spirit. Along the track I was passed by trekkers twice my age. There were Americans, New Zealanders, Australians, Germans — all streaking by me. My sea legs were slowly getting stronger but ached under the weight of my thirty-pound pack. I was always the last arrival at the overnight huts, which were scattered along the trail for those who preferred slower treks. They were simple log cabins, filled with cots, firewood and, at the lower altitudes, nestled near freshwater creeks.

Stopping at a cabin seemed the ultimate in luxury, especially if no one else was there. It felt homey enough and took a good deal of urging in the mornings to get me away from it.

Having reached the summit puffing and out of breath, somewhere near 8,000 feet, I looked over the narrow ledge into the magnificent Eden below. I suffered a momentary rush of fear; there was perhaps one foot between the edge of my muddy boot and the ledge that fell away to the valley floor. I suddenly locked up; every part of me was frozen. Then I let myself free-fall, summersault through the air, falling helplessly into the abyss. There my magpie came up underneath me, winging me back to the ledge of safety where my strength returned and I was able to move along the trail again. The magpie, of course, only partly existed.

As I descended, gradually leaving the timberline and winding back through thick rainforest, each vision was as beatific as the first. Finally, I reached Milford Sound with its cascading waterfalls, pristine glacier lakes, majestic fjords winding through hard granite passes... Still, I was not lulled by the beauty, comfort, or generosity of the people and their land. I kept on... kept on moving anxiously from one place to the next until after many months of roaming, I understood. It was time to return to sea. Whatever demons pursued me on land, they could only be tamed by the sea's sheer brutality.

Chapter Thirteen

PIERCE

And there it was again, Auckland Harbor, alive and charged by the flux of foreign ships and yachts coming through almost daily. I breathed the same air the sailors breathed, that fills the lungs and palpitates the heart, that keeps one striding the wide boulevard by day and evening, looking seaward in advance of the next adventure.

Soon enough I was standing over a classically designed forty-foot wooden yawl, which had been sailed out from San Francisco. I signed on as crew for a couple heading north to Brisbane, Australia. I assumed sailing with a married couple would save me from being trapped in any more precarious relationships. I thought I would be safe.

I had my usual internal debate: Why would someone consider going to sea again, knowing full well what lay ahead? There was only more of the Southern Ocean, the Tasman Sea and the Pacific — another two thousand miles or so to contend with. Why go back to it? I ached just thinking about how cruel the sea can be. Why choose it, if I can stay warmly and safely ashore where there is struggling enough? We sailors, silly fools, think of escape and only of escape. But escape from what — to where?

We say to ourselves:

> *I will not be bound by land. I will not be pressed to pay any taxes nor endless bills. No phone to interrupt my reveries. No morning paper to address the tragedies throughout the day. No rising prices to pay, no endless lines to stand in. No honking horns…*

If you look into the desperate heart of a sailor, you will find a vexed spirit, a boiling pot of fermenting passions, runaway dreams, a nomad from the old world...

We had seven successive gales those twenty-three days at sea with one morning of sun. Damn that cruise ship off our starboard bow. Ladies dressed in fine black gowns. From my position at the helm I can see them two ship-lengths away, their diamonds glistening under flooding decklights. Damn the sea breaking over my shoulders, my hands frozen to the tiller; Antarctic cold spills through the slightest gap where my hood snugs closed under my chin. Damn the cold ocean trickling between the cleave of my breasts, the warmest spot turned into a sharp ache. Damn their music, the civility of it all: women bare-shouldered enfolded in men's arms, swaying to the gentle rhythms of a waltz, oblivious to the surge of dangerous sea below their feet.

There were four of us on board *Salida*: Pierce, Jesse, Checkers and I. The yacht was American by its papers; the husband, Australian by birth; the wife, American by coincidence and the cat — black and white.

The gales set in as soon as we departed; there were few moments for shared conversation. I came to rely on the cat for updated weather reports. A loose coil of checkered fur lying about the cockpit meant fine weather indeed. A more tightly coiled kitty, with her tail tucked up between her legs, forecasted increasing winds over fifteen knots. A sulky kitty in the main salon signaled impending bad weather, the severity of which redoubled as the coil, the kitty and the tail disappeared below the covers on the main bunk. I soon realized her behavior was far more reliable than the humans on board.

I had scant clues as to who my skipper was or what he looked like behind the red-tinted, black-framed glasses he wore. The fact that I never saw his eyes kept me on guard. Occasionally I tried to catch glimpses of them as he wiped his glasses clean of salt spray, but I was never quick enough. I could discern, from one vantage, the deep-cut lines flaring out from the corners of his eyes. They were lines of age and the lines of a sailor who had squinted against the hard glare of sun. Pierce's hair was thick, jet-black, with dashes of white streaked through his sideburns; it gave him a deceptively distinguished look.

Jesse, on the other hand, looked like she'd just left Woodstock. She had that blissed-out, bra-less, scraggly blonde appearance. Maybe I saw something of myself in her. After all, I'd been to Woodstock. The summer of '69, I snuck off to Woodstock (disregarding my parents threats), just after it had been declared a "Disaster Area." It was my seventeenth birthday and I couldn't imagine a bigger birthday party. I have fond memories of slogging through the mud and seeing lots of nude people. There was music out there somewhere, but there was no chance of getting near enough to hear it over the slosh of rain.

I looked at Jesse and saw the sixties embodied in her blank stare. She was there, but not there. Jesse looked like one lost little flower child, all cuddled up in her blanket with nothing short of our sinking to persuade her above deck.

It was clear she hated the sea. She told me so herself not long after we had shipped off. She hated it with a consummate passion, feared it more than anyone I have ever known. Her fear intrigued me. It was not that she was uncommonly frail, prone to seasickness, or disinterested in the whole process of sailing, but she lazed about much like Checkers. There was one telling difference. Unlike Checkers, Jesse was never seen on deck, not in twenty-two of our twenty-three days at sea. That's why she had beautiful skin and dirty hair. So, it was clear to me from the start that the responsibilities of sailing and cooking would fall to Pierce and me.

I made no attempt to intrude upon their privacy until one moonless night when the Fates forced us together. Pierce and I were both low on sleep from the thirteen previous days of gales. The seas were rising steadily. Preparing to shorten sail, we were slow to react and clumsy moving about on deck. Everything moved in slow motion.

Pierce was forward grappling with the jib, when I heard the roll and thunder of a mountainous wave somewhere aft our stern quarter. The stern rose up and crashed down, sending a long shuddering tremor throughout the wooden frames on the boat. Our full sails were pitching us harder into the troughs and I lost sight of Pierce altogether. I switched on the overhead deck lights, which strobed through the night, flashing everything into a stark splintering white. Over all the screams of the night, I heard, "Free the sheets!" But no one belonged to the voice. There was nothing ahead of me but glittering diamonds of water exploding everywhere.

"Goddamnit, free the bloody sheets!" I heard the command again. The message slowly snaked through my system as I fought off a fatal lethargy. My left hand reached for the cleat, freeing the sheet. In the snap of a second, the line whipped through my hand, pulling my hand into the winch as the line flew off it.

I soon felt my hand burning raw against the lashing. Then I heard the cracking and snapping of my fingers caught between the unraveling line and the winch. Everything went numb and queasy as the small bones in my fingers broke under the pressure. Pierce came aft, having finally freed himself from the flogging jib.

"By Christ, what happened to you?" he shouted at my blank stare.

"Think I broke these fingers." I held up my limp, mangled hand.

"Christ, what a mess," Pierce yelled over the thundering sea. "Go below then. Tell Jesse to get into the supplies. No more than two at a time. I'll still be needin' ya."

"What?" I asked dazed.

"Go on, just tell her."

I climbed down the companionway, steadying my hand against my chest. Jesse lay in her bunk with Checkers snugged up against her belly.

"Jes," I said, nudging her shoulder until her glazed eyes recognized mine. "I broke some fingers. Pierce says to get into the supplies. No more than two at a time."

Jesse straggled out of the bunk, motioning me to lie down in her place. She went forward to the v-berth where she pulled out a large satchel. It was so heavy that she had to drag it aft. She strangely took on the demeanor of the most adoring mother and knowledgeable nurse. Ever so gently, she splinted and bandaged my crushed fingers. Then she gave me two capsules from one of the fifty or so bottles in her medicine chest. Dumbfounded by the size of the cache, I stared into the chest of illicit drugs. Before I could react, all my world went soft and hazy. Jesse swallowed two blue capsules and whispered to me, "Nothing will hurt us now."

By our sixteenth day at sea, I had gathered enough clues from Jesse's pill taking to understand something of their curious habits. As Jesse explained to me in her matter-of-fact manner, Pierce had been a hairdresser in San Francisco. Apparently he had plenty of spare time. Several times a month he piloted a plane at low altitude over the Mexican border, carrying a cargo of various illegal drugs back to the States. After minimal surveillance, I discovered that we were bucking along in a well-stocked drug store. We had enough red, white and blue pills on board to keep a crew load of people either very awake or soundly asleep, for a very long time.

Pierce and Jesse had escaped imprisonment by sailing away, and now I, as their crew, was linked to their crimes. I was forced to consider my options, neither of which seemed favorable. I could arrive in Australia on a boat laden with illegal drugs, or not arrive at all.

The random movements of the heavy medicine chest helped explain the uneven rise and fall of moods around me. One moment Pierce was a ruling tyrant and, in the next moment, a hovering, over-protective father. At times he was so restless that he moved about the deck and cabin like a caged animal, only to drop off into a stupor in the middle of plotting our position.

Meanwhile, Jesse lay like a corpse frozen in time without fresh air, water or food. Sometimes her own drug-induced hallucinations jerked her alive, but only long enough for her to take another blue capsule.

I retreated into a desultory silence. It suited me. I gave up thinking about anything. I no longer imagined the comfort of a motionless, dry bed, or the taste of fresh food. I no longer prayed for the sight of land nor for the gales to stop. I waited witlessly for the Fates to show me some sign of deliverance. I waited... and waited.

A sign came. Pierce and I sat topside enjoying a moderating sea. Jesse had risen from her bunk below and was preparing a real breakfast of powdered scrambled eggs.

Suddenly my view of vacant sea was invaded by several whirlwinds of water spinning straight at us.

"Pierce, wha— what is that?" I gulped down my coffee. I wasn't sure what I was looking at — an advancing front line of spiraling water, a deadly battalion of water-spouts twisting through the air sucking up the sea as they went. The tornadoes marched toward us with a weird exploding sound, like an army of black-hooded soldiers preparing to obliterate us.

Pierce followed my squinting stare. "Bloody hell, mate, WATER-SPOUTS. Jesus bloody Christ!"

Hurling his plate overboard he yelled, "Pull down every bit of cloth, secure everything on deck." Then he lunged down the companionway still yelling, "NOW!"

I heard Pierce below, swearing and cursing as he manually cranked the engine. It ticked over dead at every turn. As the menacing legion of spiraling black water-spouts twisted toward us, I fastened down everything. In a second glance, I saw that they were still on course and nearly within striking distance. I shouted, "Pierce, they're right on us, coming right at us. What'll I do?"

"Down here, mate. Batten down the hatches."

I saw how the end would be. Their advance was certain as we sat idly by. Nowhere to go, nowhere to hide. I slid down the companionway awkwardly, one hand bandaged and nearly unusable.

"What do we do now, Pierce?" I asked in a jittery voice.

"Do? Bloody hell, mate. We sit on our backsides and wish we were at the bloody pub."

We closed up all the hatches and waited. The sweat trickled off both of us during the confinement. The air was so close and damp. Sensing impending disaster, Checkers shivered inside the dead weight of Jesse's arm. She was wrapped in a deep sleep, oblivious of the imminent devastation.

"Pierce," I whispered insensibly, "I'm scared — scared as I've ever been. I don't like being closed in. I can't stay in here like this. I want to go topside."

His voice was gentle on the return. "I don't blame ya, luv, but she'll be right. She's a sturdy ship. She'll get us through."

To distract me from impending panic, Pierce told a story from his boyhood in Australia. He spoke softly about his father's farm, and how it went on forever and he never did see the end of it...

Then I heard them coming — the sound of water hissing and steaming like a boiling pot. It felt as if the boat was being picked up and hurled into the eye of a hurricane, yet we must have been absolutely stationary. All around us was an explosion of fissioning water sucking us in and swallowing us. I felt our stern being swept along, down into the gaping wide hole of sea, down into a black world of demons and corpses, where Jesse and Checkers were frozen and motionless.

I fell into the center of the earth where I was forced to disinhabit my being and leave it behind forever. My breathing stopped. I no longer groped for air through the water. I drowned.

All my world grew lighter, sweeter, gentler, more inviting than ever I'd known it before. I did not exist nor had I any wish to. I was finally of air and water. My spatial being was no longer enclosed, but expansive, reaching far beyond the small meteor of earth. I was not alive. But I was not perfectly dead either.

> *BUBBLE AND SQUEAK*
> > *BUBBLE AND SQUEAK*
> > > *BUBBLE AND SQUEAK*

The sound of bubble and squeak in the pressure cooker brought me around much later that night. I simply could not believe my misfortune — forced back to earth, after such a pleasant journey.

"You had quite a spell there, luv." Pierce handed me a bowl of steaming hot cabbage and potatoes. "This'll set ya right."

"What happened?" I slurred drowsily, "Thought I'd drowned." Pierce chuckled at my histrionics.

"Half your bloody luck, mate. The spouts went 'round us like two bulls in a pen."

"But— I heard them coming and the boat lifted up and spun around, dropped into the sea. I— I—"

"Steady on mate, just got a little close in here for awhile. Reckon you just had a spell."

I sniffed my bubble and squeak trying to get used to the idea of being alive, while wondering why the steam of boiled cabbage and potatoes smelled so good.

That last mirage of ocean lasted just short of an entire lifetime. The sea, the wind, the waves, the currents, all conspired against us. Beyond our immediate futile slogging upwind, the center frame, holding the keel to the boat, began to leak. In order to keep the yacht afloat Pierce and I had to manually pump the bilge 'round the clock.

For three sleepless days and nights, we alternated the chores of pumping, cooking, mending the sails, navigating and steering. Pierce took pills to stay awake, while I exhausted my body's supply of adrenaline. Jesse and Checkers slept on.

Nothing distinguished our nights from day, except the deepest black of night devouring the lighter shades of day.

As the sun rose on our twenty-third day at sea, I slowly turned westward, following the expanding light rays over the water.

"Jesus bloody Christ! Where are we?" I mimicked Pierce's curses.

"Oh my God, it's not Australia! There are two islands — three islands!" I talked to myself, trying to calm a rising panic.

"Pierce! Pierce!" I screamed hysterically.

Pierce struggled on deck, rubbing his eyes free of sleep, while adjusting his glasses.

"Pierce, we're all bloody wrong." I babbled on breathlessly. "Look, two islands. Australia's one island, isn't it? You said so yourself. I heard you say it — one island — one big island. But look, there's two... now three."

Pierce turned steadily west. A short crease of a smile caught the edge of his sun-dried lips. Leaning over, he unclenched my fingers from the wheel, reassuring me. "Steady on mate, we're home." Pierce pointed landward where the rising sun filled in the odd-shaped landscape as it intensified.

"Those are the Glasshouse Mountains, just north of Brisbane. They do look a bit like separate islands drifting alone."

Dazed from lack of sleep, I stared at the horizon for a long time. It appeared to me to be a vacant moonscape with three protruding sculptures set on its mantle. In my sleepless state, I fashioned them from clay and saw a black-skinned Madonna staring at me. She looked profoundly sad, yet proud. I could not unlock my gaze from hers.

Pierce tugged at my shoulder. "Come along then, mate. You need some sleep, eh. I'll be needing you alert tonight. If we're lucky, we'll be heading up river by dusk."

I went below with an all consuming weariness.

Semi-conscious, Jesse rolled over mumbling, "Are we there yet, Pierce? Is it over?"

"Yes," I said, taking his place beside her in the bunk. "We're almost home."

Sleep chased away my last day at sea.

Chapter Fourteen

SAVED BY SCOTCH

"*The land need only to be low here, as it is in a Thousand other places upon the Coast, to have made it impossible for us to have seen it at the distance we were off. Be this as it may, it was a point that could not be clear'd up as we had the wind; but should any one be desirous of doing it that may come after me, this place may always be found by 3 Hills which lay to the Northward of it in the Latitude of 26 53's. These hills lay but a little way inland, and not far from Each other; they are very remarkable on account of their Singular form of Elivation, which very much resembles Glass Houses, which occasioned my giving them that Name.*"

The Journals of Captain James Cook
The Voyage of the Endeavour, 17 May 1770

Pierce wrestled me awake late that afternoon. Pulling myself stiffly up the companionway ladder, I left Jesse to the mysterious alchemy of her bunk.

"Keep a sharp look out, mate. We're right in the middle of the shipping lanes. We've got thirty miles to go upriver to Brisbane, bloody losing our light fast."

I relieved Pierce at the helm. He spoke to me through layers of nervous exhaustion, while moving below deck trying to kick- start the engine.

Aye! The sunburst moonscape had expanded while I slept and now filled my vision. We had arrived at the mouth of the Brisbane River. It opened into a large inland waterway sprinkled with odd-shaped islands. The low flat land swept around me in every direction, swept over me like a chilling wave — I had reached it! I breathed in the air as deeply as I could. It was not the wet, sweet succulence of the South Pacific — seductive and irretrievably lost. No cows grazing along this shore, only infinitely long, white sand scars snaking north and south serving as a boundary, separating the eternity of sea from the eternity of land.

We met the river's headland. It stole the last of our evening breeze; our sails sagged listlessly. We let them slide painfully down their wires, each in turn lay exhausted on the deck. For a time we bobbed in the silvery twilight, waiting for permission to trespass farther. We floated like happy tourists having dodged our tour leader until twenty stories of metal with a barber's blade for bow sheer, sent Pierce reeling back toward the engine. He cursed as he cranked, cranked as he cursed. She fired at the very last moment. We swerved recklessly in the ship's five-foot bow wake. It sent a final ocean swell over our bow, our entrance into Australia aptly christened.

As dusk gathered into darkness, I fell into a trance of sorts. The energy flooded out of my system all at once leaving my vision blurred and my hearing dimmed. The great ocean recessed behind us, our sea was now a flat slate to slip across. I sat at the tiller in a confused daze, mumbling to myself like a homeless person on the streets too long:

Red light. What next? Red light. Red — Right – Returning. WRONG. That's American. This is the English system. Red is port. Green is starboard. Red... Red... RED! PIERCE!

"Jesus bloody Christ, woman, we've come too far to run 'er up on the rocks now. Stay in the bloody channel."

I shook my head trying to break through the hypnotic stare of lights coming at me. Thirty miles of navigating upstream, buoy lights flooding toward me, six hours of flashing red, white, green, yellow, oscillating, flashing, periodic, one, two, three, four seconds. *Hold on, read the light, read the course, bear 230 degrees, stay to starboard... Make a mistake. THE END.*

Jesse slept on. My eyelids hurt. *Open, please. Green becomes red, red becomes green... only five more hours.*

We docked at the Customs pier on the Brisbane River and made fast our lines. It was well past midnight and Pierce was certain the officials would not board us until morning. Neither Pierce nor Jesse had mentioned our cache of drugs or what they planned to do with them. I might have jumped ship there and run for my life, but the Harbor Police had already notified Customs that there were three people on board the foreign yacht.

Feeling like one of the condemned, I willingly followed Pierce's suggestion to get some sleep. As I went forward to my bunk, I passed

Jesse sitting in the main salon. Giggling like a little girl who had devoured a box of forbidden chocolates, she looked glassy-eyed and well drugged.

"Get up ya slut, will ya," Pierce snapped at her. "This place looks like a bloody whorehouse, thanks to you."

I climbed into my sleeping bag with an awful sense of dread. Ever so faintly I could feel the slight rocking of my wood-planked bed as Pierce moved from port to starboard and back again, in an effort to free Johnnie Walker and his friends from the stowed liquor.

Just then, when all the clinking and rattling of glass bottles had subsided, I heard a short-syllabled, long-consonanted, tightly packed profusion of words being hurled through the night.

"Ahoy mate, preparin' to board. Customs and Immigration at your service. Welcome to Austraaalya."

"Jesus!" Pierce cursed under his breath as the two men boarded the boat. Trying to soften his alarm, Pierce added quickly, "You blokes are workin' late tonight, eh. Welcome aboard."

One of the officials immediately began to volley questions in rapid fire: "May we see yer papers? Yer Australian? The yacht's out of San Francisco? Been away fifteen years, eh?"

Then his tone became even more demanding. "Everybody up, please. We won't keep ya any longer than need be."

I was suddenly overtaken by an irrational impulse to dive deep into my sleeping bag and hide, but Jesse came forward and started tugging my T-shirt.

"Come on, they're here!" she said as if we were honored guests at a surprise birthday party.

Jesse looked as strange as I'd ever seen her. Her hair was a tangled mess as usual and her clothes were crumpled and dirty, but it was her eyes that were most shocking. They were dilated like cat's eyes groping for more light in the night. Surrounding her black pupils were jagged branches of blood-red vessels that looked ready to burst. She was sweating profusely. No one, I thought anxiously, could overlook her symptoms of overdose. I wondered how much longer she would be able to stand without collapsing in front of our interrogators.

As I stepped into the main salon with Jesse stumbling behind me, I shot Pierce a glance of desperation. He quickly grabbed a tall bottle of Scotch and offered it to our visitors.

"Awh yeah, mate, I reckon we could do with some of that." Both officials jumped at the chance of having a stiff drink.

"That's a fine mix, that is."

Pierce filled two tall mugs with straight whiskey, adding apologetically, "Sorry, we don't have any ice to go with it."

The gesture pleased the two fellows immensely. They settled comfortably into their seats, going through our passports, the yacht's papers and then our health documents.

Finally the stern fellow with the jagged scar along his sideburns turned to Jesse and said, "Yer not looking well, miss. Do you have any illness we should know about?"

"I'm fine!" Jesse blurted out. "No more sailing. No more going to sea." She sang the phrases like a verse from *Alice in Wonderland*. "I'm fine — I'm fine — I'm fine," she giggled, while applauding herself.

Pierce and I intercepted the questioning glimpses of the two men. He refilled the inspectors' mugs the moment they were empty. Halfway through their third round the two fellows turned their attention to me. Slapping his hand on the table, the drunkest of the two looked at me saying, "Is that one dumb? Does she talk?"

Leaning stiffly against the bulkhead I said, "Yes," quietly.

The other official kept up the pertinent questioning. "Will ya be staying on this yacht while you are in Austraaalya?"

I wasn't certain what answer would pacify him, so I shot Pierce another glance and he slowly nodded his head. Then I thought of the cache of drugs waiting to be discovered.

"Well, my job has ended," I stammered nervously. "We only just met up in Auckland, you know."

He cornered me with his next question. "How long will ya be stayin' in Austraaalya?"

I knew I didn't have enough money to leave the boat and satisfy their requirements for a six-month visitor's visa. Weak from nervous exhaustion, I felt confused and hardly able to muster a reply.

Amazingly, the drunk official saved me from my own sticky web. Leaning toward Pierce he chatted as if I were deaf and mute.

"Awh, keep yer eye on that one, mate. They'll be itchin' to get into her knickers. Look at those legs wouldja."

The scarred official grabbed the inebriate by the shoulder.

"Well," he said, "I reckon we've had our fill, mate. Thanks for the hospitality. Sorry we've kept you up so late." He pulled his partner out of his seat adding, "If yer headin' upriver, mind the tides, eh. The sand 'll shift on the tide and leave ya high and dry."

The unsuspecting Custom officials were not two feet away from the boat when Jesse collapsed, falling into one of her drug-induced stupors. Lifting his wife into the bunk, Pierce turned to me. "Don't look so worried, mate. We're free as bloody loris."

"Loris?" I muttered, numb from our evening's interview.

"Lorikeets, mate. Free as the bloody birds."

Chapter Fifteen

OZ

Pierce was anxious to get away from the formalities of the waterfront city, so we left Brisbane at dawn and steamed toward Surfer's Paradise as if our lives depended on it. We motored back out the Brisbane River then headed south via the inner coastal waterway. Along our route we passed a half-sunken fishing boat being towed by a bigger trawler. Checking our VHS radio, we heard the news: *The twenty-five foot fishing boat had been attacked and holed by sharks. Two fishermen were eaten; one had survived by climbing in the refrigerator used for bait fish.*

We made our way south along silt-filled estuaries with random signposts tilted in every direction. Maneuvering around small sandbars, we navigated each twist and turn with hyper-awareness. Our charts were useless in the maze-like tributaries. We crept along at two to three knots until *Salida* gave out an awful shuddering thud, bump, bang. She ran aground. Hitting an imperceptible sandbank, she fell hard on her beam. The forty-year-old ship lay on her side wheezing and moaning under the sound of cracking and breaking wooden ribs. It was like riding a racehorse to a slow death. Her innards collapsed. She drew on her last breath.

All in a matter of seconds we'd been jettisoned from our posts, flung across the yacht and snagged by her lifelines. Stuck in the muck and looking at the sky from an eighty-degree angle was not how I had envisioned my journey's end.

It seemed this last zag in our expedition severely tweaked something in Pierce's brain. Just like my former skipper, Pierce lost all sensibility and began the laborious process of damning the gods, the heavens, and every living being including the customs officials. Like Mick, and anyone else who has suffered defeat by the sea, Pierce went slightly mad.

I had learned. I understood. By then, I knew. You see a mad sailor, you clear out of his way. I went forward and sat astride the bow pulpit. Taking up my perch, I prepared myself for a special outing at the theater, *L'Humane Comedie*. And I was not disappointed by the preview.

Pierce was a frantic man. He appeared on deck brandishing a long, jagged, rusty hacksaw. He came forward, bent over my toes and started sawing.

"Christ, not my toes!" I yelled at him.

"Not your bloody toes, the whisker pole. I'll cut 'er in two and prop 'er up."

Well, that was an interesting solution considering Pierce had abandoned all reason. He cut the pole in the oddest length then tried slipping it under eight tons of broken boat in a silt-filled river. Digging a hole for the pole in an ebb tide of sand-muck was a curious process. Pierce dug the hole; the sand-muck filled it up again. He dug, and dug himself right into a nice self-filling hole. Clambering back on board after a futile hour, Pierce was suddenly enraged by the lack of cold beer. In fact, we had never had any beer on the boat, let alone a cold one. We had no refrigeration. But the true Aussie in him was starting to crack through his American facade. He wanted a beer, one cold beer.

It was about that time a fishing punt miraculously sputtered up next to us. Two crusty fishermen nudged their dory as close as they could without going afoul. Needing an assist, I could tell, was eating straight through to Pierce's gut — the Australian part of his gut. Left high and dry on a sandbar within earshot of the pub was humiliating. When the fishermen asked if "we were right," Pierce shot back, "Seems some sand shifted since I was here last."

The thin strake of a wizened seaman shook with laughter. "Less'n you were 'ere yesterd'y mate, ya wouldn't 'ave a clue. She changes on the tide. Headin' to Southport are ya?"

We hung our heads shamefully, while the fishermen agreed to pull us off the sandbar as soon as the tide rose. They even offered to guide us the rest of the way to Southport. I found the two weather-scarred fishermen hard to look at without feeling a twinge of revulsion. Their hair was matted and clumped in knotty nests of filth. Their faces were burnt beyond recognition and when they spoke their mouths opened into black caverns of pus-filled holes, barely a tooth left standing. They both wore the same green canvas jackets, rotten with the smell of fish and ripped apart by sunlight. Everything about them said they were hard creatures. Their hands were not hands at all, but misshapen claws that grabbed and tore at life. They lived on the sea, sucking its blood and spitting it back. They were rough creatures, scarred and mauled by the sea, yet they helped us, they offered us food and they gave Pierce their last cold Aussie beer. We became great friends.

By day's end we had finally dropped anchor in front of the Southport Yacht Club. Jesse acknowledged the end of our long sea journey by primping in front of the mirror. Pierce, who had been on a manic tirade all day, suddenly became friendly and effusive in his happiness to be home. Slapping me on the back, he nearly knocked me over with his excitement. "Good job, mate. You can sail with me any d'y. Good to be back in OZ, eh. Off we go for a few cold ones at the pub, eh..."

I felt irritated by Pierce and wasn't about to trust his new- found camaraderie. I was irritated by the sudden resurrection of his Aussie accent as we had neared the coast, and irritated by his high spirits and sudden transformation back into a human being. Most aggravating was the fact that he was home, in a place he called OZ, and I was not.

Though I had never said anything, I was annoyed at Jesse's constant helplessness, which had cost me an untold amount of sleep. I didn't want to be near either of them and could only think of packing my bag.

"You and Jesse go ahead. I'll stay on board for awhile," I said, anxious to be left alone. The thirsty couple was quick to row ashore.

I sat for a long time on deck commiserating with Checkers, wondering where I would be off to next. As dusk seeped into me, I could feel something of the unknown take hold. The evening air was thin, clear and brilliantly alive — clear enough to see the heavens refracting and bending around the image of earth.

I felt like a prisoner whose cell door was suddenly thrown open and couldn't quite grasp the fact that I was free to leave. Taking in long, deep drafts of fresh air, I experienced a dizzying energy spreading through my veins. For one elusive second of my existence I caught a moment of joy — pure, inexplicable joy, which I hadn't felt for a long time. I remembered with a laugh a promise I had made to myself as a kid sailing my own dinghy on a freshwater lake in Pennsylvania. It was there I promised myself that one day I would sail on a sea, pure and untainted by the sight of land. I decided then that I would set out to find a place of unlimited beauty and grace, filled with endless warmth, with no harsh winters to disturb my languid daydreams. I was twelve and my dreams were always wild and delicious.

Looking over the enormous expanse of low-lying land that stretched in front of me, I thought that perhaps my dream of finding perfect freedom was now within my grasp. For one fleeting, magical moment I believed I had finally eluded my demons and might find the serenity I was looking for in a place aptly nicknamed OZ.

I stayed wrapped in my enchanted spell for a long time, until it was broken by the unexpected return of the hapless couple. I turned to find Pierce flinging his arms wildly in the air, cursing Jesse on their approach to the yacht.

"You flamin' stupid bitch," he yelled through the still night air. "You spent all me money. How d'ya expect to cel'brate if we don't have any money, flamin' stupid bitch."

Pierce bent down and picked up his cowering wife by the seat of her pants and threw her on board. She flipped over the lifelines and slumped onto the deck with all the defiance of a shackled slave. I reached for her hand but she pushed me away, warning me of her husband's rage. Once on board Pierce shuffled toward me wreaking of alcohol. "Ya know what she did, don't ya?" he slobbered over me, while pointing his finger accusingly at my chest. "She bloody well drank up all me money."

I watched Jesse as she crawled along the deck on all fours, too beaten down to get up. "I didn't, honestly I didn't," she sobbed pathetically. "I must have lost the bill — must have slipped out of my back pocket. I only had two drinks, honestly."

Each in their turn pleaded their case to me as if I were the judge going to set one free and sentence the other. I listened impartially until Jesse struggled to her feet. Then in the single stroke of a second, Pierce turned on her with a raised fist and caught her square in the eye. She didn't scream, but whimpered like a pup whose tail had been pinched for the fun of it.

"Jesus, leave her alone," I swore at him. "Come on Jes, we're getting the hell out of here."

I'd seen enough of Pierce's tantrums to know we had to get away from him quickly. Jumping into the dinghy, I pulled Jesse's soft, malleable body over the lifelines toward me. The blood from her slashed eyelid streamed through her fingers and onto my shoulder.

Pierce continued flailing his arms. "You won't get far," he yelled. "She can't do a bloody thing without me."

I rowed through the glittery night toward land feeling her warm blood seep through my T-shirt and harden over the curve of my breasts. I was only sorry that in our great escape I didn't take any money or clothes. Nevertheless, I continued to row wearing my blood soaked, T-shirt and underpants — nothing more.

I avoided the Yacht Club dock and dragged the dinghy up a muddy bank next to it. Pulling Jesse from the boat, I wondered what I could possibly do now to help her.

We began our pilgrimage to town. There was the familiar sound of cars careening around tight curves. Their headlights cast weird, elongated shadows of our bodies along the road. Jesse stayed close to me, swaying into the cleave of my shoulder, knocking me off balance as we went. I couldn't imagine what we must have looked like to those driving by. I vaguely hoped that someone might offer help.

"I've got to stop, got to sit down for awhile," Jesse pleaded with me as if I were now her keeper. "I'm so tired. Please, can't we just stop and have some coffee."

I agreed to stop at the small roadside coffeehouse a short distance away. We went in with Jesse in front of me, while I tugged at my oversized T-shirt trying to make it into a very short dress. I immediately felt the stares from the truck drivers and mumbling drunks crawl all over me. We slid quickly onto the ripped vinyl chairs, hoping to hide my naked legs under the cold metal table.

"Good Lord!" the buxom waitress exclaimed loudly. "What on earth happened to you two? Look worse than what the bloody cat dragged in." Her deep voice brought another round of gawking stares and muffled laughter from the men around us.

The heavy-set woman looked at us quizzically with eyes that were big, round and slightly tarnished gray.

"I reckon you two are in some strife and need lookin' after. That punched-up eye there needs a stitch and a tuck, I'd say." The waitress leaned over and leered at Jesse adding sympathetically, "Look luv, I know how it is, bloke comes home at night, whacks ya a few times and if yer lucky you get out. Heard that one a million times." The woman kept on, probing for the truth.

"We're all right, really," I lied. "If you could spare some coffee and ice, we'd be very grateful."

The woman rolled her eyes upward. "Good Lord, Yanks as well! Suit y'rself, luv. But wherever ya both come from, I wouldn't be in any hurry to get back to, eh."

Jesse ran her hand along the ridge of her pale eyebrows, just above the gaping flesh wound. She swayed her head back and forth moaning in pain. "I've got to get back to the boat," she said, wiping the crusting blood from her cheek. "Pierce will be so worried."

"Pierce!" I yelled at her in disbelief. "Pierce worried! Are you crazy?" I said, pounding my fist on the table. Taking in a deep breath I tried to calm myself. "You can't go back to him, not after all that. Jeez Jes, if you could see yourself. You've got to get away from him. You'll be drugged and beaten up for the rest of your life. Is that what you want?"

Jesse broke into tears. "That's easy for you to say, you don't know what we have together."

"What you have! What *do* you have?" I asked, exhausted by her twisted logic.

Watching Jesse sink inside her fear, I sat numbed and caged in by my own memories. They tore into my gut and started pummeling me. I gasped for air, my heart raced as the memories came at me, suffocating me. It wasn't Mick threatening me with a knife, but my own husband.

> *"Oh," they said in hushed tones at the wedding, "What a beautiful young bride. What a lovely couple..." That very night he grabbed a handful of my hair and smashed my head against the wall. He turned into a greedy, hungry animal, ripping and tearing at my insides. No marks on my body, only memory, only fear and anger, and no one to tell. "Don't tell anyone," he had threatened his young bride. And I never did. One day I ran away and I just kept running. I kept moving day and night because I never felt safe enough to stop.*

The waitress arrived back at our table. Still under an assault, I snapped back into reality as she set down some ice, coffee, scones and a ten-dollar Australian note.

"No good goin' walkabout at this hour," the matron said. "Here's a few quid to get ya started. You look a decent sort."

"That's very kind of you," I said. "I can repay you tomorrow."

The waitress glanced back at us. "Not to worry, luv. Better just work on gettin' y'rself some proper clothes, eh."

Jesse continued to pout about getting back to the boat. I knew she was right. We had to get our clothes, money and passports.

Leaving the coffeehouse I said to her firmly, "We'll go back to the boat, but only long enough to get our things." I took Jesse by the shoulders and made her look into my determined eyes. "All you need are some clean clothes and your passport," I said very slowly. "Remember your passport, OK?" Jesse shrugged vacantly.

Once aboard I ushered Jesse below. Pierce was sitting at the settee, slouched over a mug of coffee.

Looking up at Jesse, he crooned, "Awh, Jes darlin'. I'm so sorry. I've been worried sick about ya."

Jesse pushed past me and fell into his arms. Not a word, not a moment's hesitation. The final act was played out.

I gathered up my bag, and squeezed past the couple draped adoringly in each other's arms. Reaching for the top of the companionway ladder, I looked sadly at Jesse and said softly, "Good luck, mate." But she didn't hear me, so I kept the good luck for myself.

Poking my head out of the companionway and into the fresh night air, I felt safe. Finally, I was free. Freer, I thought, than I'd ever been before.

PART TWO

THE LAND OF OZ

AND THE VAST, UNINHABITED LAND
FRIGHTENED HIM. IT SEEMED SO HOARY
AND LOST, SO UNAPPROACHABLE.
THE SKY WAS PURE, CRYSTAL PURE AND BLUE...
AND THERE WERE GREAT DISTANCES...
HE LET HIMSELF FEEL ALL SORTS OF
THINGS ABOUT THE BUSH.

IT WAS SO PHANTOM-LIKE, SO GHOSTLY...

WAITING — WAITING — THE BUSH SEEMED
TO BE HOARILY WAITING. AND HE COULD
NOT PENETRATE INTO ITS SECRET.
HE COULDN'T GET AT IT.
NOBODY COULD GET AT IT.
WHAT WAS IT WAITING FOR?

D. H. Lawrence, *Kangaroo*

Chapter Sixteen

NO DIRECTION KNOWN

Lifting up a glass of rum at the Southport Yacht Club bar, I toasted my survival with an uncustomary morning drink and swore that I would never go to sea again. The sea had betrayed me at every turn, pained me — all her deceptive beauty; she was a cruel woman in her heart. I wanted no more of her. Tossing back my head, I gulped down the stinging hot rum thinking wryly, "...sailor home from the sea."

Through the fish bowl distortion of my rum glass, I noticed an oddly contorted face staring back at me. Startled by the sudden intrusion, I nearly rocked backward off my chair.

"Sorry, didn't mean to rattle you," said the young man, catching my fall. "Do you mind if I join you?"

I set down my glass and in place of the distortion stood the handsomest man I'd seen in a long time. I nodded *yes* against all my better instincts. A throng of inner voices started yelling at me: *Don't be a fool. He's probably from Immigration. He's too well kept, too handsome. Don't talk to him.* All the voices raged on behind a stony, blank stare.

"Sorry," the young man repeated the apology, "I saw you sitting here and the barman said you were off the American yacht. She's a beauty."

I looked out the Yacht Club window at the classic wooden yawl I'd just been freed from. "Oh, she's a beauty all right." It slipped out with a guttural sound more akin to a dying man's last gasp than my intended chuckle.

The young man said his name was Richard. I didn't mean to stare so intently at his face, but his features were so soft and gentle and welcoming. He had trimmed light-brown hair and large brown eyes, which gave the impression of directness.

"You've come from America then?" Richard's face beamed with excitement.

"S'ppose you could say that," I answered flatly, thinking of the months and months of sailing.

Then Richard leaned closer to me, as if I was on the verge of disclosing an immense secret. He looked into my eyes without ever letting his attention stray. "I think it would be absolutely wonderful to take off, just as you have. Pack it all in..." Richard continued on, explaining that one day he, too, would like to set off. He wanted to know what it was really like at sea, what storms I had encountered, what food I had eaten, what exotic ports I had called into.

I couldn't imagine him at sea; I didn't want to. I liked the look of his smooth skin, clean-shaven face and manicured nails. Everything about him was polished and protected from the corrosive effect of the sea.

Richard watched my expression closely, still waiting for the moment when I might disclose the sea's heady rapture. Instead the grim memories shot through me in rapid succession: the threat of prison, Clari's spitefulness, William's promises, being left in Fiji and sailing with Mick. The memory of Pierce and Jesse, so fresh in my mind, circled around me like hungry buzzards ready to pick apart my insides. Staring off into the distance I answered dryly, "It was interesting."

Overtaken by a sudden self-consciousness, I turned my attention to the dirt underneath my nails and played nervously with them. My two broken fingers skewed off in different directions, undoubtedly repulsed by the sight of each other. It would probably be another six months before the blackened nails would fall off and regenerate something akin to a fingernail. I had downright ugly hands. Tallying up my losses, I followed the ragged line of my tattered shorts to my scraped knee. Then, turning up the edge of my blue-purple elbow, I remembered with a wince slamming into *Salida*'s bulkhead. All told, it had been a rough ride. I wished I had been well scrubbed and smartly dressed.

"Well," Richard said, "you must be tired. Are you off the boat now?" He motioned to my worn-out backpack propped up against the table leg. I nodded vacantly.

"So, where are you off to?" He kept pursuing me.

The question, the possibility of a new direction, charged me with renewed vigor. There I was, nothing in the world to hold me. Where should I go? What should I do?

"Well, actually," I said, finally mustering the strength to respond, "I thought I might — head north."

"Going by train, are you?"

"Hmmm, no, I don't think so."

"Going by motorcar then?"

"No, not by car."

"Well, then?" Richard pushed on further, leaning even closer, gripping the table, anxious for an answer.

"By bike," I decided on the spur of the moment.

"Ah, motorbike, then?"

"Nooo… I mean bicycle."

He suddenly took on the demeanor of a concerned father. "A pushbike! Good Lord, you've thought this through, have you?"

"Ah, no, actually, I just thought of it now."

"Do you have any idea of the distances, the condition of the roads?" Richard's eyes widened with apprehension. "We have multitudinous creatures that can kill you instantly, not least of which is the average truckee!"

I was determined not to travel by any conveyance that required being caged in with people for any length of time. On the other hand, I didn't have enough money to buy much more than a "pushbike." I looked at Richard with a coy smile. "You don't happen to know where I can get a good second-hand bike, do you?"

Within the hour I was the proud owner of "Red," a rusty old two-wheeler with wide-rimmed tires and a saddlebag. We loaded the bike and my pack into the back of his sports coupe and headed toward the General Post Office in downtown Brisbane to pick up my mail.

Richard continued his questions about sailing as I laid my head back in the wind. I caught glimpses of him as he drove expertly down the road. He had a perfectly sculpted profile, dominated by high cheekbones and a firm jaw. I thought I might fall in love with him and his gentle, soft brown eyes, which seemed to harbor no demons, only dreams. I was already in love with the comfort surrounding him, our ease of motion. I liked the road, that particular road — it was long, straight and narrow. The speed was so intoxicating. I felt as if I had never gone so fast... so fast. All the verdant colors streamed by in one magnificent collage.

Richard took me in, fed my soul for a few hours, helped me on my way. I wished he'd put his arm around me so I could feel safe, snuggled against the warmth of his yellow cashmere sweater. *Perhaps I should postpone my journey for another day.*

As if overhearing my thoughts Richard suddenly interjected, "This is probably quite mad of me, of course, but I'd love to show you around Brisbane. There are some interesting things to see. I'm an architect by trade and some of the buildings..."

An architect. Of course, his hands are so delicate. Couldn't I stay in Brisbane, just for one more day? Couldn't I? There's nothing pressing ahead of me. I don't know anyone else. There's no reason not to.

Suddenly, I jerked myself back into reality. I stared at Richard — charming young man, intelligent, good-looking. *If I stayed the afternoon, wouldn't I stay the night? What then? Go on, get on your damn bicycle, get moving now, while you still can... nothing more dangerous than falling in love with a stranger.*

I picked up my mail at the G.P.O. still avoiding Richard's open invitation. We sat on the sandstone steps of the immense Post Office building huddled together like old friends, sharing the excitement of news from home. From among all the letters, a telegram fell out of the bundle. I was immediately seized with fear thinking it must be bad news from home. I picked up the slender note and handed it to Richard. "Will you read this?" It was an odd impulse, I thought, trusting a stranger so implicitly with a personal message.

Richard opened up the telegram slowly, thoughtfully. "Good Lord!" he muttered, covering his mouth with one hand. "If I understand this correctly, a friend of yours, Katie, has lost her boat on a reef just north of Bundaberg, and she's asking for your help — is how I read it."

"Katie?" I snatched the paper from him, trying to figure out who Katie was and why she would ask me for help. Slowly, a vision of Katie revisited me. We had both embarked from Hawaii over a year ago on a great sailing adventure. She had sailed off with her boyfriend on his boat, while I had become a sea-going hitchhiker. Turning to Richard I asked, "Where's Bundaberg?"

"Oh, I'd say about four hundred kilometers north of here. You're not seriously..."

But I was serious. I viewed the telegram as a personal message from the Fates. It was certainly odd that this plea for help should suddenly fall into my hands. How could Katie have possibly known I had sailed to Brisbane? I hadn't spoken to her since leaving Hawaii! There was no doubt in my mind I was supposed to head north, and I couldn't let Richard dissuade me.

"I should get going," I said with renewed determination. "I'd like to be clear of the city before nightfall."

"No, you mustn't!" Richard jumped up, blocking my way. "I mean," he added in a gentler voice, "you should find a nice Bed & Breakfast just at the outskirts of town. There's not much after that. I could help you—"

I took in a long deep breath while searching for the right answer. "I loved meeting you, but I need to be on my own for awhile. I'm afraid I've been at sea for too long." I smiled, trying to lighten the situation. "The noise, the city, it's too much for me right now. I hope you understand."

Richard put his hands on my shoulders. "I've got to say, I really don't understand." He looked at me intently. "I've enjoyed your company immensely. You're so — different."

I waited for him to pull me toward him, to wrap his arms around me for one lasting embrace, but his expression changed.

I started to lean forward to kiss his cheek, to finally touch the inviting tenderness that had pursued me all day, but he backed away from me saying, "Good Luck, then, eh. Look after yourself."

He turned and walked quickly down the steps without looking back. I felt panicky. *You crazy idiot. You always let the best in life slip away. You idiot! Stop him!*

"Richard!" I yelled as loud as I could, but the crush of city noise overpowered my hesitation.

Couldn't I stay just one more day?

Chapter Seventeen

PHANTOMS

By dusk I was on my way, rolling past the city limits and onto the main road heading north. The narrow, two-lane highway stretched before me for another two thousand kilometers.

As all the colors of the day dissolved into winter light, I could barely separate the coal-black bitumen from the bush around me. Open country in every direction, immeasurable vastness; it was immense like the sea. For the first time, I felt the freedom I had sought, the freedom that had always eluded me. From the moment of setting my foot on the pedal, I was completely and perfectly free.

There was, however, one new problem. In my haste to get out of the city, I had neglected to pack any food other than some chocolate bars. Richard's concern had been genuine. After biking nearly seventy kilometers, assuming at every turn there would be a Milkbar, Take-Away stand or Petrol station, I found nothing but bush. There were no shops, no signs along the road, no boarding houses, no sounds of distant cars... nothing, except the impenetrable solitude of night closing in over the wilderness.

Under threat of darkness, I gave in to the splintering cramps in my neck and back and pulled into the heavily wooded forest, hoping to find a bed for the night. At first it looked like God's own private residence — splendidly framed by tall gum trees and giant palms rising skyward, towering above everything. Their long branches braided through each other forming a natural thatched roof to nestle under. I stepped carefully over the ground, remembering Richard's warning about dangerous crawling things. Just ahead of me I heard the scurrying sounds of small animals clearing a path. The farther I ventured into the woodland, the more distinct the various sounds of animals and bird life became. As the cool winter darkness pressed in around me, the wild chirping, squawking, buzzing and croaking seemed to expand with the night into a wild native chorus.

At day's end the forest had looked an inviting dreamy Eden, but as night approached it became a frightening place. The trees I had so admired in the light, now locked me inside their oppressive walls of darkness. The native chorus settled into a hypnotic hum as I climbed into my sleeping bag and laid on the leafy ground feeling alone and vulnerable.

I'm just a kid from New York, really. What do I know about the bush? Nothin'. And Mick was right — I don't know anything about war either, or survival training, or how to protect myself. I know how to sail. That's about it. Richard was right — there's nothin' out here — I'm sleeping on the ground in the Australian bush? I could be at a Bed & Breakfast. Why? What am I after? There has to be a reason...

I pulled my head into the bag like a turtle drawing into its protective shell and lay there, half-dreaming Richard and I were in an intimate restaurant, chatting affectionately over an exquisite dinner. His hand was entwined in mine and his touch made me feel safe. *I could be in Brisbane tonight. Ah, that would be sooo nice...*

Just then, I heard a soft rustling, like the whispering of a breeze escaping through the branches above me. Yet it was more than that. It shook me. Then came the most gruesome of female cries. It slashed through the dense underbrush like a machete, cutting a path toward me. It was high-pitched and hideous. The clawing, thrashing sound of struggle grew louder. I sat upright, consumed by fear. With my heart thumping madly, I reached for the marlinespike knife in my pack and crouched cautiously. Stepping lightly through the bush, I hoped to catch a glimpse of my assailant.

Gradually the rustling in the bush settled, the screech grew raspy, more akin to a death cry. I listened closely for the sound of its shallow breathing to guide me. Then came a noise from over my shoulder and I turned quickly. A pair of striking yellow eyes stared intently at me. The imposing owl loomed above me on a branch of a giant gum tree. He stood unflinching, his eyes fixed on mine.

Have I trespassed? I asked, wondering if I was on sacred Aboriginal land.

No answer.

Is there danger here?

No answer.

Why have you come here? I asked the bird, convinced he had something to tell me.

The bird slowly unfurled his wings and with one powerful flap, he vanished. There was a ghostly silence all around me.

I slept restlessly in the bush that night assailed by a dream that kept the owl perched on the branch, staring at me. He never flew away in the dream. As I watched him, he slowly changed from a good omen into something frightening — a scavenger bird scouting its prey. At one point in the dream, he dove at me. I curled up in a fetal position to protect myself and flailed my arms in the air to fend him off. Screaming a hideous cry that was not my own, I thrashed in the bush, fighting off the avenger in complete darkness.

I awoke with a start in the morning soaked in my own sweat, exhausted by the feeling that I had been battling something equally beautiful and terrifying all night.

Unable to shake a feeling of dread, I began to re-experience the anguish of my dream. I had looked inside myself in the dream and saw a horrifying emptiness laid bare by the devouring predator bird. I was seized with revulsion. Clutching my stomach, I rolled back and forth on the ground as memories dove at me, one after another, relentlessly attacking:

My childhood place, the Eden itself, beauty beyond touching. All that was good and pure and safe in my life left behind, so long ago. Beyond the tall fence of our grounds, the outside world threatened to invade our peaceful home. Each day when I ventured out to school, the nuns, hiding inside their black gowns, awaited with subtle tortures. I must give up my lunch money to the poor souls in purgatory, or "You will burn in hell," said the jolly, red-cheeked nun taking my money. The smell of vomit was everywhere in school. It was the smell of fear. Endless punishments were

*meted out. My ears tweaked, knuckles rapped and my
tongue forced to stick to the dry, chalky blackboard for a
misspelling or incorrect answer. The nuns told me that my
insides were all black and rotting from Original Sin and I
could never, ever rid myself of it. I went to church every
morning throughout grade school, hoping to expel the
blackness within. But once a week the priest reminded me in
confession that it was still there — I was riddled with horrid
sins — and there was no amount of Penitence that could
save my diseased soul. I would always be a Sinner and I was
damned to hell. Amen.*

The cyclone of emotion subsided, leaving me exhausted on the leaf-strewn floor of the forest, staring unfocused through the looming trees.

The morning sounds of the forest gradually re-awakened me. All around was a symphony of birds erupting into a chorus of song. I didn't know them by name then, but I could hear the lyrebirds, wrens and warblers piping their melodies, while the bellbirds sounded their chimes and the whipbirds accentuated the crescendos. The gentle morning breeze rustled the palms; they twisted and swayed like invisible maestros.

Leaving the forest I felt weak and out of sorts. Twenty-four hours had passed since I'd had anything to eat. By the time I was on the road again and cycling north, everything around me looked slightly surreal and out of proportion. I pedaled through moments of dizziness in which I thought I saw the road merging into one dangerously narrow lane, finally disappearing altogether.

At every turn a new vision greeted me — the bulbous curve of a bottle tree, the tail of a huge lizard dipping off the road, or a field full of wild scrub called wattle.

As I came around one curve a shimmering mirage appeared before me. An expansive plain of wheat-colored grass swayed back and forth in the gentle breezes like rhythmic seaswells. Scattered among the tall grass were glistening black volcanic hills. I stopped pedaling and looked over the plains for some time, mesmerized by the largest of the hills. I remembered with a start how, from a great distance at sea, I had viewed a hill, which stood out so markedly from the lowlands, thinking it looked like a black-skinned Madonna. Was this the same majestic peak that had held me so transfixed? Like a mother with her children at her feet, she sat in the center of the wide plain surrounded by a family of smaller mounds. From the edge of the road I could follow the dark beauty of her ancient features rising toward the heavens. I could see how the hills might have erupted from the earth a millennium ago, after a violent tremor broke the earth open reforming the barren wilderness.

Just ahead of me there was a small fruit stand. An old man snoozed in a chair tipped back precariously against a small shed. At first I assumed he was a black man because his skin was so thoroughly black, but soon I realized he had white skin baked black under years of sun. I wheeled up to him disturbing his midday nap.

"Excuse me, sir," I said, as I snatched one of his plump oranges. "Could you tell me what those mountains are called?"

He shook himself awake, startled by my sudden appearance.

"Eh, eh... mountains?" He straightened up and followed the point of my finger. "What're ya on about? Gave me a start," the old man said, watching me eat one fruit after another.

I felt the sweet fruit juices dribble down my chin and onto my T-shirt so I wiped my chin off, while handing the old man a ten-dollar Australian note.

"Sorry, I haven't found a restaurant in two days."

"By Christ," the old man laughed, "yer lookin' fer a proper restaurant are ya... must be a bleedin' Yank, eh?"

The old man spun around and offered me his jug of warm water. "Need a refill?" He handed me the large plastic container. "That's a nasty bit of business, I reckon, ridin' a pushbike up this way."

I thanked him with a smile and emptied some water into my bottle, then pointed again to the mountains. "Those mountains," I repeated, "what are they called?"

The old man shoved his wide-brimmed hat back, shading his eyes as he looked across the open plain.

"Depends."

"Depends on what?"

"Depends on who yer askin'. If yer askin' Capt'n Cook, I reckon he'd tell ya, they're the Glasshouse Mountains; if yer askin' an Aboriginal he'd tell ya, it's some kind'a female spirit, who begat her children out there on the plains. So it depends. Map'll tell ya somethin' altogether different."

That was the first reference I'd heard regarding the Aboriginals since my arrival. My only knowledge of their culture stemmed from dated articles in National Geographic with photos of primitive, spear-chucking, war-painted people.

"I don't know much about Aboriginals," I admitted to the old man. "Do they live around here?"

"Depends." The cagey old man pointed out the dichotomy again.

"You ask a whitefella and he'll tell ya he owns all this land, but if you ask a blackfella, he'll tell ya all Australia belongs to him. Not that he paid money for it, you understand, but that he *is* the land." The old man then hesitated for a moment, looking confused by his own words.

"Never mind, it's not for the whitefella ta know."

The old man sat down in his chair and rocked back against the aluminum-sided shed as if he were preparing to close the conversation.

"Well," I said nervously, "are there places I shouldn't go, things I should know before I ride farther on?"

"Depends," the man snagged me for the third time.

"On what?" I said impatiently.

"On where yer goin' and what yer doin'."

I was tiring of the man's double meanings. The acid from all the fruit I'd eaten was starting to burn my stomach lining. I kicked a stone irritably with my foot. "I'm going to Bundaberg," I muttered. "After that, I don't know."

The old man pulled the brim of his hat down toward the tip of his nose, no doubt tiring of life's endless riddles.

"I'll tell ya this," he said. "I don't understand much of what the blackfella says, his Dreamtime and all, but I can tell ya, there's a strangeness in this land — a power. The farther north ya go, the deeper into it yu'll get."

The old man's voice lowered as he chuckled to himself. "By Christ, a Yank... a sheila on a pushbike. What next?"

Hoping to catch the old man before he drifted off I asked insistently, "Are there any shops or—" But he interrupted me before I could finish my question.

"There's plenty up the road." The old man laughed again. "But no fancy restaurants, if that's what yer after." Then he added in a serious tone, "Just keep an eye out, eh."

"For what?"

The old man didn't answer. He didn't stir. I decided to move on.

Finally sated and lightheaded from all the fruit, I rode slowly along the long stretch of empty highway. I'd never heard of the Dreamtime and had no concept of what it meant, and yet I thought it curious that the Aboriginal and I had both imagined a female, surrounded by her family resting out on the plain.

As the road spun underneath me, I kept rerunning the old man's words with the same monotony. *What did he mean by the Aboriginal IS the land? What power did the land possess? He couldn't have fallen asleep so quickly. He just didn't want to answer my questions about going north. Cagey old fellow.* Then I started thinking about the sudden appearance of the owl in the forest, how it had unleashed a flood of memories. I began to feel that the old man and the bird were trying to show me something I couldn't quite grasp on my own. I wondered if mystical experiences hinted at something existing beyond my immediate sensory perception. Without all the civilized interference, I felt as if I could actually hear and see and feel so much more. The intensity was sometimes overwhelming.

Chapter Eighteen

HELL FIRES

I had cycled more than four hundred kilometers when I set off from Maryborough one invigorating winter morning. Brimming with a sense of purpose, I anticipated the happy reunion of sailing friends in Bundaberg. I hadn't really planned to cycle the whole distance in one day, but I was propelled forward not so much by my own will, but by the very shape of the earth.

By late afternoon seventy kilometers had disappeared at a good clip. Then, rather mysteriously, the flat terrain began to swell up into small evenly spaced hills. After pedaling uphill for a short distance, I found I could glide effortlessly down the other side. The rhythm created in the groundswell meant I never had to push the pedals again after that initial rise. Those perfectly spaced hills continued on for miles — glorious miles. Without having to pedal, I marveled at the land unfolding before me. The bush had been scythed back in every direction. In its place were fields of golden feathers waving in the pristine breeze.

The sun slipped lower wedging itself between the trees and casting long shadows over the road, playing a kind of hide-and-seek with me. With the wind chasing the shadows, I imagined kangaroos leaping across the road. I'd seen enough smashed "roo" alongside the road that I eventually saw them behind every tree, jumping out of every shadow.

Hints of an evening mist began to settle on the fields as the golden light melded into an evening's silvery gray. Lulled by the rhythm of the road, I slipped into a dreamy hypnotic state.

Suddenly and inexplicably, the undulating landscape burst into flames all around me. I felt caught in a war zone with bombs exploding in every direction. Brilliant orange-yellow flames enveloped the earth sending up plumes of sickeningly sweet black smoke. I gagged and coughed uncontrollably. The fires swept ruthlessly across the landscape, moving from behind me and swallowing everything on both sides of the road.

The twilight sky was now streaked by clawing fingers of toxic flames. I rode on, desperately following the narrow black path that divided the inferno. I felt as if I was riding from heaven straight into the hell fires. Armageddon had arrived.

I was convinced that I had cycled to the very doorstep of hell. Then I saw the sign:

CARAVAN PARK

OVERNIGHT

TENTS – CARAVANS

I stared at the sign for some time trying to discern which way the arrow pointed. Noticing a rickety caravan (trailer) off to the side of the road, I followed a pebbled path to it. An ancient, rusty sign pinned to the ripped screen door read *Manager*. I went over and frantically knocked on the door. I could feel the caravan jostle on its frame as someone moved about inside.

"Hang on, hang on, I'm comin'," came a muffled, gravelly voice.

The manager opened the door. He was an odd-shaped fellow. Dragging one leg behind him, his whole body looked permanently twisted from the crippling effect of his dead leg. A dirty yellow beard covered his face. Yet, aside from these oddities, there was something cheerful about him. At the sight of me, his eyes widened in surprise. He looked ready to laugh at any moment.

"Gawd, what do we have 'ere? A bird on a pushbike! Where've ya come from, luv?"

His manner was so calm and controlled I thought he might have slept through the nightmare that raged outside.

"I— I— came through the fires," I stammered, trying to control my panic. "They're everywhere, all around us."

"No way 'round 'em that's fer sure." The manager said this with so little concern I thought him suicidal, calmly awaiting his own annihilation.

"Where d'ja say you came in from?" he asked again, motioning for me to come in.

"Brisbane — but the fires—"

"Long way fer a gal to be ridin' all alone, I reckon."

"The fires are everywhere!" I shouted hysterically at the man, while slapping the makeshift desk with my fist. The whole caravan gave out an awful sigh.

"Hmmm, yeah, that'd be about right," the twisted man assured me, still unperturbed by my ravings. "T'is the season!"

"What?"

"Burnin' off the sugar cane and Bundy ain't nothin' but. Yer Yank, ain't ya?"

I stared at him in disbelief before nodding.

"Reckon you could use a good scrub, eh. A two-dollar note will get ya a caravan fer the night and a key to the washroom." The man pushed a key toward me as if urging me to get hold of myself and recover my sanity.

"That'd be fine, thanks." I took a deep settling breath. "Then, what you're saying is that all the fires... those hell fires I've just come through... are meant to be here?"

"Hell, yes, they're meant to be here! This is sugar cane country, luv. The only hell fires around here are what we put in the rum! So where ya headed?" The man pricked up his ears as if preparing himself for the punch line of a good joke.

"Bundaberg."

There was something in my answer that made his jaw fall open with laughter. He gripped his belly, jiggling happily in response. "Good luck to ya, luv. Drop off the key before ya leave, eh."

I stumbled down the uneven steps of the caravan, my legs shaky and weighted with fatigue. Turning back to the homely man I asked, "Well, how much farther is Bundaberg?"

The old man kept on giggling. "Reckon yer here, luv. If the fires don't get ya, the rum will!"

Chapter Nineteen

BLUEY & THE ROAD

"You'd be a fool through and through if you rode over *Horror's Stretch*," the mail clerk warned me in Bundaberg. "No water, food or petrol for two hundred mile or so... nothing but a few hungry buzzards waitin' to peck out yer eyes." On his advice, I boarded the train in Rockhampton, hoping to avoid the *Horror*, while still heading farther north.

It was the night of a full moon. I had no inclination toward sleep and relished the idea of tracing every mile of the forbidden route. Unfortunately I saw only long thin fingers of moonlit rays showering mile after mile in silver dust. There were a few lonely thin trees standing abjectly in an otherwise barren wilderness. The *Horror* stared back at me, echoing the warning from the old man at the fruit stand: "There's a strangeness in this land, keep an eye out."

Uncrinkling the note from Katie, which she'd left for me in Bundaberg, I reread it dejectedly as the old train creaked and moaned northward:

Dear Neva,
Sorry to have missed you. We've been deported by the Australian government. Lost all our documents with the boat on the reef. I enclose the newspaper clippings, which will tell you all about it. I'll be glad to get home — had enough sailing to last me a lifetime.

Gotta catch the plane.

Take Care, Katie

I had been so sure the hand of Fate had been carefully guiding me north toward old friends. I had envisioned helping her and Tom rebuild the boat, and I had even gone so far as to daydream about sailing with them. Staring out into the shadowy emptiness of the *Horror*, I thought of Richard and how feeble my excuse to leave him looked now. Why couldn't I have stayed?

I had to keep moving, I rationalized. I must be free, not shackled by anything, especially silly romantic notions. Edward was right. Loving anything or anybody only caused pain, endless suffering. He couldn't bear watching his mother suffer with cancer, just as I couldn't bear my father's paralysis. Every word father spoke, every breath he took required such strength. I doubted my strength. I thought myself weak and cowardly and was never sure why. Or, maybe, I did know.

I had to keep moving. I ran away from things. I feared not having my parents' courage to face adversity. I loved them with all my heart, but I feared I was a terrible disappointment to them. I was the youngest of four, yet the first to marry and the first to divorce and run away from it. Though I always had good grades in school, I never felt "smart." I had that resounding damnation in my head: *Stupid, Ignorant Child...*

Being a loner by nature, I was never part of any cliques. The nuns had done an excellent job of teaching me that I was not worthy of love or respect. The priest had stamped my soul *Unforgiven* — I was just an itinerant sinner.

I looked out at the *Horror* and searched for hidden clues in its bleak nature. It stretched on for miles. Each rickety clatter of the rails sounded like an uneven heartbeat. I wondered if people just naturally feared being alone and anything resembling solitariness was frightening. What was out there, really? Like the odd-shaped shadows cast on my wall by moonlit nights, I still felt the child within me cowering from undefined phantoms:

> Cobalt blackness confused by light, splintered, broken... chasing, chasing, chasing me. Who is out there? I whispered into the Horror. Spirits, God, Demons or Ghosts? I am the Sinner chased by the Devil himself. Little girl cries out in the night. What? What memory is that? Why must I keep the knife by my bed. Mother, Mother wipe my tears away, keep me safe. He's coming to get me. Who? Who is out there?

Gazing out into the vacuous moonswept wilderness, I realized that it wasn't the empty stretch of land I feared as much as that long stretch of highway called Memory. I *had* to keep moving. It should have been clear to me then that there was no escaping the demons that pursued me, but it wasn't.

We rattled along until daybreak. The morning sun transformed the moondust into golden feathers of sugar cane.

I got off with my bike at McKay dazed and sleepless. Sniffing the early morning air, I found it repugnant. It was that sickeningly sweet smell of burning sugar cane again, clouding the pure air. Anxious to be on my way, I lifted my leg stiffly over the crossbar and pressed my foot hard on the pedal.

I rode as far as I could that day, fueled only by the desire to get to the next campground and recoup the night's lost sleep. The road was flat and straight as a ruler, cutting a monotonous path through the cane fields. I was growing weary of my repetitious thoughts and revolving door of memories. I was tired of watching the black rim of my front tire draw weird circles on the pavement. After weeks of being alone, I was bored with my own company.

After eight hours of cycling, I pulled up next to a dilapidated sign for the Proserpine Caravan Park. The sign lay smothered in an overgrowth of cane; the campsite, obviously, choked out of existence by its profusion. There was nothing there.

Tired, hungry and frustrated, I dumped my bike on the ground and sat down on a large stone to sulk with the cane toads. I lectured myself — *Come on, things could be worse. Slept on the ground before, no big deal. Got enough crackers.* I was preparing to discuss matters with the spider making his way up my rock seat when I saw a giant double-axle red truck steaming down the road. The sight cheered me enormously. It was the first intrusion that day, blotting out the monotony of the highway.

The giant truck pulled up next to me and stopped. Surprised, I slipped off my stony perch as the curly-haired, freckled driver leaned his head out of the window.

"In some strife are ya, luv?" He called to me.

"Actually I was just looking for the Caravan Park." I pointed to the sign. "But it's not here anymore." Standing up, I dusted myself off.

"Hasn't been fer donkey years, I reckon." The truck driver scratched his flaming red hair, implying that I should have known that. "Need a lift, then?"

I hesitated. "No thanks, I'm just resting." I straightened my shoulders and slipped my hands into my pockets reconsidering the offer. I was desperate to talk to somebody, anybody!

The truck driver swung down from the cabin like a deft monkey. I was amazed to find him nearly a foot shorter than me, after he had appeared so tall, elevated in his large truck.

We stood awkwardly facing each other. Automatically extending my hand, I remembered belatedly that Australians don't shake hands as a greeting. My hand sagged uncomfortably in mid-air.

The truck driver grinned. "M'name's Bluey — Bluey—" he pointed to his head with a wide grin. "It's on account'a me red hair. By Christ," he chuckled, "yer a tall stretch of a Yank at that."

"What makes you think I'm Yank?"

Bluey doubled over in laughter. "Think yer Yank! Bloody hell, nobody else would be silly enough to be out here ridin' a pushbike. No bloody Aussie sheila, I'll tell ya."

I didn't really take offense, but my expression must have said so. Bluey was quick to add, "Don't get me wrong, luv, the Yanks are a good lot. We never forget they helped us out in *The War*, eh."

"*The War?*"

"Bloody World War II, mate. If it weren't fer the Yanks we'd be Jap, I reckon."

I was too tired and too hungry to get into any lengthy discourses about war again. It was always a touchy subject, regardless of the vintage of *The War*, so I nodded my head in agreement to whatever Bluey said about *The War*, and left it alone.

Bluey had jade green eyes, a straight-boned nose and a fixed broad smile, all of which gave him the friendliest appearance.

"Where ya headed?" he asked.

"North," I clicked like an automaton, wishing I'd said something more purposeful.

Bluey dug his hands deep into his back pockets with a quizzical look. "North?" He rubbed his chin thoughtfully. "That would take ya anywhere from now through a lifetime to get to, I reckon."

He shook his head. "I'm headed up Townsville way. Yer welcome to come along. It'll be hot as the Nulla' from here on up."

I hesitated, but I liked Bluey and I couldn't find anything about him that sent out a warning of distrust. So I nodded and we loaded the bike and climbed into the cab. It felt just fine sitting high and comfortable above the heat of the highway.

"What brings ya up this way? Can't say as I've seen many Yanks lately. Not since *The War* anyway. It's all Greeks and I-talians... and a few of us Irishmen." Bluey laughed heartily.

From there we launched into a non-stop conversation. I soon realized that Bluey was much older than I first thought. He said he'd been driving that route for thirty years, longer than I'd been alive!

At one point he reached over the back of our seat and pulled out a tall bottle of Coca Cola. I began to salivate at the sight of that familiar red label. He took a big swig and handed it to me. "Here, this'll set ya right."

I tilted my head back letting the sugar-water flood into my mouth. Instead of the bubbly sweet relief that I expected, a fiery brew stung the back of my throat and I gasped for air. Bluey smacked his lips as a sympathetic reaction.

"That'll take the sting out of the road, two-thirds rum. Bundy, of course, best bloody stuff in the world, I reckon."

After the first taste of rum, it settled in my desperately empty stomach, leaving me in a calm and dreamy state. The miles began to disappear as Bluey continued to intrigue me with stories of his travels around Australia. He knew more about Queensland, its history, residents and by-ways, than anyone I could have hoped to meet. He also had an encyclopedic memory for the names of plants and animals, of which I knew very little. He went on to describe in lurid detail the various deadly snakes, stinging red ants (whom I had already met), and a gaggle of spiders, including the lethal red backs. "Mind you don't rattle the bandicoots, tease a roo or swim with a box jellyfish..." Under the influence, it was hard remembering the names and descriptions of all the creatures that could kill me — "not least of which," Richard had said, "was the average truckee!"

The miles began to disappear at a reliable rate as I sunk into the dizzying comfort of Bundy, while sticking to the thick cushion which propped me up to an astounding view of the Australian countryside. Moving faster and sitting high above the road, I could better appreciate the subtle changes from the cane fields to what was, ever so discreetly, slipping into the myriad shades of the tropics.

Instinctively trusting Bluey, I found myself telling him about some of my experiences: the volcanic peak I'd envisioned as a female spirit, my conversation with the old man at the fruit stand and my nights in the bush, especially the visitation from the owl.

Bluey listened intently to everything I said. His expression gradually changed from lighthearted to serious. "You've been touched, have ya?" he asked, looking askance at me.

I interpreted "touched" as touched by madness.

"You think I'm nuts?" I winced at Bluey.

"I didn't mean wacko. I meant touched — touched by the land, its power. Magic. Call it what you will. One way or another this is Aboriginal country. They were here eons before the whitefella and I reckon they know what it's about. I reckon the whites came along and mucked things up."

Bluey continued in a serious tone. "The Aboriginal has been ruined by the whites, locked 'im up in his own country. Mind you, I'd never say that to any of me mates. Sympathizing with the blackfella is not looked upon kindly. But, By Christ, I've spent me life drivin' over the outback. I've come to know a fair few blackfellas."

"Do you know anything about the Dreamtime?" I asked, remembering the old man referring to it as we talked at the fruit stand.

Bluey looked curiously at me and gripped the wheel harder. "The Aboriginal has an incredible sense about the world around him, but there's no way into it for the whitefella. Just the way it is, I reckon."

Bluey fell silent for an unusually long time and then he turned to me, making sure I was still listening. "I've seen magic out there. I can't explain what I don't understand, but I reckon you've already seen something of it." Bluey looked back at the road. "So you watch out fer yerself, eh. It could lead a whitefella into some awful strife."

Bluey seemed nearly in a trance just from speaking about the Dreamtime. All his talk of magic and doom made me want to get back on my bicycle and ride away.

My fright turned real when a kangaroo leapt out from the side of the road, darting into our path. Bluey didn't swerve the truck but held her steady, just as I might have steered a boat into a giant threatening wave, hoping to avoid its overwhelming power.

The animal's muscular hind legs catapulted him clear of danger and Bluey relaxed back into the curve of his seat. "Christ, mate, there's a lesson for ya. Like I said, you've always gotta keep an eye out," Bluey cautioned me again. "You'll be movin' along smooth as silk and then there'll be this reminder."

"Reminder?" I asked, not exactly sure what Bluey was getting at.

"Reminder," he insisted. "We're just intruders. The land doesn't really belong to any of us."

"Like the sea," I reflected, watching the afternoon heat shimmer over the blacktop as it cast off wavy lines of merging light bands. The road looked like a long, slithering serpent, clearing a path to the north. I shut my eyes, trying to rid myself of the image, but it stayed with me even as I slept.

After arriving in Townsville late that night, Bluey pulled his laboring truck up next to a Caravan Park. He asked me one more time if I wanted to head on to Mt. Isa with him. I liked the notion of going to Mt. Isa, of sitting high and lofty off the road, sipping hot smacks of rum while watching the black bitumen peel away for thousands of miles. But I had this needling thought that I had to get North, that something was there, just ahead of me. I had to go North. So I climbed down from the cab and looked at Bluey for the last time. Before I could raise my hand to shake his, Bluey leaned over and handed me a slip of paper saying, "Here's me address. Drop me a line, eh. Picture postcard 'll do. Just let me know how ya get on."

"Thanks so much," I said. "I won't forget—"

Bluey interrupted me, "Take care of yerself now."

"Thanks Bluey, I'll write," I said sincerely, knowing I wouldn't. That was the one thing about the road we both knew — you carry your friends with you as long as you can, then you let them go.

I watched Bluey's rear lights shrink into imperceptible dots before I wheeled into the Caravan Park. It was one big lot full of parked cars surrounded by a sleeping town called Townsville. There were no tents and no grass for tents, so I laid my bike down and threw out my sleeping bag on the hard blacktop. I wondered why I hadn't found my spot yet, the place I was going to stop and relax and spend some time in. I had this picture in my mind of sitting on an island making my own campsite, living off fish and reaching back into my soul for a moment of peace. It must be farther North.

Meanwhile an Aussie accent flared up at a dog barking at my shadow cast long and lumpy near their caravan. I fell into an uncomfortable sleep thinking that Bluey was probably right: "It's a bloody long way, ridin' a pushbike to the Never-Never."

Chapter Twenty

JAMIE & THE ROAD

I kept pedaling north, north through the tropics, through blasts of heat followed by sudden rain squalls. I might have made Cairns in one day; instead I stopped for the night in Innisfail, hoping to find a warm bed out of the rain.

I didn't see anything in the small provincial town resembling a Bed & Breakfast, so I stopped in front of a modest brick building with a worn-out sign announcing *Women's Hostel.* I imagined it was a place where women enjoyed a warm, convivial environment, where I might stretch out and dry my chapped derriere and sip tea, while chatting about women's things. I thought I might find a longed-for retreat from the lonely road.

Swinging open the weak, wooden front door of the hostel, I expected a greeting of some sort. There was none. I ventured down the narrow hallway; the doors were closed all along the corridor, so I continued to the end of it. There I found a small kitchen with an old-fashioned iron stove and a sturdy wooden table. How quaint, I thought, just as I'd imagined.

I was suddenly aware of someone standing next to me. From over my shoulder came a deep, harsh voice addressing me. "What would ya be wantin' here?"

I turned to find a middle-aged woman glaring at me. Her eyes were dull, red and puffy. Her unwelcoming expression was molded by a sallow, pitted face. She looked as if she never ventured outdoors for a breath of fresh air.

"I'm just looking for a room for the night."

"A room fer the night, eh?" She leered at me suspiciously. "Yer bloody car broke down or somethin'?"

"No, I just need a place to sleep out of the rain, that's all. This is a women's hostel, isn't it?"

"Awh yeah," she drawled, while crossing her arms impatiently. "But I don't reckon it's the kinda place you'd wanta stay in. That is, if you had the choice."

"Are you the manager?"

"I can set ya up if you like. Three dollars 'll get ya a room, use of the kitchen and bath down the hall. The doors lock at ten and open at six-thirty in the mornin'."

Put off by the manager's suspicions, I agreed reluctantly to the stipulations and followed her down the hall to my room.

"Will my bike be safe outside or can I bring it inside?

"Bike? What kind'a bike."

"Just a pushbike."

"Nothin's safe nowhere as far as I'm concerned. Do what ya like, you can sleep with it under yer pillow, if that suits ya. Just keep it out of my road."

On that note I slouched into my room, and a sorry sight of a room it was. I had become accustomed to a certain amount of inconvenience and discomfort on the road. Sleeping in the bush, in fields, atop red ant hills, near the road, on the road, on the beach, etc., but nothing was as depressing as this. The room was small and stuffy, and painted gray with despair. No amount of my jimmying could pry open the painted window, which afforded a smudged, square view of the entrance into the dingy place. The bed had collapsed on its wire springs long ago, so it barely cleared the floor. After the woman left, I couldn't stop myself from tearing off the stained white cover and hurling it into the corner. There was a nightstand pressed against the opposite wall, but it wouldn't do as a writing table. Its legs teetered and shook on their arthritic hinges.

I sat on the sagging bed for some time and stared at the broken lines of silver rain, driving into the hard ground. Beyond the constant patter of rain, I slowly became aware of the sound of someone weeping. Tip-toeing down the hallway, I came to a darkened room with its door left slightly ajar. The sobbing, like the rain, kept on incessantly. As I strained to see who was whimpering inside the bleak room, another voice caught me off-guard.

"The ol' widda can't speak English. They left her here."

I turned toward the voice and found a young girl standing next to me.

"No place to put 'er, I reckon. She falls down a lot, lands on her head."

I guessed the girl was about fifteen years old. She had dancing bright eyes and a quick smile. Less appealing, a dirty cotton dress hung from her shoulders and drooped down to her mud-capped knees.

"Have a cuppa?" The young girl invited me to the kitchen for that cup of tea I'd longed for.

Her long peach-blossom curls bounced at the back of her head with a life of their own. She laughed gaily while introducing herself. "I was supposed to be a boy." She skipped about the kitchen, preparing our tea. "So me dad named me Jamie." Stopping abruptly, she turned to me. "You from Eh'merica then?" Jamie whispered in her Australian twang, coveting the word "America" as if it was sacred.

I nodded.

"Awh, I'd love to go to Eh'merica. Get out of this bloody dump. Bloody loony bin this is." Jamie paused for a moment, savoring her daydream. "What in the bloody hell you doin' 'ere anyway? Not many Eh'mericans call into Innisfail."

"I've been riding a bicycle along the coast, just having a look," I said defensively.

"Ridin' a pushbike up the coast! What in bloody hell for? We've got ourselves a proper train, ya know. Never mind, I'll be out of this place tomorrah... never comin' back."

"Why are you staying here, if you don't like it?" I asked Jamie naively.

"Stayin'! Stayin'!" She scowled. "You must be bloody jokin'. You think this a bloody guest house, don't ya? I watched ya come in. Couldn't believe me eyes, lettin' Miss Philes give ya a room. Bloody hell!" Jamie pointed to the hallway. "You'd be as mad as them, I reckon."

The kettle whistled. The girl whirled around and grabbed the pot in one motion. Then she slopped the boiling water into the teapot for steeping. Jamie poured it so recklessly that hot water and tea leaves spilled onto the counter-top, then to the floor, where they made a brown wading pool.

"Hey, you better slow down there," I said, trying to avert an accident.

"Never mind," she laughed at my cautioning. "Me ol' man 'll be 'ere tomorrah. One way or other, this'll be me last night in this dump."

Just as Jamie swung around with the cup and saucer, the cup flew off and shattered on the floor. The crash brought Miss Philes into the kitchen.

"You clumsy little bitch you. Get out of here." Miss Philes lunged at Jamie, wagging her finger at her. "S'ppose you've been pinchin' me tea again. Aren't ya, you little scoundrel? Get back into that room of yours and don't peep a word until your bludger of a father comes tomorrah."

Jamie skipped out of the room quite cheerfully. Turning to Miss Philes she said, "Well, it ain't gonna be me that's gonna die here like a shriveled-up old lizard."

Miss Philes turned to me with renewed vehemence. "Gawd, that girl's more trouble than she's worth. You'll be clearin' out of me kitchen soon, won't ya? I got preparin' ta do. Got a family to feed. Can't be wastin' me time jawin' with the likes a you."

I thought I might win her over with some sympathetic conversation. "So you have a family?" I asked. "Are they nearby?"

Her voice raised a decibel. "I said I can't be wastin' me time with you lot."

I rinsed my cup and turned it over on the dish rack in surrender. Miss Philes kept on about what a nuisance people were and how nothing was ever the way you wanted it; people were always barging in and getting in the way.

I left the kitchen, but as soon as I turned the knob on my door, I heard Jamie's muffled giggle as she followed me into the room.

"Don't take any notice of her," Jamie scoffed. "Miss Philes is mad as a bloody hatter. She'll be fixin' supper alright, for the next two or three hours, jawin' away. She sets the bloody table, talks to her whole bloody family. Only trouble is, there's nobody there."

I moved about the small room feeling caged in and claustrophobic. It took me a moment to understand what Jamie meant about Miss Philes and her make-believe family. Turning to Jamie I changed the subject abruptly. "How long have you been here?"

"Well, let me see." Jamie sat on my bed, rubbing the buckles on her shoes together. "Me Mum died when I was born and me Dad tried carin' for me but he was no good at it, on account of him gettin' on the grog and all. He brought me here when I was ten." Jamie suddenly jumped up off my bed and went to the window. "Tomorrah's the day. He promised." Jamie reiterated her statement as if trying to convince herself.

"You got any family in Eh'merica?" Jamie asked, peering out the window.

I nodded. "My parents, a sister and two brothers."

Jamie seemed to have a hard time believing this. She shook her head in disbelief, just as I had a moment before, thinking about Miss Philes.

"Gorblimey! You gotta family and place in Eh'merica and left?" Jamie glanced at me with a look of desperation. "I'd never leave home if I had one."

"It's hard to explain." I stumbled for words, trying to defend myself. "I got married too young — it was a terrible mistake. I felt ashamed and I ran away."

"There ya go!" Jamie piped in excitedly. "We're not so different after all. I'm ashamed too, ashamed of being born and of bein' a girl. I killed me own mum."

"Oh Jesus." I collapsed on the bed, overwhelmed by Jamie's confession.

"Jamie, being born a girl is not a crime." I shook my head, trying to ward off my own self-doubts. "Surely you didn't hurt your mother, you didn't *kill* her?"

"That's how me ol' man puts it. Says I killed her just as sure as I put a knife in her belly. But me Auntie says she just died for lack of help when I was born."

"So your mother died while giving birth." Feeling despondent and not wanting to imagine a world without my mother, I defended Jaime. "But none of it was your fault. You must understand that." I felt useless in the face of real tragedy. "Things happen, Jamie, far beyond our control. My god, you were just a baby. Whatever happened wasn't your fault."

Jamie turned to me, her high spirits spiraling toward sadness. "She was beautiful. I'd a loved her so much. I'd never hurt her." She sank onto the bed next to me and I put my arms around her. We both sat there on the sagging bed sniffling and shivering. Through it all, we could still hear the old widow whimpering in her dark room and the rain falling relentlessly outside.

The next morning was cast in the same mold as the day before — gloomy and forlorn. I laid in bed for a long time lulled by the continual tapping of rain as it trickled down the eaves.

It wasn't until midday, when I was finally preparing to leave, that I heard the iron gate bend back on its rusty hinges. Then came the long strain of the bell blaring down the narrow hallway. I heard Jamie's light footsteps tapping down the hall toward the door.

Choosing not to open my door and get mixed up with goodbyes, I sat on my bed, peering out the window at Jamie's father. He stood slightly hunched over at the door, well-hidden inside his canvas coat and wide-brimmed hat.

Their muffled conversation went on for about ten minutes. Then, through my rain-soaked window, I saw Jamie trailing after her father with her suitcase in hand. She tugged at the sleeve of his overcoat as he pushed open the wrought-iron gate.

"Please take me with you. *Please.*"

The man walked on, never looking back.

Jamie stood in the rain soaked to the bone, her voice growing weaker with each step her father took away from her.

Frozen in anguish, I waited for the sound of Jamie's footsteps, wondering if I should try to console her. My mind churned over useless banalities: "Everything is going to be OK... the women's hostel isn't so bad... your father will be back to get you as soon as he can..."

In the next moment, I heard Jamie running down the hallway to my room. "I've changed my mind," Jamie said solemnly to me. "I want to go to Eh'merica with you."

"Jamie," I began slowly. "I wish I could take you with me—" Feeling like the ultimate betrayer, I continued, "but look, soon you'll be old enough to leave here on your own."

Jamie stared at the floor and then straightening up, she said, "Never mind, it was just a thought. Dad said he'd be back next week, after he'd fixed the place up a bit, that's all."

Rubbing Jamie's shoulder, I tried to reassure her. "It won't be long." She turned away from me and went back into her room.

I gathered up my bike and wheeled it down the hallway past Miss Philes preparing tea for her nonexistent family. I wheeled past the old widow in black, rocking her chair and weeping incessantly. I pushed my bike through the doorway and past the wrought-iron gate. As the latch clicked shut, I thought of Jamie and her aloneness, which I had freely chosen.

I hesitated, drew in a deep breath, and wheeled on. I could so easily escape what they could not.

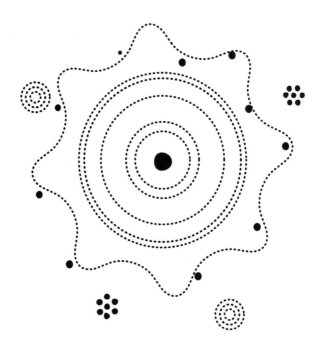

PART THREE

DREAMTIME

THIS WAS WAY BACK,

AT THE VERY BEGINNING.

THE LAND AND THE PEOPLE

WERE CREATED BY THE SPIRITS.

THEY MADE THE RIVERS,

THE WATER HOLES,

THE HILLS AND THE ROCKS

AND ALL THINGS LIVING.

THEY GAVE US HUNTING THINGS,

THEY GAVE EACH CLAN THEIR LAND,

THEY GAVE US OUR TOTEMS

AND THEY GAVE US

OUR DREAMING.

Carolyn Windy, Docker River, Northern Territory
The Aboriginal Children's History of Australia
(Written and illustrated by Australia's Aboriginal children)

Chapter Twenty-One

CHASING

What a strange ending, I thought, as I sat on a bench facing the Coral Sea. I had biked two thousand kilometers to Cairns, hoping to find some purpose in my journey, but my intent, like the marshy tidelands that stretched out before me, was still murky and undefined.

While cycling I had longed for the road to turn back toward the coast so that I could be near the ocean breeze again and be comforted by the constant lapping of waves. Having finally arrived back at the shoreline in Cairns, I was disappointed to find the tide at low ebb, leaving almost a mile of stagnant mud flats stretched out before me.

As I sat on the bench I could hear an amusing sucking and popping sound all around me as the mud shifted. Small holes opened up in the mud where tiny crabs excavated below. After a time the surface bubbled, then broke, leaving a hole for the crab to scurry up to the surface for some fresh air and a bit of sun.

For a time I shared their sense of relief at having surfaced from the darkness below. But my relief was for the crabs, not for myself. I had traveled so far but I hadn't really arrived anywhere — only another park bench. My aching need to keep moving cheated me of any sense of calm.

I wanted to stop. I wanted to prop my bicycle up against the park bench and leave it there. I wanted to walk down the street, turn the corner and see my childhood home in New York. I wanted to run hard with my arms outstretched, ready to fall into the gentle comfort of Mother's embrace. Perhaps she would have forgiven me by now for leaving a husband and running away. I wanted to be forgiven and I wanted to feel safe again.

I was tired of the demons chasing me; their voices crowded around me at night, staring into my bed, staring at the child cowering within. Perhaps I had thought that by not having a proper bed I might escape them, but no, the ghosts were clever creatures. They could find me anywhere, at any time. Running was no good. The demons ran as fast I did. They all wore black — black as the moonless night, black as the ocean depths starved of oxygen, black as the priest's cloth spread over me, suffocating me.

I felt the old paralysis start to creep up my spine. I must stand up. Father always said to keep moving. That's what you must do to outpace the paralysis. He couldn't, of course, but I could. I stood up.

I felt a sudden tug at the back of my shirt and thought of Jaime. Jaime wanted to escape with me. "I'd never leave a family, if I'd a had one," she said.

A mad rush of bird squawking suddenly broke through my barren thoughts. In the mud flats, just in front of me, a small riot had broken out. Two large pelicans were having a go at each other, fighting over fish entrails that had no doubt drifted down from the docks where the fishing boats were tied up. A raucous pack of jealous sea gulls cheered them on with wild screeches. Finally, a large heron intervened, sauntering over to inspect the leftovers, followed by a small fleet of delicately limbed sandpipers stepping in time behind him. I couldn't help laughing at the endless antics of the small crabs scurrying around, chased by the graceful heron and bullied by the greedy sea gulls.

In the distance half-submerged rocks glistened with silver splashes of light. They danced in front of my eyes like fireflies. I couldn't see past the shimmering, blinding white light that exploded off the sea in the far distance. With one hand shading my eyes from the penetrating sunlight, I thought, this is as good a place as any. After all, the paved road ended just north of Cairns. The thought of bumping along some red dust road leading me deeper into bush country, only to end up in another Never-Never, seemed ludicrous. Why not stop, I thought. I had been on the road long enough — more than a year had passed since I'd left Hawaii and sailed across the Pacific. I had somehow managed to lose eight months just wandering about New Zealand, and another few months sailing to Australia and pedaling along its northeastern coastline.

Looking over my shoulder in the direction I had just come from, I saw the majestic Tablelands rising above the plains to the west. I had taken the detour via Innisfail and ridden along the plateau. Those lush green mountains towered above the plains like an ancient protective totem, spreading their lavish arms, guarding the virgin territory below. There was nothing for me to do now, except stop and admire their sacred beauty.

Cairns seemed a friendly enough place, I reasoned, while wiping the sweat away from my eyes. Gazing down the tree-lined esplanade that ringed the seaboard, I followed the road as it gradually curved toward the small port bustling with activity. Fishing trawlers of all sizes were busy off-loading their catch. This was a good enough spot to rest.

What I had seen of the town appealed to me. The low-lying buildings appeared to be an unusual hybrid of Victorian and Wild West architecture. I had a momentary vision of Richard and I walking hand-in-hand along the esplanade. He might have explained the ironic mix of Cairns' gracious and bawdy character.

I felt almost giddy at the thought of settling in for awhile. I would finally sleep in a bed and have regular meals, find a job and talk to people about everyday things. I had come to the end of my journey, I'd find a place of my own and cast off my strange weave of memories into the sea and let them go.

The tide was changing. The long, subtle process was reversing itself. The reluctant wavelets slowly edged their way back toward shore. It would be a long journey home.

I promised myself I would change. Just like the tide, I could cover up all those sunken mud holes of memory with a beautiful shimmering sea of life. And I went on and on, mumbling to myself, thinking once again that I had won, that I could outpace my demons.

Chapter Twenty-Two

CAP'N BOB

Set on staying in Cairns, I bought the local newspaper and scanned the classifieds for a job and place to live. I read the "adverts" amused by the variety: TOBACCO PICKER up in the Tablelands, CLERK at the newspaper, COOK on a prawn trawler, MAID at a Bed & Breakfast. I decided on MAID — a job I felt fully qualified for and it offered free room and board.

Hoping to find a place to stay before nightfall, I called the number immediately. After a sequence of harsh buzzes, a husky guttural voice answered, "Ah-low."

"Yes, hello. I'm interested in the job advertised in the paper. Just wondering if—"

The deep male voice interrupted me. "You get seasick?"

"Pardon?"

"I said, do you get seasick?"

"Ah, no sir, I don't but—"

"Well, the job won't be open much longer. Come straight away if you like, 156 Grafton, three blocks in from Main."

The receiver clicked and I was left staring quizzically at the phone. I couldn't imagine why seasickness played a major role in cleaning a small hotel, but I thought I might as well give it a try and headed off to Grafton Street.

The single-story building looked more like a travel agency than a hotel. A poster in the window pictured divers snorkeling over the Great Barrier Reef; its colors were faded by the sun, turning the Reef into a drab and murky underworld.

I had almost forgotten my purpose, when the glass door swung open and a heavy-set fellow leaned out. "You the ly-dee that rang?"

I nodded.

He raised his thick, hairy hand and waved me inside.

I looked around the room expecting to see a lobby of some sort — a clerk, check-in counter, tourists bustling about — but none existed. It was a dark room with an empty desk and two chairs. The walls were covered with mock-wood veneer and in one dreary corner hung a stuffed fish with bulging eyes. The frightening moment of death had been garishly preserved. I turned quickly for the door, but the man's questions caught my attention again.

"So, ya don't get seasick, eh?" He screwed up his thick, black eyebrows.

"No, I don't." I turned to the man slowly. "Well, only once, but it was something I ate. It wasn't the sea exactly, it was—"

"How much time 'ave ya spent at sea?" The big man interrupted me.

"Some." I stared at him blankly, still wondering what the sea had to do with cleaning a hotel room.

"Think ya can handle it?" He slapped the empty desk with the flat of his hand.

"Ah, yes, of course. Handle what?" I tried to concentrate, but the man started talking so fast, using Australian slang, I couldn't make sense of it:

"Alotta sheilas go up there thinkin' there's quick money to be made, but it's no good to ya if yer spewin' all over the decks. No good to nobody. We put the money up front. It's a few bob, I'll tell ya, just to 'ave ya spewin' and turnin' yer tail back to the big city. So, if ya think ya can handle it, the job's yers. We'll send ya up on the afternoon mail run."

The man drummed his fingers impatiently on the desk. "So, ya game?"

I nodded, still searching for the clue that would tell me exactly what it was I was game for.

"It *is* cleaning?" I asked. "I'm just going to be cleaning... like the ad says."

"By Christ, you'll be cleanin'!" He slapped the table once again. "Righto." The man spun around enthusiastically and took some papers out of his desk drawer. Then he strode over to me and pushed them into my hand. "I've got yer ticket. Yu'll be off this arvo. Remember my name, eh, Cap'n Bob. Tell 'em Cap'n Bob sent ya."

"Captain?" I muttered as the big fellow turned toward the door. "Where is it exactly that I'm going?"

"Weipa," he said, pronouncing it Wee-pa. "It's on the inside of the Gulf. Someone'll be there to pick ya up and take ya straight away to the *Northern Pearl*. No worries. Everything 'll be taken care of."

Cap'n Bob pushed open the door, speeding my departure.

"What should I take with me?"

"You won't be needin' much. Too hot fer clothes and nowhere to go."

The big man swept me hurriedly out of his office. Before I knew it I was standing in the street, clutching an airline ticket and the ad from the newspaper. I held them both up, hoping the information from one piece of paper might shed some light on the other. The plane ticket read:

> BRAFFORD BROS. - depart Cairns - 1400 hours -
> 18 July, 1977 - destination - Weipa, North Queensland

Then I turned to the classifieds. There it was, right above the HOTEL MAID ad:

> COOK: WANTED IMMEDIATELY - 110 FOOT
> PRAWN TRAWLER - NORTHERN PEARL -
> IN THE GULF - COOKING AND SEA
> EXPERIENCE NECESSARY

Cook! He bloody well didn't say anything about cooking! Oh, well. What the hell. I've never been to Weipa.

Chapter Twenty-Three

BEYOND THE STARK
NEVER-NEVER

Weipa, North Queensland, I was told, was a mining town. As we landed on the clay-red earth, Weipa was nowhere in sight. The "airport" was a small hutch in the middle of the stark Never-Never. I don't even know why the small lean-to existed. No one was inside it and no one walked over to it. As I clambered down the short boarding ladder, my legs wobbled badly from all the vibration in the deep-bellied propeller plane. I'd had two large oil drums for company, which had threatened to crush me if I mistakenly shimmied in their direction.

I searched for the welcoming face that Captain Bob had assured me would be there, but all I could see was a flat horizon of dust and flies stretching to infinity. Hardly an imaginary place, the Never-Never did exist in Australia, and I was staring dead center into it. Instead of a welcoming face, I was met by a blast of equatorial heat so powerful that I gasped for each scorching breath of air.

The bulbous cargo plane turned and taxied down the runway, kicking up clouds of dust as it took off. The flies swirled up my nose and into my ears, no doubt looking for safe harbor. The plane quickly evaporated like the last drop of moisture in a desert pond. I stood alone, overwhelmed by the merciless invasion of heat, flies and dust.

Somehow the situation seemed remarkably familiar and ludicrous. I laughed, recognizing my penchant for traveling long distances and ending up even closer to nowhere. I laughed because I didn't know what else to do. Four hours earlier I had promised myself a normal life. Now I stood in the middle of a red-clay desert so enormous, so inconceivably vacant that after turning 360 degrees, I felt sure that I was at the center of an otherwise uninhabited universe.

Captain Bob's promises were as empty as the dirt track that stretched before me. Swatting at flies and choking on the dust, I started walking down a "road." The only telling clues that it was supposed to go somewhere were tire marks cutting zigzag patterns into the rich, red earth.

An hour passed before I felt a hopeful rumbling in the earth. It was followed by the sight of a large truck bumping down the road, heading in the same direction that I was walking. At first it looked like a weird aberration, advancing inside a cloud of red dust. But by the time the truck pulled up next to me, I could see the large shadow of a man behind the wheel. The door of the cab flew open and the driver cheerfully called out, "By Christ, you look as lost as an Abo gone walkabout in the big city, I reckon."

As I looked inside, the driver leaned toward me. "M'names Lucky, headin' down river to Weipa. Reckon you could use a lift, eh."

Gawd! He was an awful looking creature. His wild eyes were too frenzied to ever be reassuring. He was a big, hairy beast of a man. His excess body hair ran down his neck and onto his unshorn shoulders, ending in clusters under his soiled T-shirt. His ape-like arms hung clawing at the wheel.

In defense of the brute, Lucky did have that friendly Australian smile I'd become so familiar with, but it wasn't one I would cling to for safety. I stood speechless in the dust, swatting the flies and considering my few options.

"S'truth!" Lucky bellowed with a rap on the wheel. "I ain't seen a sheila up 'ere since the last rains. You'd be up fer one of the Brafford boats, eh?"

I nodded uncertainly.

"Been prawnin' before, 'ave ya?"

I shook my head.

"Cat got yer tongue, eh." Lucky continued on, without waiting for my reply. "I'm a nice fella, no worries. Another few hours out 'ere and you'll be black as an Abo and diggin' fer grubs, I reckon. Come on."

I took a deep, soldering hot breath and climbed into the truck. As we set off down the track I held onto the blistering hot dash with one hand and the searing metal door handle with the other, praying for Weipa to appear.

Lucky must have thought my anxiety humorous. He laughed and whistled a tune as we drove. After giving me a side-long glance he cheerfully added to my distress. "There'll be blokes up 'ere ya gotta watch out for. Some fellas been up 'ere a long time. Know what I mean? Some never been to town at all. They're a shifty lot 'specially on them fishin' boats." Lucky shook his head, chuckling.

Meanwhile, I was busy choking on the dust, trying not to show my mounting fear.

"You need to look after yer'self," he warned again. "Need a strong fella like Lucky to look after ya."

I flushed crimson red, wondering if Lucky was looking for a job as my bodyguard.

"This 'ere's a town of five thousand minin' men, and as far as I know, there's only two ly-dees, and they're bloody spliced — keep to themselves. It's a bloody dog's life fer a woman up 'ere, mate. No place, I reckon, fer a sheila."

Lucky suddenly changed the subject. "Where ya from?"

"America," I coughed.

"Christ! Yank as well."

"Is that bad?" I sputtered.

"It ain't the worst ya could be. Asian be the worst and there's plenty of 'em around, I reckon."

Lucky started to look genuinely worried about me and that made me all the more tremulous.

He drove on, jabbering away about the local points of interest, which were limited at best. Every mile or so an alloy-roofed house would crop up out of the red dust, perched rather forlornly on five foot stilts. Lucky pointed out that it was for the "wet." It was hard enough to conceive of any form of moisture, let alone a wet season, but he assured me there was one and it rained enough for the lowlands to flood. He said that the earth was so hardened and cracked by the sun in the winter that it could not absorb the downpours during the cyclone season.

We came to what appeared to be a main street of sorts, though there was no sign willing to admit that we were in Weipa. Our dusty track was now flanked by a few whitewashed buildings with aluminum-ridged roofs, replacing the desperate emptiness of the flat, burnt country. The sudden proliferation of alloy roofs made sense. As Lucky explained, we were in bauxite country from which aluminum oxide is derived. Lucky's pronunciation of aluminum tripped me up a bit and I had to practice it several times to get it right. "Al-loo-min-e-um, al-loo-min-e-um..."

It was the bauxite ore that made the earth glow like a red-hot branding iron. The alloy made good roofing material in the tropics, shooting the hot daggers of heat back toward the heavens, delineating the boundary between heaven and hell. Overall there was not much to recommend the place.

With some relief, I recognized one building as the G.P.O. owing to the Australian flag out front and the word TELECOMMUNICATION posted over the doorway. I immediately thought of my parents. I hadn't had time to write them about my new job before leaving Cairns. I had planned, of course, to sit down that very night and write a long account of the end of my bike trip and how I'd gotten a job as a maid at a Bed & Breakfast. I was going to confess to them that I was growing tired of the road and the loneliness of it, and I was looking forward to the security of my new job and settling down in the quaint town of Cairns...

Watching the G.P.O. disappear in the rearview mirror, I felt the last trappings of my civilized self being crushed under the heavy wheelbase of Lucky's truck. Any thought of home slowly suffocated in the dust as we drove on.

Lucky must have seen the look on my face as we passed that last outpost. "Never wrote a letter in me life," he admitted cheerfully. "Can't write and nobody to send it to, I reckon."

I tried smiling sympathetically at his admission, but I couldn't fend off the thought that he was probably a fair representative of the other five thousand men who inhabited this remote corner of the world. Beyond the swirling red dust and flies, I didn't see a square inch of it that I thought I could easily fit into.

Lucky hung halfway out the window as he drove, lashing out profanities at his mates, who happened by in hauling trucks or jeeps. No one went on foot. As Lucky said, "Got to be a bloody goanna to survive up 'ere."

The road dead-ended at the water's edge. I felt some relief looking at the narrow, silt-filled estuary, which I knew must eventually wind into the Gulf of Carpentaria and ultimately to open sea. It seemed like a plausible escape route, now that I'd had a good look at Weipa and a handful of its inhabitants. It was hard to imagine the place sustaining any humans, let alone the amount of men Lucky had mentioned, but he did retract that by saying they were a "shifty lot, always coming and going all the time." He might have meant that fifty men came and went one hundred times a year. That made sense.

Nobody appeared to work in the afternoon heat. That made sense too. "You'll find most blokes at the pub," Lucky said, explaining the vacuous, forsaken feel of the place.

The air by the river was cooler by a degree or two and heavy with the smell of saltwater. Two small fishing boats were tied up to the dock, momentarily obliterating my full view of the larger vessel. I could barely make out the letters etched along its bow — Northern Pearl.

"Which one 'll be yers?" Lucky leaned over the wheel, straining to get a look at the boats.

"The biggest one. She's 110 feet... should be that one." I pointed nervously at the *Pearl.*

"Awh, she's a beauty, mate," Lucky said, noticing my shaky hand. "Look, if anybody gives ya any strife, you tell 'em Lucky's yer mate, eh. If word gets out, yu'll be right as rain."

Climbing down from the cab of the truck, I thanked Lucky for the ride and his words of encouragement.

"You look after yerself," Lucky called out, trying to reassure me again. "Remember... Lucky's yer mate."

I waved to him and turned toward the boats, wrestling with something akin to blind terror.

Chapter Twenty-Four

ME MATE SQUIDS

As I approached the *Northern Pearl* my fear threw a calm and civilized sunset into a dizzying palette of colors. I walked slowly toward the large fishing boat thinking it looked enormous — enormous and empty. The generator's angry drone felt like a warning of some sort. I stopped, turned away and headed back toward land. Just then I heard someone yelling.

I looked up and saw a young man, wearing only his briefs, standing at the *Pearl*'s boarding ladder. He appeared to be signaling me to hurry up. "Bloody hell," he scolded me, "been a bloody fortnight since Cooky left. Nearly starved to death, we did."

The young man was no more than a teenager; he didn't look like a rough veteran of the seas. His build was relatively small and fragile. Only his red hair hinted at an unruly nature. It was so tangled and wiry that he appeared to have just narrowly survived an electrocution. His body was covered in freckles. Altogether he was as red as the sunburned, clay-covered earth.

At the young man's insistence, I returned to the boat and started up the boarding ladder with my heavy pack swinging from side to side. Wearing a pareu was not the best choice of attire. As I climbed, it unwound. Grabbing the loose piece of material, I lost my balance and slammed against the boarding ladder, all the while my pack threatening to hurl me overboard. The young fisherman only continued his prodding. "'aven't 'ad a proper ly-dee on board since Carolyn left, the Cap'n's wife, and a right bitch she was too."

With a final mighty heave, I flung my unraveling self onto the deck. The fellow made no attempt to help me; he just kept talking. As I lay sprawled before him, he finally shut his yapper and softened a bit. Then his verbal engine fired up again.

"M'name's Squids, Squids-Jason. Jason's me Christian name but nobody goes by their real name up 'ere. They call me Squids on account a me bein' small and spoutin' off all the time."

Squids ushered me along the deck. Pointing to an open-slatted door he said, "There's yer dunny, it's private enough."

Squids talked nonstop as we went toward the bow. Next he pointed to my cabin. By then I was feeling a little delirious. Part of it was the heat and not having eaten all day; the other part was the realization of where I was — far beyond the Never-Never.

Squids slid open the door to an eight-by-six cell. I gasped, reeling from the pungent mix of damp wool blankets, diesel fumes and rotting fish. I almost fainted, but Squids steered me toward the bunk. "Jesus, if ya don't look like yer gonna spew already. No need to worry about makin' tucker tonight. I reckon everyone 'll be ashore 'avin' a bloody great piss-up, last night in port and all."

I wanted to scream SHUT UP! He just kept yakking on and on. His nonstop blathering, together with the constant roar of the generators, gave me a blistering headache.

Watching my stuffy new world spin around me, I dropped into the bunk with my pack still slung over my shoulders. It was obvious I was much longer than the bunk. As if listening to my thoughts, Squids looked at me with some concern.

"Ah look, it's not so bad. You'll see. Christ!" he suddenly blurted. "What's yer name?"

I looked at him, hardly able to muster a word. He answered for me, "Cooky, I reckon."

Confused, I shrugged my shoulders.

"Doesn't matter," he went on. "They'll call ya Cooky just the same." The young man turned to leave. "Come 'round to the galley when yer ready. We'll 'ave a cuppa and head fer the pub, eh."

I fell back onto the bunk dazed and stared at the ceiling. My mind was so numb all I could hear was my own familiar refrain: *Oh my God, what have I done this time?* Naively, I had envisioned basking in the sun on a 110-foot motoryacht, lying about on deck in my bikini and reading all day. I knew now that my daydreams bore no relation to reality. This was a working fishing boat and I was Cooky! First things first, I thought. Meeting the rest of the crew over a refreshing toddy might calm my nerves.

Reluctantly, I got up, went to the galley and found Squids brewing some tea. My spirits rose considerably as a cool blast of air hit me. The galley was air-conditioned! This unexpected luxury slightly offset the horrifying sight of dirty dishes piled nearly to the ceiling on every available counter.

"Not to worry, mate," he said handing me a cup of tea. "I'll help ya sort these out."

Nodding toward the mess he added, "We get a little carried away when there's no missis around. She'd be nippin' at us like a bloody croc."

Once the tea had settled into my system, I started to liven up a bit. I finally felt capable of speaking.

"So, where are we off to tomorrow?" I asked, feeling like a shy schoolgirl inquiring about a field trip.

Squids looked at me quizzically. "Yer accent, it's different from them other sheilas. Reckon you've been to a proper school or somethin', eh?"

I smiled at Squids. "I'm not Australian. I'm American."

"Christ!" he exclaimed, as if I had confessed that I was from outer space. In another moment, Squids shoved his tea aside and stood up excitedly. "Come on, come on then. Let's fix up these dishes and off to the pub, eh. Last night ashore for bloody weeks."

When I stood up all the fatigue from the day suddenly made me feel weak again. I fell back down, thinking I should just sit there and drink tea and go to bed, but the thought of retreating to my smelly quarters set me back on my feet.

Together Squids and I cleaned up the galley. He gave me a full run-down of my duties, though I understood little of what he said. There was one thing I was sure of. Fishing and sailing shared only one commonality — the sea. I took some comfort in that.

As Squids and I left the ship, I felt refreshed by the warm tropical breeze. Dusk had settled over the raw landscape, softening its hues from burnt red to deep bronze. I listened to the rustling of the bush in every direction. A multitude of cicadas entertained us as I stepped more carefully along our narrow path. The stars of the far north were so bright that whole constellations were clearly visible just after dusk. It made the heavens appear to hover just above our heads. I followed the curve of the Scorpion's tail with Antares burning red at its darkening heart. Lower on the horizon rose the distinct Southern Cross, a dignified emblem hovering over the burial ground of sea.

I could hear the soft swooshing of water as it followed the meandering curve of the river. Amid plumes of spray, giant pelicans swooped down, crashed into the water and flew off with their prey. Adding to the wild commotion, squawking sea gulls circled and dove for their share of the fish.

I noticed a peculiar hum surrounding me. Twinging with an eerie shiver, I felt a vibration of some sort come up through the earth. I thought perhaps it was a convoy of large mining trucks moving about in the distance, but their work day had long since ended.

I turned to Squids. "I can feel something strange." I hesitated, wondering if he would laugh at my allusion. "Is it because we're so far away from civilization, you can hear everything?"

Squids was slow to answer. "There's a strangeness up 'ere alright." He spoke in a low voice. "It scares most people away. This is blackfella country, though they've mostly been shoved off it and sent to the missions." Squids spoke quietly as we walked along the dirt path. "They say the spirits live 'ere, everywhere. I reckon there's somethin' to that. The Abo's call it Dreamtime."

Jolted by his reference to the Dreamtime, I stopped walking. There it was again, lingering in front of me like a talisman.

Squids went on guardedly, as if he were harboring a secret. "I'm from the bush, ya see. I was practically brung up on the Dreamtime. The Abo's believe it's a part of everything. Those stars up there..." Squids pointed. "This clay, the pelicans divin' in the bloody river. It's in everything."

Squids glanced around as if sensing someone nearby. "The Abo's have alotta strange ways. I used to hide in the bush and watch their corroborees — their clan meetin's. All sorts of strange stuff goes on."

He continued to talk secretively even as we neared the pub. "Ya see, they tell stories about how everything came ta be... how the stars came into bein' and how the rivers were made..."

After listening intently to Squids, I finally interrupted him. "What's Dreaming? Is it the same as sleep dreams?"

Squids seemed unsure of the answer. "Not the same, mate," he drawled slowly. "Each Abo has his own Dreaming. They believe that without a Dreaming ya have nothin'. It can be a bird, fish, animal, anything."

I looked at Squids quizzically.

"Say it's Kangaroo Dreaming," he explained. "Then yer related to the kangaroo and everyone else who has Kangaroo Dreaming. Your Dreaming tells ya who you are and where ya belong."

I laughed quietly at the thought of having an animal reflect who I was. What would I be? Something that's scared of it's own shadow and always keeps moving — maybe a rabbit.

"Wonder what my Dreaming would be," I said half kidding.

"Oh, that's just it, mate, you'd be..." Suddenly Squids stopped talking as the boisterous clatter from the pub drew his attention. He fell strangely silent for a moment and then lapsed back into his louder, nonstop chattering. The hum of the land was muted, the spell of the Dreamtime broken.

Chapter Twenty-Five

THE CREW OF THE *PEARL*

The "Pisshole" was a four-poled, cabana-style hut with its shag pandanus roof camouflaging a badly bruised, wooden bar. The rest of the Pisshole consisted of four metal tables sitting on a crusty patch of clay, all of which was enclosed by a miserable looking chain-linked fence. We madmen were on the inside swatting at flies and mangrove mosies, while the nocturnal sounds of bush backed up against the fence posts. Any creature wanting to crawl in or out, could.

Squids bought me a beer while I watched the bawdy crew of the *Pearl* douse themselves in grog. All eyes suddenly turned to me as one tipsy fisherman rose in a toast:

"Cooky's 'ere... Cooky's 'ere," he chimed in an off-key, singsong voice.

They all joined in. I stood there, glazed in embarrassment and generally feeling completely stupid. Squids nudged me to sit down.

The introductions began. Squids called everyone by their nicknames. Matty, the Irishman and RF, the Kiwi, smirked at me. India John rolled his eyes as if he were going to pass out. The two most disagreeable characters, Crazy Duck and Branch, ignored me altogether. Squids explained why the two Asian crew were not there. "The chinks don't go to the pub, can't hold their liquor, I reckon. Turns 'em green instead of yella." The slur brought an excessive round of laughter.

The one furthest into his cups, India John, finished his toast:

> "Cheers! To a dyin' man,
> And 'appy I am to be one.
> It's a dog's life,
> Without a wife,
> But worse
> I mighta 'ad one."

India's eyes swirled over his whiskey. He fell off the bench and rolled onto the dirt. No one seemed to care. Squids turned to me. "Don't mind 'im. He's as mad as a Dingo. Been in and outa jail all his life."

As I sat on the feeble bench watching their faces merge into one collective image of someone so foreign to me, I was racked by a severe loneliness. It seemed as if the person I had once known as *me* was no longer. There was no more sailor, Yank or American. No longer "sheila," "bird" or "ly-dee," I was "Cooky," and I was not well acquainted with her position in life.

My thoughts were suddenly interrupted by a shrill cry in the night. It shot through me like a hypodermic needle overloading my system with adrenaline, snapping all my reflexes into awareness. Squids didn't seem to hear the high-pitched scream. I shook his forearm. "My God, what is it?"

He answered blankly, "Reckon it's the Abo's 'avin' a tiff. None of our business. We don't bother with 'em on any account. It's better that way."

I heard the scream again. Barely human, I thought. "Christ," I swore at Squids. "I can't stand it."

I got up and bolted past the bar. There was an outside flood light, beaming down from overhead, illuminating the figures that were otherwise as dark as the night itself. Sitting on the hood of a dented pickup, a black woman was shaking so badly that the truck rocked underneath her. Next to her, a tall black man was standing with his fist raised above his head and aimed directly at her face. The powerful fist came down and she screamed again with that half-animal cry. In the next moment, I had her in my arms. The black man's fist stopped an inch away from my jaw. I held her there. Her small fragile body quaked inside my arms. I stared up at the clenched fist and then into the Aboriginal's angry dark eyes.

> *No more, I thought, No more.*
> *Stop the angry torment. Leave me be.*
> *You're not stronger.*
> *I'll show you.*
> *I'll show you who is stronger.*
> *And so I didn't react,*
> *but turned in silence, never to see him again*
> *(husband of mine).*
> *The child had died within, but the woman was free.*

The black man said, "White girl, no business here."

My eyes remained locked on his. Then, ever so slowly, he unclenched his fist. The woman, whose trembling had subsided, leaned close to my ear and whispered, "Thank you. Now, go away quickly... go."

I turned to find all the crew of the *Pearl* lined up. They stood absolutely motionless until I was back at their sides. RF grabbed me roughly by the elbow, twisting my flesh as he flung me around and headed me back inside the pub.

"Jesus bloody Christ, woman," RF cursed me. "Who the bloody hell do ya think you are? Ya could'a got us all in a bloody great punch-up. We don't mess with the Abo's business."

I stammered, confused at the violent turnabout. "I... ah... he was going to beat her up... couldn't just stand there."

"Couldn't ya just. Bloody meddlin' Yank."

All the men went back into the pub. I turned to Squids for support, but instead he brushed past me. "RF is right," he said. "We don't get mixed up with 'em."

"I thought you liked the Abo's," I snapped.

"The men 're no good on the piss. It's just the way it is."

I could feel my heart pounding as I sat down at the table. I hadn't thought about my actions, I had just reacted to the violence. I had wanted to stop it.

Nothing had frightened me more than looking into the eyes of that Aboriginal man. There was so much anger and so much power in them. I had felt his warm breath on my shoulder as he panted through his flared nostrils. I had watched the veins in his arm expand as he reached up to hit the woman. I was deathly afraid of what might have happened if he had turned his anger toward me. But beyond it all, my own anger still raged against memory. I knew I couldn't outrun it any longer. Somehow I had to stop and face it.

Chapter Twenty-Six

COOKY

I was attempting my first meal as Cooky when I heard the galley door open. There he stood, his large frame filling the doorway. The black hair, thick prickly moustache, big flabby belly overloading a thin leather belt — all belonging to Captain Bob! My jaw dropped in surprise at the sight of him – Bob... travel agent Bob... employer Bob... Captain Bob!

While I stood in stunned silence, wondering about the man with the hairy hands who had recharted my life back in Cairns, he, in turn, ignored my surprise completely.

"I see ya found the galley all right. Good on ya, luv. I'll be takin' all me meals on the bridge, eh." And with that cheery statement, Cap'n Bob left the galley.

I soon found out that Captain Bob was the skipper of the *Northern Pearl* and that we were leaving port that afternoon for an indeterminate amount of time.

I set about preparing a meal I thought most suitable for our dietary requirements, taking into account the impressive heat of the far north. I was determined to make the best of the situation, and feeling inspired by the heavy responsibility of my new job, I laboriously produced four different salads: fruit, tinned bean, potato and mixed green. I also made something akin to cornbread, an offering to the gods to help sop up the residue of alcohol from the previous night's debauchery. Stepping back from my creation at the galley table, I admired my work, thinking, perhaps, I did possess some talent in this direction.

The six ragged fishermen filed in, jostling and shoving each other like school children in a lunch line. I became distracted by the thought that I wouldn't get my letters off the ship before leaving port and so ignored the grumblings of the crew.

They had barely found their seats when a salad bowl was hurtled through the air, landing at my feet. It was the mixed garbanzo and kidney bean salad (one of my favorites) which had found immediate disfavor, splattering on the floor in an oil and vinegar mess.

The scurrilous Branch had tossed my salad, yelling madly, "What kinda fuckin' fodder is this stuff, Cooky. We ain't vermin, ya know."

Squids came to my rescue, or so I thought. "Shut your gobb, Branch. Cooky don't know."

I could see the thick muscles in RF's shoulders tighten as he reached over and grabbed Squids by his freckled neck. "And who are you, mate, bloody Cooky's protector? Cooky speaks fer 'erself and we wanta know, what's after fodder?"

"Fodder? What's after fodder?" I stumbled along, hoping for a fainting spell. "The salads... you don't like them?" I cleared my throat. "In California..."

"Cooky don't know." Squids tried again to subdue the mutiny, but it only aggravated the situation.

"We'll feed Cooky to the bloody crocs if she don't come up with somethin' better than rabbit fodder." India John flew at Squids, knocking RF, the stout Kiwi, off his feet. Then Irish Matty entered the fray, trying to hold back India from choking Squids. For all his anemic-looking skin and bones, India John was surprisingly strong. Squids' face looked about to pop, when RF changed alliances and yanked India's arm behind his back, threatening to break it in two. After RF and Matty joined forces the commotion settled down. But instead of going back to their lunch, the disgruntled six filed out of the galley, cursing me as they left. I followed Squids to the galley door, asking for a translation.

"We don't eat rabbit food," he snapped. "Meat is what we like — steak'n chips, sausages — that sort of tucker."

Then Squids softened a little and smiled. "India, Duck and Branch don't 'ave many teeth left, ya see. They're like sharks, they like to tug and gnaw at their tucker." He made it clear to me that there was not much variety in what they did like.

"There'll always be somebody who it don't set with. Take RF, feed 'im mutton and he'll take yer head off. Says he's 'ad enough sheep meat to grow his own wool. Then there's Matty. Serve 'im up some potato mix he ain't used to and he'll curse you night 'n day. India wants his sausages, all greazzzy (he exaggerated the sound) and slippery — somethin' he can put on the back biters and gnaw at, or you'll be croc bait. Just the way it is, I reckon."

Squids had one more thing to add. "And besides, nobody ever heard of your Cal-i-fornia, so what you eat there don't count fer much." Most of all, he cautioned me before he left, "Everybody hates fish. We never, *ever*, eat fish, 'cept the chinks and they cook their own tucker."

Though the two engineers were not Chinese, they couldn't escape the label "chinks." Joe Sun was Taiwanese. I took to him immediately. He had a very soft and gentle face and a warm, kind smile that put me at ease. His English was very broken, but we got along quite well with gesturing and half-words. The Singaporean, Lee, was much smaller than Joe Sun and considerably more nervous, perhaps just around me. He wore a pair of fragile, wire-rimmed glasses, which he constantly took off and wiped clean with a small hanky he kept neatly folded in his pocket. Lee appeared to serve as Joe Sun's protégé, never overstepping an imperceptible boundary. As ship's engineers destined for the engine room with all its grease and oil and stench-ridden fumes, they managed to maintain perfect decorum. Unstained, white T-shirts tucked neatly into white cotton pants were worn during the day, with the addition of white, starched, Nehru-collared jackets at night. I admired their cleanliness and their sober dedication to their grimy job.

After the scuffle in the galley, Squids apologized for not finishing our tour of the trawler before the previous night's "bloody great piss-up." He asked me to follow him so I could see where the meat was stored, thereby saving me from the crocs.

He lead me aft along a narrow passageway on the main deck, where we passed the men's quarters. I quickly averted my eyes. I didn't care to see how the likes of the drunken India John, or the silently doomed Branch, or the Crazy Duck lived with each other in the fumous confines of the ship. Instead, I watched the ebb tide swirl brown mud pools in the narrow estuary. Squids caught my attention fixed on the brackish inland waters.

"Don't go gettin' any notion of swimmin' in these waters, mate. Last bloke that did went floatin' by us on the mornin' tide, I reckon."

"He drown?" I asked, repulsed by the image of a dead body floating by the boat.

"Christ, no," Squids said. "Bloody croc ate 'im. All that went by was a few bits and pieces, I reckon. We knew it was 'im because of his hat."

We went farther aft and stood amid the maze of fishing gear. The labyrinth of mechanical lifts and drums of coiled wire, elevated sorting trays and huge bulk of netting, set my head spinning. I felt the same dizzying confusion as my first sight skyward in downtown Manhattan at the age of three. Like those imposing buildings, the fishing gear towered over me like misshapen monsters. I had the same sense of some enormous, imposing power of which I was totally ignorant and subservient to.

Squids handed me what I can only describe as an antiquated spacesuit. Laughing at my bewilderment he prodded, "Here, try this on fer size. Time to cool off."

I wriggled into the legs of the silver-gray suit sweating profusely. Next I tugged on the long sleeves and zipped up the spacesuit to my chin. "This better be good Squids, this thing is hotter than hell."

Lifting up a hatch cover that appeared to lead down into the dark bowels of the ship, Squids handed me a flashlight saying, "This is where yu'll be doin' yer shoppin' from now on, mate, down there. Bread, milk, beef, chook, all ya need." He pointed down the steep metal steps. "Go on, 'ave a look. Christ, don't forget to wear these gloves and boots."

COLD. COLD vaporizing moisture blew up the companionway as I began my descent into the frozen, misty catacombs. The cold grabbed my lungs, choking them, making it nearly impossible to breathe. It was an eerie sight framed by my own frozen sweat dangling icicles from my eyelids. Animal corpses were flung in large heaped pile — slabs of frozen beef, upper thighs, loins — then, other ice-encrusted piles that looked like a variety of frozen fowl. This enormous freezer section took up the whole aft end of the 110-foot trawler.

When Squids closed the hatch over me, cutting off the hot drafts of tropical heat and sunlight, I clutched my chest, gasping for air. Feeling imprisoned by the space suit and suddenly very claustrophobic, my heart raced as I started to wheeze in the cold, dry atmosphere. Fending off panic, I tried calming myself by repeating what Squids had said to me. *I'm OK. It's just a little dark and a little cold. I'm just shopping... I'm just looking for...* Then I yelled at the top of my lungs, "*SQUIDS, GET ME OUT OF HERE!*"

The curly-topped, freckled Squids looked down the open hatchway laughing at me. "What's up, mate? Don't forget the sausages, eh." He howled with laughter.

I shuffled over to one bin and pulled out a long link of frozen sausages. As I started my slide, skating back toward the ladder, I slipped forward, catching hold of the metal railing on the rebound. My glove was snap frozen to the metal bar. I was stuck to the rails like a guilty shoplifter, spread eagle and frozen in my tracks. My bare hand stung with the cold as I lurched up through the hatchway, leaving the glove behind. Once back in the 110-degree heat, the fringe of my hair melted, re-drenching me in my own thawing sweat.

This time I cursed Squids. "Jesus bloody Christ, it's like a mausoleum down there."

Squids laughed again, enjoying my hysteria. "Well, then, no more rabbit fodder, eh. You best get back in the galley fer tea time."

"Tea? You guys drink tea?"

"Nah, mate, I meant suppa. Yu'll be needin to fix suppa..."

"I just finished cleanin' up the mess from lunch," I protested.

"Well, what did ya bloody well think you were gonna do 'ere, polish yer bloody nails all day?"

By the end of my sentence as Cooky, I overcame my vegetarian disposition and learned how to cook a roast, medium done with its red juices weeping out of its innards, streaming down the delicate crevasses of the poor by-gone beast — and in a raging sea if I must. Under threat of being tossed to the crocs, I learned. I also mastered the art of drenching potatoes in lard, so their crusts were crackly, while their puffy white insides were mushy and sweaty with steam. By God, I learned. Over a period of time, I gradually won over the most resistant crewman with my cooking. Perhaps my admiration for the engineers was skewed by the fact that they asked me very politely *not* to cook for them. In return, they taught me how to prepare delicious concoctions using a variety of fish that the other crewmen referred to as "garbage."

As part of being Cooky, I had to bury memory. I had to forget table manners — sitting quietly with my back straight, no elbows on the table. I also had to repress all the years of my strict Catholic upbringing and the dress code that went with it. In the brutal heat of the tropics, I had to tuck away the memory of soft white gloves and patent leather shoes bought at Saks Fifth Avenue in New York. Instead, I wore a tattered T-shirt draped down over my briefs.

Most painful of all, I had to cut away the most delicious part of my youth — the beautiful home spread over a luxurious green landscape. I had to forget about a loving mother and father, and my brothers and sister. The mere thought of them brought a flood of warm memories, a sense of comfort and safety I couldn't afford to own on a fishing boat.

Frustrated by the thought of my parents' continual worry, I spent coveted moments writing them long letters, describing the tedium of my day-to-day existence. I knew well in advance that the exercise was fruitless; Squids had already told me we'd be at sea for months.

No one on board cared a morsel about who I was, or where I came from, so I had to bury me and just learn to be Cooky.

Chapter Twenty-Seven

DECKIE

I stood at the rails of the *Pearl* as if I were a passenger on a luxury cruise ship admiring exotic ports. It was an enormous relief to be untied from land and gliding down river into open sea. Still, it was a strange unknowable land to me. There was something forlorn, or was it forsaken, in the vacuous northern air. We passed the sunbaking crocs in their lairs of weedy marshes surrounded by a hum of insect and bird life. The clawing thicket was alive, steamy, jungly, yet the broader landscape was still largely vacant. Birds of prey gawked and flapped over our empty afterdeck, enraged by our lack of spoils. The birds angered, engines droning — a deceiving combustion of noise beyond which lay a threatening silence.

The landscape absorbed the afternoon light leaving gradients of hardened earth colors. There was nothing soft to look at, nothing gentle to rest the eyes on, only hard contours and unforgiving sharp edges of light. We chugged along, touched by the sea breeze created by our forward motion. *What sea is this?* I wondered. *Where am I?*

I sniffed the air now filled with moist sea breeze. Sweet, like a liqueur, soothing my senses, washing over me like a cool wave. *Sweet like—*

"Bloody hell, mate." Squids rushed by me, twisting my elbow off the rails, "Ya seen Branch or Duck about? Matty thinks they buggered off in Weipa."

I smiled, smiled a long deep satisfying smile — they're gone, the worst of them, the two bent-over drunks rotting from the inside out — they're gone. Wonderful! Two less mouths to feed.

Cap'n Bob came steaming in behind Squids. "Seen 'em yet? Bastards. Well then mate, yer it." The good Captain looked at me. "Better get tea done with. Yu'll be on deck tonight."

With that command Cap'n Bob pushed off and left me with Squids. "What was that all about?"

"Without Branch and Duck, mate, yer it."

"I'm 'it'?"

Squids seemed to relish this part. "Yer the new Deckie."

"Deckie?"

"Deckhand, mate. Yer the new bloody deckhand. So get tea finished with and up on deck ya go."

Squids had made his point. I understood. Deckhand. I'm the new deckhand.

Cooking was certainly a stretch of my skills, but I'd never entertained the notion of actually fishing. Experiences from my youth had already proven how inept I was at it. My previous fishing résumé consisted of dangling a stick with a piece of string tied to a hook. A big wad of gooey white bread was smashed over the small hook. This all happened at the end of a dock perched over a very small body of water. I was not actually out to catch the curious creatures, as much as entertain myself during the long, languid summer afternoons spent at our lakeside cabin. Having fully lowered the hook and line into the delightfully clear water, I actually had the bad luck of catching a few small perch. I'd carry the slimy trophy around until I found someone to unhook it and throw it back into the lake. I never knew what drove my compulsion, as the fish were too small and inedible, and I hated watching defenseless creatures die. In any case, there was nothing about my new job description that suggested I was going to like prawning any better.

Our ship slipped through the night vibrating with its own droning engines. We swayed back and forth over the low sea swell. Only the clinking of the yards and the sliding of the ship's stores could be heard over the engine noise. It was eerie to me, as if we were an old battleship trying to sneak up on a foe for a nocturnal attack, ill-equipped and unmanned. There was no hint of land around us, only the odd-shaped flickering of navigation lights from other fishing boats.

I stumbled along the deck next to Matty as the overhead lights cast weird, elongated shadows over the strange equipment. He tried explaining the whole process of prawning to me, but I understood little of what he said, partly because of his Aussie-slanged Irish accent and partly because I didn't want to know.

"You stop 'er from payin' out, 'ere's the brake. Mind yer fingers, they'll be gone..."

In the middle of my lesson an ear-piercing series of buzzes sounded. Matty looked at me, cursing the buzzer. "Awh bugger it, mate," he said, abruptly ending the lesson. "Learn as you go. Yu'll be needin' a jacket then, gloves, and grab them boots, same pair every time."

I heard the galley door wheeze open and spring shut as Squids, RF and India John joined us on deck. I put on the yellow foul-weather jacket, cotton gloves and cumbersome rubber boots. The night had only slightly cooled, so standing in our fatigues, preparing for battle, I was soaked in sweat without ever having moved.

"We're going to shoot. We're going to shoot," Matty yelled.

Squids and India John took their positions on deck near the sorting trays. I hung close to Matty listening to the engines being throttled back to a smooth, quiet crawl. The powerful overhead floodlights illumined the deck and Cap'n Bob standing on the bridge. His huge belly cast broken pools of black shadows over everything. He gave the order: "Cast away."

RF and Matty were at opposite sides of the boat, each at their wheel. On command, they worked in unison, watching each other disengage the gear levers, while backing off the brake wheel. The wire cables began to pay out, lowering the huge nets with their weighted boards into the water. The winches groaned miserably as they ground against the gears. The nets slowly disappeared into the black sea, mysteriously falling away into the dungeon depths. Then the brakes were locked and the men retreated into the galley. The process was completed in a few minutes; it all seemed disappointingly straightforward, all the cautionary advice a little overdone.

Squids brushed by me saying, "You can 've a kip if you like, not much sense in it though. The nets are down fer thirty, up they come — sort, wash, stow 'em, clean the deck and we drop again."

The galley door wheezed shut and I was left standing alone in my oil skins, cotton gloves and huge boots, feeling like the great war had been fought without me. Scanning the horizon for any hint of our next maneuver, I dug my hands deep into my pockets. I felt a little pinch and, jerking my hand out, I found a friendly little crab gripping on to my cotton glove for dear life. Shaking him loose, I knew exactly how he felt.

Since I'd already spent enough time in the galley, I waited on deck for the next event. Staring at the winch drums as if they were gruesome monsters about to stalk me, I waited like an ill patient prepared for the worst prognosis.

Twenty minutes later the buzzer sounded again. The men came out on deck, throwing their cigarette butts overboard and mumbling about something. Matty and RF released the brakes and set the hydraulic winches into action. They, in turn, started grinding away, pulling up the cables with a terrible twisting and cracking sound, winding back onto the drums. Then came the huge nets palpitating with life. The sight of it all — fish of all sorts and sizes wriggling and squirming, caught in the mud-muck with its putrefying smells of the underworld — was overpowering. They were all in their death throes, gasping for air, their eyes bulging through the stringed traps, dying all of them, twisting and choking, squirming and flapping, their once brilliant colors draining out of their oily skins. My stomach wrenched tight at the sight of them.

The men swung the nets over the sorting trays and left them dangling there. Squids and India climbed up on their trays. They tugged away at the bottom strings holding the nets closed. As if the belly of the sea had been slit open, an avalanche of smelly spoils flooded the ten-by-ten-foot trays. Matty's Irish brogue suddenly cut through the night air. "Bloody Jesus! Get that damn sea snake."

No one moved. Matty pushed past me and leapt onto the sorting tray. His silver knife blade slashed through the night, slicing off the head of the sea snake. Blood splattered everywhere as the headless snake tossed in its final quiver of death. Matty pulled the long ribbon of entrails from the net and flung it overboard. With blood dripping down the front of his open jacket, he turned toward me. "Bloody sea snake, mate. Kill ya, thirty seconds, if yer lucky." Matty wiped the bloody knife on his T-shirt. "Mind the stonefish too, they'll kill ya just as quick."

I could not get my hands to stop trembling as I sorted out the prawns from the unwanted fish and sludge. Hypnotized by the writhing coil of creatures passing down the shoot back into the sea, I sorted slowly and carefully, trying to recognize the lethal ones. I had to learn quickly. Grabbing the wrong fish could kill me. Matty called the prawns "tigers." Maybe it was the way they resisted capture. Each palm-sized shrimp squirmed in my hand, drilling minute holes with its pincers. The cuts burned in the saltwater as I dropped the prawns into crates at my feet.

We spoke little as we sorted. Now I knew this was a serious job. We sorted through the muck, the fish, crabs, lethal box jellyfish, crushed seashells and miscellaneous flotsam, to pluck our innocent jewels from the mess.

As soon as we finished sorting, we cast the nets back into the sea, washed down the decks and all the equipment and carried the cartons of prawns down to the freezer in the ship's hold. When those jobs were done, the men filed off to the galley for more coffee and cigarettes. We were all bathed in the essence of fish guts.

I went to my cabin and fell onto my bunk. Even the suffocating stink couldn't keep my eyes from slamming shut with fatigue. Just when I started to doze, the nerve-wracking buzzzzzzzzzzzzz sounded again. I leapt from my bunk, fighting off the image of being trapped inside those nets.

We did this five times that night and every night thereafter. We worked through the funereal night to the first light of the equatorial sunrise. The whispering glow began at the edge of the horizon and gradually worked its way through the colored spectrum of perilous purple-grays, into the spectacular morning rise of rich scarlet to burnt orange, to flaming yellow — come to save us from the night.

By 8:00 A.M. the crew was scrubbing themselves down with saltwater, trying to rub the stink from their skin and hair while growling about "breaky."

"Where's bloody breaky?" they moaned. "Slower than a lazy croc, she is."

Their day ending, mine just beginning. Unlike my crewmates, my chores were not over until breakfast was cooked, the dishes washed and the galley restocked. They ate breakfast and rolled straight into their bunks. I cooked and cleaned and donned my spacesuit for an outing below deck. Luckily, no one broke their sleep for lunch so I was saved from that chore. I crawled into my bunk about noon. There, my world slammed shut for about four hours.

I soon learned to function on four hours of afternoon sleep and to cook in a trance-like state. More than once, I was found half-asleep in pancake batter, or worse, I'd fall asleep next to the stove waiting for muffins to cook. Joe Sun kindly pulled me off the oven once, my eyebrows singed back and crusting off. He advised, "You need mow slip, missy. You be fried like squid." Though not wanting to awake, I quickly responded to the title "missy." It sounded familiar and friendly and comforting.

Sleep became my god. The idol I paid homage to. Sleep became the grand prize for all my efforts — the narcotic I craved to escape the drudgery of endless chores.

Chapter Twenty-Eight

SLAYING DEMONS

I struggled with sleep those days, wrestled with it to exhaustion, trying to eclipse the daylight from the cracks in the portholes. Losing my battle with the searing heat, I laid on my sheets soaking them in sweat, never able to stop the depletion.

I dreamt... dreamt of sea snakes coiling around me like the wires around the drum. They wound out of the darkness, at first, wrapping themselves around my legs then spiraling upward. I saw them as I did when I was a child kneeling frigidly before the statues at church, or illumined in the mosaics of the stained glass windows. Here they were again to torment me, just as they had then.

There was no sense of time passing at sea. My afternoon nap became my night and night started the working day. I drifted along in my sleepless state like someone under a spell. After a time I gave up going to my cabin in between dropping the nets and, instead, shuffled behind the men to the galley. They continued on with their stories, cursing and swearing, completely indifferent to my existence. As a female cook and deckhand, I clung precariously to the lowest rung on the social ladder.

I learned a little bit more about my crewmates, but not much. Talking about the past, or life on land, seemed taboo. They knew I was Yank and ate rabbit fodder. On some occasions, for no apparent reason, I suffered under the nickname "Sepo." Not clear on the derivation, I learned from Squids that it was cockney rhyming slang for "Yank."

"Sepo, Septic Tank, Yank Tank. Get it?" Squids looked at me as if I was the thickest-brained human on earth. Why didn't I understand my own nickname?

Of my crew mates, I found RF, the well-muscled Kiwi, the most disturbing. He was tall, blond, with bullish eyes and a bad turn in the ridge of his nose. Quick tempered, he almost always looked mad about something. I heard bits and pieces of his story: He was so in love with a girl back in Cairns that she drove him mad, literally. He said he loved her so much, he couldn't keep himself from strangling her. RF was hand-rolling a cigarette at the time and stuffed it into his mouth without ever letting slip how the love story ended.

Matty, on the other hand, was a much more likeable sort, having an easy, relaxed manner about him. His features were gently rounded and well sculpted, his clean-shaven face was smooth and unscarred. His eyes were green-gray with a curious orange streak flaring out from the center, strangely, like mine. The edges of his lips turned up in a cocky half-smile, which came naturally to him, and which he used when he wanted my attention. Wavy black hair flopped around on his head in all directions; most remarkably, it was almost always clean. He looked at ease with himself, though something simmered underneath his pale Irish skin.

On one rare occasion we sat alone in the galley. Matty turned his cigarette paper over between his thumb and forefinger, never quite getting to the job of actually putting tobacco in it.

"I know it's a bit rough at first, but after you settle in, it won't be so bad. Still, nobody lasts very long up here, 'specially the women. Anybody gives you any trouble, you tell me first…"

I was tempted to like Matty and trust him; still I couldn't think what to say to him.

"So, how long have you been up here?" I asked.

"Hard to say." Matty finally opened his tobacco tin and rolled the cigarette. He drew his head up, his eyes shifting to mine and I reckon, at the edges of them, I caught a glint of sadness.

"So, you like this way of life?" I prodded.

"Like it? No. I wouldn't say that. Like it?" My question seemed to catch him off-guard.

"You don't have a choice. Once you've gone off to sea, there is no other life. Life on land's impossible, not room enough. I've been a merchant seaman most me life. You live on the sea because you have to."

Fixing my eyes on his, I felt like he had just told me the most terrible of all truths.

"It gets in your blood," he continued. "You can't get it out. It's a disease, sure as any, that'll kill ya."

I'd overheard a lot of Matty's sea tales. They took place all over the world, and like Melville, Conrad and London's stories, things start out OK, but then they slowly dissolve into horrifying tales of characters gone awry.

The rest of the crew fed on Matty's stories, never getting enough of the lurid details. I usually sat in disbelieving silence, not wanting to see the brutality of the male world, where knife fights and slicing open someone's belly brought cheers from the crowd.

When Matty asked me what I was doing on a fishing boat in the far north, I answered blankly, "I'm sailing around the world and the Gulf was sort of on the way."

"Sailing are ya, on a fishing boat?"

I didn't answer him. I just smiled politely.

Matty's voice trailed off until he was mumbling to his cigarette: "...have me a wife, damned if I'll ever see her again. Bloody I-talians and all..." Matty mumbled on and on and I couldn't make out the story, though Squids filled me in later. Matty had married a girl in Townsville and when her brothers found out she'd married an Irish fisherman they went after him, threatening to kill him. Matty was shot twice through the shoulder and left for dead. That explained why he was elevated to First Mate and did less of the heavy lifting. His scars were hidden underneath the sleeveless white undershirt he always wore.

Then there was Squids, me mate. Like a younger brother, he was always hanging around, trying to be helpful, but always getting in the way. He was funny, annoying, and smart in a way I couldn't calculate. I liked him, but he always talked more than I could tolerate. Still, he didn't mind when I threw him out of the galley; he always left laughing and baiting me on. I already knew Squids' story — a kid from the bush who ran away from home and never went back.

I didn't have much interest in even thinking about India John and his life. I didn't want to know his story and could barely watch him talk or eat without praying that he might accidentally fall overboard. He was a wretched human being as far as I could tell, never had a good word to say about anything.

"He's a no hoper," Squids explained. India was a thief by trade. "Been in and out a jail most of 'is life. Only fishes to escape the coppers." For many of the fishermen of the far north, their career choices consisted of escaping to sea or going to jail.

Joe Sun, Lee and Captain Bob kept to themselves. The Asians cooked their own meals when I was out of the galley and quickly disappeared back down into the "dungeon," where they lived and worked.

After I came to terms with the fact that Cap'n Bob wasn't a travel agent playing tricks on silly yank sheilas, I found him to be a convivial sort and more than welcoming of my company. I daresay he was more content snoozing in his bunk than at the wheel of *Pearl*. After my first introduction to the wheelhouse with its assortment of instrumentation (gear levers, wheel, radio, radar screen, depth scanner, autopilot, compass, etc.), he was quite amenable to my taking the wheel at any time day or night. As I had my own chores to tend to, I could only manage the wheel in the earliest hours of the morning. I'd appear about 1:00 A.M. and, without saying a word, the Cap'n would roll into his bunk for a quick kip. He didn't seem in the least disturbed by my grimy appearance and overpowering fishy smell.

Those nights on the bridge where absolute magic. I loved steering the boat through the darkness, monitoring the radar screen, depth scanner and compass, while watching the parade of boat lights. The profusion of different colored navigation lights was, at first, disorienting, but after a time I learned how to mentally untangle the myriad lights of trawlers crossing each other in various directions. I could then tell which ones might keep paralleling our course and which ones might suddenly veer off to cross our path. Deciding which course to take through the coal darkness required vigilance and a sixth sense. I reckon Captain Bob gave credence to a woman's intuition, because I certainly didn't have the Captain's license to go along with my job.

Those precious moments were mine, belonged to me, but there was always an end to it. The fatal buzzzzzzzzz trilled up my spine, launching my skipper bolt upright onto his heavy haunches. Lumbering down the ladder, I reluctantly returned to my "deckie" persona and the grumbling crew fighting over fish slops.

The farther away from port, the farther away from the grog, the more deranged the crew got. As our time at sea stretched from days into weeks, we all achieved a certain sullen plateau.

One night we came on deck in particularly foul moods. Our nets had been empty for several days, except for a few bottom dwellers. The men were silent as the nets came up from the sea. But this time the nets were full to bursting. Now an experienced deckie, I jumped up on the sorting tray and untied the nets. Matty yelled at me, "Get that sonofabitch out of the net, NOW!"

I turned and saw a sea snake winding his way out of the net toward me. I grabbed him the way I had seen Squids and Matty do it — grabbing him by the tail and pulling his whole slithering body out of the net to fling him overboard. I tugged and tugged with all my might, but I couldn't untangle the four-footer from the weave. I heard Matty cursing as Squids yelled to me, "Back off 'im mate!"

Aye, and then I saw it. I'd grabbed the small end thinking it was the tail, but it was his head. His jaw twisted in every direction trying to get hold of me, trying to dig his curved fangs, dripping with venom, into something fleshy. His small deadly jaw snapped frantically, trying to get hold of me. I held him, unable to move. We stared at each other — frantic prisoners locked in survival mode. I didn't breathe; I didn't move. Then it came down through the night. The glistening silver blade slashed through the night and sliced off the sea snake's head. Blood splattered on my face, all over my T-shirt and jacket. I thought I was dying. The head still squirmed and quivered in my hand. It was alive and I was dying. No. Matty had killed the snake. I stared at its bloody head.

"For Christsake, throw the bastard overboard," Matty cursed.

I couldn't move. Matty stepped in behind me and raising my arm, he flung it for me as if trying to improve my pitching style. My hand, against all my paralyzed will, finally released the quivering, shrunken head.

Watching my glazed stare, Matty said in the gentlest voice, "It's dead mate. It's gone overboard." Turning me toward my cabin he added, "Have a kip, sleep right through if ya like. We'll get ya in the mornin'."

Walking away like a dead man, I heard India giggling in my wake. "...seen blokes bigger than 'er drop dead at the sight of 'em."

I lay down on my bunk just as I had stood — staring straight ahead and motionless. The snake blood crusted hard over me.

Maybe I slept, I don't know. The same image came back to me over and over again. As I lay on my bunk, I could feel the snake coiling around my feet and slowly winding its way up my legs. When it twisted around my stomach and bound my chest, I started gasping for air. I tried calling for help but no one came. By then the snake was slithering around my neck and I could feel its moist cool skin wrapping itself tighter. When I was eye-to-eye with the thing, its jaw, as wide as my head, opened, ready to swallow my head whole. In this dream-image the knife is poised over the snake's head, but it never lowers. The snake doesn't die. I die.

The morning after the incident, Matty sent Squids to rouse me. "And you lived to tell the story, mate." Squids laughed.

I propped myself up on my elbows, still dazed. Squids looked genuinely relieved that I was alive.

"I never seen anyone meet a sea snake and live to tell about it. You'd be quite dead now if that snake hadn't let you live."

The thought that I had been lucky — that the snake had let me live — had never occurred to me.

I shivered slightly. "Squids, I've never been so scared in all my life. The snake—"

"You've got it all wrong, mate." Squids grinned. "He saved your life."

The snake dream revisited me every time my eyes began to shut. It was not always the same. Sometimes the images reached deep into my childhood memories, exposing some earlier terror. Once in my dreams I saw a sea snake winding through the net. As I grabbed for its tail, the net became a stained glass window. The church window bore bloody images of Christ being crucified. As I reached for the snake, the window shattered pouring blood all over me. I woke up feeling drenched in blood, though it was really my own tears and sweat.

One morning Squids was helping me carry some stores up from below deck. I asked him what he had meant by the snake saving my life. "It's like I told ya, mate. If you were an Abo, you'd see that snake was yer Dreaming. He's there to protect ya, not kill ya. Would 've been easy to kill ya, I reckon."

Squids seemed sure about this. It was clear and simple to him and yet I couldn't fathom what he meant. The image of the snake, any snake, filled me with an insane fear.

I went on deck each night dizzy from lack of sleep. As the nets were hoisted, I didn't see nets at all but huge monsters clawing their way out of a slate-black sea. I held onto a shovel to defend myself against the monsters and didn't let go of it until their bellies were slit open and all their slimy innards had fallen onto the sorting tray. Then I sorted the prawns, cursed them, and shoved the rest of the dead muck back into the sea as quickly as I could.

My status on board elevated slightly when I learned how to run the winches, which paid out the nets and boards into the sea. For the most part, the job required staying awake long enough to keep one's fingers away from the uncoiling wire drum, and out of the braking lever. My new found skills meant that we could rotate our positions, so the fastest sorters could pluck prawns, while I manned the winches. It seemed like quite a luxury and gave my swollen, perforated hands a chance to heal. Baited by exhaustion and loneliness, life at sea took on a surreal cast. I fell mindlessly into the shipboard routine.

Chapter Twenty-Nine

CALL ME ISHMAEL...

One night the monster came, such an ugly head had he. No one said it was my fault directly, but they cursed me just the same — the night I hauled up a hammerhead shark in the net. He was fourteen feet of raging anger. His wide tubular head, with eyes peering out from each end like a squashed telescope, stared at me through the net. He looked at me and twisted — he fought, thrashed, battled hard to cut through the mesh with his sharp-toothed jaw.

Amid the battling on deck, the overhead glow of lights suddenly cast a full-length shadow over the tortured creature. There our Captain stood, lifting his double-barreled shotgun to eye level. The gun blast exploded in the night, blowing apart the shark's misshapen head. Convulsing in death, the shark snapped its tail against the net. Trembling and flapping, even in death it struggled to free itself from captivity. The Captain said no prayers, but blasted him again and again, spraying the deck and crew with blood. Blood everywhere. His guts splattered in my hair, ran down the ridge of my nose, dripped off my chin, down my neck... I had the sour taste of his blood in my mouth for the rest of the night.

The Cap'n shot the shark.
They boiled his jaw for teeth.
The Asians boiled his fin for soup.
I have a tooth. I sipped the soup.

After that night I quietly yearned for land and began to plan my exit at our next port. Our holds were filling up; we'd off-load soon.

I became impatient, cursing the slow cooking beef, burning it because I'd fallen asleep. The crew cursed me, I cursed them. I avoided going up to the bridge, except to give the Captain his meals. He'd ask, "You right there, luv?" and I'd slam his dishes down and leave. No more midnight watches for me. I couldn't untangle the lights anymore; I couldn't even tell one color from another. They were one psychedelic blur.

I was no longer patient with Joe Sun's broken English and flung overboard the carefully prepared fish he offered me. I took up talking to the fish, befriending the beautiful and tormenting the ugly among them. If Squids was snagged by a catfish, he'd pick it up and break its spine, and so I delighted in the practice too.

I slowly became aware that I hated them all. I hated their smell, their touch, their taste, their life and their death. Yet, I became more an ardent fisherperson, than less of one. I became, as we all were, deliciously greedy; I no longer saw what it was I was after. I took and took, and tallied up what I took, and hated what I loved taking.

I began to lose my taste for sleep. Pushed by adrenaline through the night, I rallied my energy: *What's out there tonight? Sharks, snakes, deadly fish at my fingertips, raw prawns — money, money, back on land, I'll be rich...*

Back on land, out there, somewhere.

Chapter Thirty

TUGS

The *Northern Pearl* puffed along like a pregnant cow, clipping back the seas with her deep sheer and fat belly. Since the *Northern Pearl* acted as the mother ship for the whole fishing fleet, we stayed at sea the longest. We were low on our lines and our hold was full to bursting with frozen prawns. Squids yelled out the rumor that we were on our way to Karumba, "a snake-pit of a town." But first we'd be taking on extra crew.

I had the insane thought that maybe Cap'n Bob had requested extra crew, so I could have a rest as Deckie. I even went so far as to imagine the crew might be a replacement cook. Perhaps a new "sheila" was coming aboard because the Captain recognized that I was suffering from battle fatigue. I hallucinated at regular intervals. I didn't tell anyone, but they couldn't help watching me duel the deck-light shadows while yelling, "Get back, get away from me." Twenty minutes of sleep could no longer tame the monsters. They always came back.

I longed for female company. I longed for the sort of private conversations that women share, sometimes reaching into the soul, other times just silly. I imagined conversations about broken fingernails, hair destroyed by saltwater washings and too much sun, and the inconvenience of having to deal with menstrual cycles and mad fishermen at the same time. Having no hope of sanitary supplies, I caught my blood with a diaphragm, then watched the sharks kill for it when the blood got flushed into the sea. The fishermen knew nothing of this and when the sharks became frenzied around the boat, it began the myth all over again — the sharks carried my curse.

Beyond anything, I wanted to feel some form of acceptance. I wanted to look into someone's eyes and see something other than cross-cuts of madness and savagery.

I felt the push and shove of another trawler coming alongside. Then Squids told me there would be an extra mouth to feed — a deckie was coming on board. He told me to fix another meal, offering no other information about our new arrival.

When the crew filed in for their evening meal there was a strange uneasiness about them. They looked at me anxiously, as if trying to warn me of something. Then I turned toward the galley door and saw the fisherman standing there. The man's huge body completely filled the entryway. His muscular torso was so broad that he had to turn sideways and stoop to fit through the opening. He towered above the rest of us with an animal-like presence. I couldn't look beyond the bizarre contortions of his eyes. You could see the blood pumping through his bulging red capillaries, streaking out from his dilated pupils. They looked like a pool of venomous snakes winding frantically out of a black cave. The fisherman's hideous eyes looked ready to explode under some unbearable pressure. When the enormous man started to sit down, I noticed his hands were tied behind his back.

India John was the only crew member who did not seem threatened by the man's presence. India looked around the table, trying to gain everyone's attention, but no one looked up from their plate.

"Come on now, mates," India plead on behalf of the fisherman. "Bloke's gotta eat. He can't eat with his 'ands tied."

Everyone kept staring at their plates, ignoring India's words, so he leaned over and untied the giant's hands. "There ya go, mate. Have some tucka." India invited the brute to eat with an uncommon amount of sympathy. I imagined that it was due to his innate understanding of being a prisoner.

The rest of the men ate in a desperate silence. They shoveled down their food as quickly as possible and left the galley. Squids was among the first to leave. He turned to me as I rinsed the dishes saying, "Be quick about it, eh."

As usual I didn't know whether it was one of Squids' sarcastic remarks or a serious warning.

The galley was soon empty, except for the man whose hands were still untied. I nervously stole quick glances of him as he ate. He devoured all the leftovers, slurping his food like a ravenous dog. When his meal was done, he picked up his plate and headed toward me as I stood at the sink washing the pile of dishes. He moved slowly, laboriously.

"M'name's Tugs," he said, getting closer to me. "I can help ya there, with all them dishes."

My back was to him, yet I could feel the increasing heat of his body begin to choke off the air around me. My legs began to tremble, so I leaned heavily on the sink for support. His voice, like his body, moved with a heavy brutishness. When the sweaty smell of him wrapped around my body, I felt nearly suffocated.

Somehow I summoned the courage to let go of the sink. Turning to face him, I felt sick at the sight of his distorted eyes and immediately looked away, panting for air. By then my back was pressed hard against the sink with the massive fisherman completely surrounding me. There was no way to move in any direction.

"Didn't mean to rattle ya, luv." Tugs leaned over me. "Just good to see a sheila after all these bloody months at sea."

My whole field of vision was now taken up by the broad sweep of his shoulders. The stink of his sweat mixed with engine oil dirtied the air between us. I was eye-level with a tattoo on his chest. An angelic figure was trapped inside a red heart and, at each breath, skewered by a dagger.

"You let ol' Tugs give ya a hand," he said, grinding his teeth. "Reminds me of home, it does... and me sista. Ya look just like me sista, I reckon."

As Tugs' massive chest expanded, the tattooed sword lifted, then lowered over the angelic figure. The angel was stabbed over and over again as he breathed.

Tugs raised his bestial paw of a hand and brushed my cheekbones with his thickly callused forefinger. I watched the tattoo pulsate as he pushed my tangled hair away from my face. With all my will I resisted looking up at his eyes again. I was afraid that he would see the terror in mine.

Lowering his hand to my throat, he rubbed it back and forth as if sharpening a dull blade.

"Awh yeah, yer a lot like me sista, you are. We used to play a lot. Know what I mean? We was real close until..."

Tugs kept rubbing my neck with one hand. I could feel the press of his other hand at my hips rising slowly.

I knew he fed off my terror, so I had to find a way of appearing less vulnerable. "So, that's nice... nice to have a sister." I panted against the pressure of his forefinger slipping along the v-cut of my T-shirt. "I have a sister too."

"Me sista," Tugs continued over my quivering voice, "She was, I reckon... she was the only... real mate I ever had."

Just then the galley door flew open. I heard Captain Bob's deep voice come from behind Tugs. "Back away from her, Tugs. I got both barrels aimed dead center of ya."

Tugs was slow to respond to the Captain's threats. His hand gripped my neck. He stood motionless. "Tugs don't harm nobody," he said, letting his hand slip from the nape of my neck over my breast. "I never meant to hurt me sista, so soft and sweet she was..."

I heard the Captain step through the galley doorway and move closer to us. "Two seconds, Tugs, and I blast ya from here to hell."

The Captain's words hung in the air. I took a deep breath. One thousand one. Dive to the floor. One thousand two. No gun blast. Cover my head. No gun blast.

I looked up and saw Matty and RF jump toward the dullard, each grabbing one arm and forcing it behind Tugs' back. Tugs didn't resist. Matty twisted the rope hard around the fisherman's wrists until they began to bleed. Then they took the witless fisherman away.

I heard the Captain yell at Squids, "Look after her." I cowered on the floor, shaking like an animal cornered in fright.

Squids knelt down next to me. "Sorry, mate. I didn't know."

"D-didn't know what?" I stammered, hardly able to speak.

"Didn't know what had happened on that bloke's boat." Squids voice was tinged with excitement. "Tugs bashed up the skipper and broke the skull of the first mate. Took four blokes to wrestle him down and tie 'im up."

Squids took little notice of my shaking. He continued on excitedly. "Cap'n says no fishin' tonight. We're waitin' fer a boat to come by and take him in."

I stared at Squids, trying to absorb what he had said. In response to my stupor, he spouted the familiar Aussie adage, "No worries, mate, you'll be right."

"I suppose," I stammered, still shivering uncontrollably, "you're going to tell me that Tugs could have killed me if he had wanted to, but he was really here to protect me, like the snake."

"Awh no, mate." Squids looked at me square in the eyes. "We all reckoned Tugs was goin' do ya in, no worries."

I lay in my bunk for a long time staring senselessly at the cabin-top. I saw a strange mix of coiling black serpents metamorphosing into human hands wrapping around my neck. Each time the pressure got unbearable, I tried to call out, but I couldn't form the word HELP.

I must have fallen asleep. At one point, I saw myself reach for a door handle, yelling HELP over and over again. I was young, perhaps twelve years old. Panicking, I turned the door handle. *HELP ME, PLEASE, SOMEBODY.* Everything around me was pitch black. The door opened very slowly. I heard a soft voice say, "Come in." The man sitting in the chair was a priest, the Monsignor of our Catholic parish. I feared him. I had always feared him, but he held out his hand, inviting me to sit down. I moved toward a chair, but he told me to come closer. He wore a beautiful black rosary around his neck; the silver cross shimmered under a beam of light. He beckoned me to sit on his lap. I always did what the Monsignor asked of me. He represented God on earth. I trusted him.

> *Tears form at the corner of my eyes as the priest lifts my school uniform and strokes my bare legs. His hands feel like a tightening coil of snakes wrapping around me. They move over my legs along my thighs and then something inside me breaks. At that moment, something deep inside me is lost forever, destroyed. The door closes; the memory goes black.*

There is no end to the dream-memory, no resolution. The snakes coil around the memory, always trying to protect me from the truth. I can't see past them.

After that long torturous night at sea, I finally understood what Squids had meant — the snake was indeed my Dreaming. The snake had led me back through the darkest corridor of memory. It had wound deep into my soul, trying to expose the fear that I had buried there — the memory I had fought so hard to escape. The priest, so trusted, so revered, had violated more than my body; he had crushed my soul with his bare hands. He had desecrated my trust, betrayed my beliefs and broken my spirit. I had become a lost soul drifting in a sea of remorse, surrounded by deadly water serpents.

I was nearly killed by a sea snake and a mad fisherman named Tugs. Yet, they helped me see the truth.

Chapter Thirty-One

LEAH

In the middle of the night, a boat came alongside to take the mad fisherman to shore. I couldn't sleep with all the commotion going on, so I joined the men in the galley. Our spell had been broken. The men were in high spirits, laughing and telling stories. The air that had felt dense with malevolence was light again. Squids, of course, let me in on the sudden turn.

"*Cape Direction* is steamin' our way, mate. Cap'n reckons we can have some grog cuz we're steamin' straight into Karumba after that."

Throwing my head back with a great laugh, I clapped my hands, thanking the snakes and fish and God all at once. No one need know, but my bag was packed and I was ready to jump ship just as the two scoundrels, Crazy Duck and Branch, had done in Weipa. The men would go straight to the pub in Karumba and drown themselves in drink and I would simply escape.

I had wished we weren't going to be delayed by that other fishing boat rafting up. I asked Squids why the delay, why couldn't we just steam into Karumba and have our "piss-up" there. Squids, having an answer for everything, said that Captain Bob and the other skipper were good mates and we'd reached our prawn capacity so we could celebrate.

"Then we go straight into port to unload, right?" I asked Squids.

"I reckon, mate, except for one thing," Squids said hesitantly. "We'll be headin' in, but not before yer traded over. The cooks 'ave been jumpin' ship like bloody flyin' fish. I reckon they're desperate to keep ya away from land."

"What do you mean, traded over?"

"They trade ya at sea, mate, so you can't jump ship in port. A sheila who don't spew and can cook at sea is worth bucket loads of prawns, I reckon. And the Cap'n told 'em you could do the winches and such."

"Told who? Who's *them?*"

"The company owners, mate, Brafford Brothers."

"But Squids, this is ridiculous. You can't take a person and trade her at sea like a tin of tobacco."

"And why is that mate? It's fair dinkum to my way of seein' it."

"Your way of seeing it!" I yelled in frustration. The idea seemed preposterous. Traded at sea. Boat to boat. They could keep rotating me indefinitely. Squids turned away from me, shrugging his shoulders like he just didn't get it — what could be wrong with getting a new position on another fishing boat? I looked around at the galley table full of celebrating fishermen and promised myself then, that if I had to swim with the "bloody crocs" to get back to shore, I would.

I turned and walked out of the galley like someone under a death sentence. I knew I couldn't take much more. It wasn't just the heat and sleeplessness and putrid fish; it was more than that. I had journeyed to the very edge of the world and while staring into the abyss, I had found my own soul writhing in its darkest memories. To some degree I had faced my fears and now wanted to stop fleeing them. I thought I might be able to start again, see the world anew without carrying the excessive burden of shame and guilt around with me. I wasn't completely sure how or where to begin, but finding redemption amid dead fish and mad fishermen seemed unlikely. I had to get off the fishing boat and back to land, somehow. Just as I began to rechart my escape, the answer came to me unexpectedly.

After *Cape Direction* tied up to us, I was invited aboard. Immediately suspicious, I thought it was a devious plot to hijack me at sea. I hesitated, until I saw Leah standing near the boarding ladder.

She was an uncommon sight. Leah stood on deck in a pair of black lace panties and a sleeveless T-shirt which just managed to cover her breasts. The rest of her shapely body was free and open to the breeze, for anyone to see. Her skin was a magnificent pale white. Leah seemed untouched by the ravages of the far northern sun. Her hair floated back in black tufts of natural curl, glistening like waves breaking over a black coral reef.

Standing next to her I felt brutish and rough. I held out my hand to greet her and was immediately ashamed of my scarred and pitted hands. Those fingers I had broken sailing had never healed properly, so they veered off at odd angles looking grotesque. My nails were dirty, chipped and broken. Leah's were perfectly manicured and polished red. She looked surprised by my outstretched hand.

"Gawd almighty," she exclaimed, "a bloody Yank!"

She tossed her head back and jabbed me good-naturedly in the ribs with the sharp point of her fingernail. "We'll have a good time of it, eh. Why I haven't had a decent tongue-wag in months. Come along then." Leah motioned me to follow her. We turned into the galley, which was delightfully air conditioned. She invited me to sit down at the galley table and immediately offered any choice of alcohol from an impressive collection.

I was in awe of Leah's beauty and then to be waited on by her. I felt suddenly transported into another realm. Faced with the longed-for opportunity to talk to another woman, I was giddy, deliciously intoxicated before I even sipped my first rum and Coke. Leah moved in next to me and we started jabbering like long lost friends having met up at our favorite pub.

Asking me a landslide of questions, Leah talked on excitedly until the galley door swung open. Behind us stood Captain Ty. He didn't seem interested in my presence. If anything, he seemed a bit irritated by it.

"I suppose you two will be at it all night then," he said sternly to Leah. "Bob and I are going a few rounds. Pass me the key to the liquor cabinet, eh luv."

At the sound of his commanding voice, Leah slid quickly out of her seat and went rummaging through a drawer. She handed the key over to the ship's captain, whose glance put me on guard. He stood an even six feet tall, well proportioned and more muscular than the general run of skippers, who as a rule, did little of the physical work. Everything about him looked strong. His eyes were direct and piercing; they beamed out a warning of some sort. Somewhere in him, I sensed an unharnessed energy that burned — burned hot and red like the dust laid down over the Territories.

I decided at our first meeting to stay out of his way. I surmised by the way Leah moved around him, pressing up against him as he handed her back the key, that they were lovers. This easily explained her elevated position on the boat.

After Captain Ty left, Leah quickly slipped back into her seat next to me. We were shoulder to shoulder at a table that could easily seat eight husky fishermen. Leah noticed my initial discomfort at her closeness. "Awh, I get so bloody tired of bein' 'round men all the time, don't you?" She laughed, expanding her beautiful smile. "They'll be in and out of here all night, I reckon, just to see what we're up to. Take my word, a man can't stand the thought that a woman can breathe without 'im."

I relaxed back into the curve of my seat, thinking Leah and I were going to be great mates.

"So, how ya gettin' on over there? Bob treatin' ya right? I know he's not much to look at, but you'd do well to take up with him."

I looked at Leah, uncertain about what she meant. "Take up with him?"

Leah threw her head back and tossed down a straight shot of rum. "Sure," she said, "that's the only way to survive up here, otherwise you'd go bloody mad."

"Look at me and Ty. All I have to do is cook breaky and tea and look after him. For that I get an equal share of the gross and off we go on holidays — Bangkok, Singapore, Hong Kong — stay in the finest hotels. Ty even owns some islands up this way. We call into them once in a while."

The thought of jumping into Captain Bob's bunk with him in it, was revolting at best and didn't even rank as a survival technique as far as I was concerned. I answered dryly, "He's married, isn't he?"

"Awh, yeah, like that would stop any bloke up 'ere." Leah poured herself another straight shot of rum. "It's not a bad life," she said, unconvincingly. "Beats marryin' some stodgy old bloke and pushin' a pram 'round the park all day."

Leah laughed. "Gawd, you don't look quite the settlin' type either." She stared into my eyes with a strangely seductive smile. "You look wild as the sea itself. All sorts of devilish things turnin' over inside ya, I reckon."

I looked away, twirling my glass between my fingers, trying to evade her knowing glance. For all Leah's concessions in life, she had a certain wisdom about her.

"Nobody ends up in the Never-Never by mistake, mate," she concluded.

My feeling of comfort and camaraderie with Leah had dulled and soon enough I began to feel agitated and uneasy. Fueled by three strong drinks, I suddenly slammed my glass down on the counter, saying through clenched teeth, "Damn it, I've got to get off that boat. I'm not taking up with Bob or anybody else. I just want to get the hell off that boat."

Leah didn't look the least bit surprised by my outburst. "Awh, mate, I know it gets a bit rough, but I heard on the radio that yer being traded to *Tribulation*. The Cap'n's a good bloke. They're a much smaller boat than the *Northern Pearl*, so they'll go into port soon enough." Leah said this, trying to console me. "I guess that's why we're raftin' tonight." She confided the truth at last. "*Tribulation* is steamin' over from Darwin now."

"And then what?" I asked, trying to quell my panic. I didn't want Leah to suspect anything.

"We'll take off at first light and they'll come in for ya."

"Just like that," I said unable to control the angry tone in my voice. "I have no say in the matter."

"Not unless you know the owner of the company and you plan to do *him* a favor." Leah gave me a sly glance. "That's how it works up here, eh."

Leah had laid out the grim facts before me. If I had "taken up" with Bob he might have kept me around longer. Now I was going to be traded and kept out at sea as long as I could cook and not get seasick.

Leah continued the flow of drinks trying to console me. "You know, the longer yer up here, the less chance yu'll wanta go back. After awhile, there's no sense in going back. Take my word, you don't fit anymore. The house, the bloody yute, the job; it doesn't add up. Look at ya, I can see it in ya. You don't belong anywhere..."

Leah sounded like Matty and Matty sounded like all of them. We were people of the sea, a secret society of miscreants, an underworld of sea creatures who couldn't survive on land. My world was beginning to spin.

The evening grew hazy as I relinquished my hold on sanity. It didn't matter anymore. I had already made my decision.

It was well after 2:00 A.M. when Captain Ty returned to the galley smelling of liquor and cigar smoke. "And what do we have here?"

The skipper looked at us. We were obviously well into our cups. "You two been on the grog all night, have ya? Look at ya, like two bloody galahs." He spoke to Leah gruffly. "Come on then, only a few hours before we get underway." The Captain urged us both to stand up. Turning to me he said harshly, "You best get back to your boat, eh, and check in with Bob as you go."

I stood up and fell over the edge of the booth mumbling, "and check in with Bob as you go, check in with Bob as you go..."

Suddenly Ty leaned over and wrenched Leah out of her seat. She was too giddy and drunk to stand up, so he picked her up roughly and tossed her over his shoulder like a sack of flour. Swinging around toward him, I had an irrational urge to go over to Ty and pry Leah loose from his grip. I felt like yelling at him, *Leave her alone. Leave her alone!* I saw myself begging him to put her down, as if she were an injured dove being crushed under his demanding urgency. But I didn't do or say anything. Instead, I tried to concentrate on my plan and stumbled back to the *Northern Pearl*.

Chapter Thirty-Two

ESCAPE

Near sunrise I heard the engines of *Cape Direction* fire up. I watched from the galley door as Matty and Squids went aft to cast off our lines. I prayed that Matty wouldn't look down at the prawn basket I had shoved to the rear of the boat. I took a deep breath, trying to clear my aching head. Matty and Squids unwound the stern lines in unison. No time left.

> *Heartbeat.* Creep over to the sorting tray. *Breathe.* Grab
> the bag from the tray. *Heartbeat.* Jump onto the basket.
> *Breathe.* Lift. On to the rails. Throw bag. NOW FLY!

I flew like a bird set free. I flew like a bird, but not quite as gracefully. There was no way to judge the distance between the two boats with *Cape Direction* powering away from the stern of the *Northern Pearl*. I stretched as far as I could but landed outboard of the rails instead of on the aft deck.

The engines churned underneath me and I knew if I lost my grip, I would be hopelessly sucked into the backwash. None of the crew dared move to help me, so I clung to the rails twisting and flapping like a dying fish. Somehow I summoned that last bit of energy to hoist myself over the rails and onto the aft deck of *Cape Direction*. Then I heard Squids yell from the *Northern Pearl*, "What the bloody hell... Cooky's jumped ship!"

I turned around to find Captain Bob peering down from the bridge. He looked irate, beside himself with anger. I knew that Ty had put the engines in full forward and that stopping and reversing the engines would take some time. I staked my life on the fact that Leah would be standing next to Ty. I prayed that she would be able to convince Ty to take me with them. Having passed those hours together in the galley, I knew she understood I was desperate and needed her help.

Cape Direction made a full turn toward the *Northern Pearl* before de-powering. I looked up to the bridge slowly, afraid to peer into the eyes of Captain Ty. Instead, I saw Leah with her hand on his forearm as if holding him back from something. He looked determined and angry. I was dejectedly folding up my escape plan when I heard Captain Ty yell over to Bob, "No worries, we'll drop off the Yank and get ya another one, eh."

I shot a glance to Leah, she returned a furtive nod. Leah came down from the bridge and walked over to me with less bravado. I expected her to be angry with me. "Well, well," she said, "half yer luck, mate, you've got legs like a bloody brolga."

By mentioning the leggy bird, I knew Leah was taking a good-natured jab at me. She was a willing accomplice.

"I'm sorry," I said quickly. "I hope this didn't get you into any strife with the skipper. I just had to do something."

Leah reached over and squeezed my forearm in response.

"Look luv, a lotta strange things go on up here. There's not much ya could do to surprise us, and Ty — owed me a favor. No worries, eh."

I felt enormously relieved at Leah's understanding, until she added a cautioning note. "Part of the deal though," Leah said, looking me straight in the eyes, "is that we'll be dropping you at Groote Island."

"Oh, that's fine. Where is it?"

"Groote's about a six-hour run from here. We'll be in this arvo. The town is run by a mining company, but it's closed down for the cyclone season." Leah hesitated for a moment. I assumed some more bad news was coming. "There's a few Abo's about," she added.

"They won't hurt me or anything, will they?" I asked naively, imagining my capture and subsequent torture by wild Aboriginals.

"No, no, but there's something else..." Leah scuffed the deck with her bare toes, continuing the delay, while my great escape was starting to look like a dangerous leap into deeper trouble.

"There's another thing." She hesitated again. "There'll be a mail plane to take you to Cairns."

"Oh, that's great!" I interrupted her. "I could be in Cairns tonight."

"Not exactly. I radioed Cairns and the plane won't be up until Saturd'y."

"What's today?" I asked, having no idea what day, week or month it was.

"Tod'y's Tuesd'y. I'll fix up some tucker. You should find water on the island." Leah turned to walk away and I grabbed her elbow.

"Leah," I said to her, "I don't know how to..."

"No worries, mate. I know if I wasn't crazy over Ty, I'd go 'round the bend, too." Leah smiled at me and added in a motherly fashion, "Mind you have your return ticket, eh. They'll want to know the trip is paid for."

I tried to get some sleep while we steamed toward Groote, but I couldn't. I lay in a spare bunk reliving my mad flight from boat to boat, each time re-experiencing an incredible mix of fear and strength. I lay there wondering about all the strange things I had experienced over the months at sea. On the verge of leaving, I couldn't envision exactly where I was going, or what I should do. I felt rather forlorn in those last hours as we powered to shore. All my thoughts reversed on me as I felt the sea slipping away. What could I do that was not of the sea? Where would I live? In a block of flats — walled in with no sea breeze to fill my lungs? What would become of me if the motion stopped — if I couldn't move ceaselessly through the day and night as we did at sea?

There I was, having manufactured my daring escape, afraid to leave my cell. Hadn't I become like all of them?

Chapter Thirty-Three

ROPER JACKSON

I stood at the edge of a long wooden pier on Groote Island, waving goodbye to Leah, trying to remember the instructions she had given me about getting to the landing strip on Saturday.

"There's only one road inland," she explained. "Follow it until you see an open, grassy field and wait."

I had four days to wait until the arrival of the mail plane and four awful-tasting Vegemite sandwiches to count the days by.

The "town" was an uncomplicated place; in that way, it resembled other bush towns. It was huddled up along the waterfront, as if its aspect toward the sea offered some recompense for an otherwise disenfranchised existence.

The so-called "company town" was nothing more than a few rickety, wood-sided buildings scattered along a dirt track. The "road" was a thin line of red dust running off into the bush. I started to walk along it, but I was overwhelmed by a feeling of desolation. It was a ghost town. The soft clatter of palm leaves slapping together in the sea breeze sounded like the chattering of ghosts. I turned toward one of the alloy-roofed rectangular houses, wondering if I should take up residence inside it. But as I approached it I felt a powerful resistance, as if something was guarding its entrance.

I looked back toward the beach knowing that I would be more comfortable by the sea, so I set off to make camp there.

Aside from the cooling shelter of the mangrove trees reaching down toward the water, the shore was not welcoming. There were sharp spiky nettles strewn all over the ground making a nasty bed of thorns. Thinking of lethal crawling things, I realized I would need to sling a makeshift hammock between two trees for a safe place to sleep.

I fashioned a small fire ring complete with a log to perch upon during the evening. Digging through my backpack, I unearthed the last of my survival equipment: a dull marlinspike knife, lightweight fishing line, hooks and sinkers (capable of towing in a minnow), soggy matches, a sail repair kit and cooking pot with requisite tea bags. My first aid kit housed two wet, rusty-looking Band-Aids, the last of my Neosporin and a quarter of a bottle of hydrogen peroxide. I also had a colorful assortment of pareus from the South Pacific to cover me at night.

Needing fresh water and hammock material, I set out from my modest campsite in search of them. Water was easier to come by than I expected. Retracing my steps back to the first vacant hutch, I came upon a large-handled spigot which dispensed cool, fresh water. It was luscious. After rinsing myself off, I filled my cooking pot and headed back down the beach.

I was nearly halfway back to my campsite when I spotted an old fishing net embedded in the sand. After tugging and pulling at the tangled mess, I finally yanked the whole thing out. Rinsed off in salt water and cleaned, it only needed a few fisherman square hitches before becoming a perfectly sized hammock.

I considered swimming, but only for a second. I quickly spotted a lethal box jellyfish innocuously floating by. Rolling up my meager fishing line, I decided that I had done enough fishing for awhile. I convinced myself a Vegemite sandwich (a taste I had yet to acquire) would have to suffice.

It was strange how the emerging evening felt cool. After such searing heat in the day, it should have been a relief, but the imposing darkness made me shiver. Perhaps it was the expansive night sky making me feel so minuscule, so powerless and alone in the giant universe.

Until that final moment of dusk, my world had been made up of the soothing sound of the sea lapping against the shoreline and the sedating heat of day. Evidence of habitation had surrounded me. However ghostly, it had reminded me that I was in a real place — a place worth sending a mail plane to.

But the night was about to eclipse any sense of reality I might have conjured up for security. The light was fading fast and in its place were deepening layers of forbidding black. Thank God for the luminous stars scattered throughout the overhanging cave of darkness.

And so I sat by the fire feeding it spare kindling while reading the sky and wondering at its enormity. I waited patiently for a feeling of drowsiness but none came. Instead, I crouched by the fire, half-alert, like an animal protecting its lair.

I slowly grew accustomed to the equatorial night. Rocking in my hammock, mesmerized by the sound of the net grinding against the bark of the tree, I began to enjoy my solitude.

As if roused from a drug-induced sleep, I heard the muted, far-off rustling of bushes. Feeling disoriented, I moved slowly, crawling out of the hammock and grabbing my dull marlinspike at the same time. Crouching low to the ground, I strained to hear any sound, but there was none. Then, from out of the dark wall of mangrove trees, I heard a voice. Looking around to find its source, I felt completely exposed and unprotected.

"Not meanin' to frighten ya," the voice said softly. A black man stepped out of the bush and into the light of the fire.

"We hear the white girl been left here 'til the iron wings fly to get her," he said calmly.

The Aboriginal had the kindest, gentlest expression; my initial fright faded, though my heart continued to race. He was wearing a regular button-down shirt and shorts; nothing seemed unusual about his appearance. He had no war paint on him or spear at his side, though he was carrying a long wooden tube. I thought it must be a didgeridoo, the Aboriginal's musical instrument. Squids had talked about it when he had described the clan meetings he had witnessed in the bush.

After a long, awkward moment of my staring, he introduced himself. "M'christian name's Roper Jackson. What's yours?"

Roper Jackson stood some distance from me. I didn't know what to say. I couldn't even think of my name. "Cooky?" "Deckie?" Those were the names I had gone by for months at sea.

"Neva," I finally blurted out. "My name's Neva. I'm Yank," I said defensively, hoping to justify my predicament.

The man moved toward me and I momentarily felt threatened again. Thinking I must be an idiot to trust this black man out here alone, I stepped back from him.

But the thought slipped away as the man's face became fully illuminated by the fire. Everything about him looked gentle. His brown eyes were soothing and he kept a constant expression – a half-smile seemed a part of his nature. There were a few streaks of white running through his jet-black hair and down his beard. Sitting down cross-legged on the sand, he looked like a wise old man. "I been sent by Andilyaugwa tribe to see how ya gettin' on. Not eaten by crocodile yet, eh." Roper Jackson rocked back on his haunches laughing, exposing a perfect set of gleaming white teeth.

I quickly scanned the beach to see if Roper was looking at something I didn't know was there. Noticing my anxiety, Roper stopped laughing. "No worries, I've only come to help ya," he said kindly. "If ya need help. We hear of you from Aurukun."

I just kept staring at the old man, having no idea what an "aurukun" was.

Before I had a chance to ask him anything, Roper Jackson said matter-of-factly, "You protect Aminya from blackfella anger."

By then I was sure the old man was confused, perhaps a little too old to be telling stories. But I was wrong — quite wrong.

Once again he did not wait for me to answer, or ask a question, which seemed in order at this point. Instead, he seemed insistent on relaying his cock-eyed story to me. "Aminya is from my clan. She's at

Aurukun Mission. We hear how the blackfella come to hit her and you come between them. This is a great power — to stop his anger."

"Stop his anger? I didn't stop anybody's anger."

"Many saw the power and now you are here. We protect you in the same way."

Then I realized he was talking about the incident outside the pub at Weipa. How he might have come to hear that story was beyond my imagination. A long time had passed since then. I had been at sea for months. Groote Island was isolated and many sea miles from Weipa. How? I could only assume that the story had gotten twisted around a bit in the telling. I thought I should at least try to untwist it for Roper.

"No, you see, I didn't want the girl to get hurt, so all I did, really, was stand in between the man and the girl, and he stopped — it was nothing I did—"

Roper had a peculiar look on his face. He looked surprised at something I had said. "You don't know. He could have killed you, like this." Roper swung his arm as if imitating the fall of an axe against a tree limb.

I suddenly felt winded and fell back from resting on my knees to a sitting position. Roper and I were then face to face cross-legged in the prickly sand. My heart started to race again. I was held by something, only for a moment, but in that moment I saw the shark in Penrhyn, Mick's knife pricking my throat, the owl in the bush and lastly, the snake entwined in the net. My chest tightened with each memory. It felt like Tugs' repeated stabbing of his tatooed angel.

I closed my eyes and took a deep breath. When I opened them, Roper was smiling. Neither of us spoke.

"I've seen things I don't understand. I just can't explain—" I started, hoping Roper might jump in and allay my fears. Instead he laughed whole-heartedly.

"If you see them, then you know," Roper said cheerfully.

"Know what?"

"Whatever you need to know."

I smiled back at Roper, but it really came from a cynical thought and not from any mutual understanding. His riddle seemed like the kind of dead-end reasoning I always came up against whenever I tried to understand the world around me.

Not knowing what to say, I sat staring at the intricate design on the didgeridoo Roper had laid over his lap. He held onto it with both hands as if it were something of great value.

The Aboriginal followed my stare explaining, "I'm the clan healer." He tilted the tube toward the light of the fire so I could see it more clearly. "And this is my healing stick."

Lifting the didgeridoo even closer Roper nodded, urging me to touch it. I leaned toward it and started to run my fingers over the elaborately designed wooden tube, but I drew my hand back when I realized that the complex series of white dots formed the image of a brilliantly colored snake, winding its way up the musical instrument.

"Rainbow Serpent," Roper said. "Don't be afraid. Healing Serpent. Snake Clan, my Dreaming," he added.

I recoiled from Roper. "Snake Clan!"

The image of the convulsing snake in my hand flooded through me. It began again. The paralyzing feeling of fear and revulsion. I started shivering, remembering how the severed head of the venomous snake had thrashed and squirmed in my hand as his blood dripped down my hair and over my face.

"Touch the serpent," the old man repeated, pushing the didgeridoo next to me. "Don't be afraid of your power."

I could barely bring my shaking hand to touch the painted totem and yet I did. All the images quickly receded and I took a deep breath of relief.

"They won't come back again, unless you forget," he said, reassuring me. "The snake will carry the bad spirits away from you. You will be strong enough for your journey."

"Is Snake my Dreaming?"

Roper laughed again. "Your Dreaming is who you are."

I got up and brushed myself off. It was more like hitting myself in frustration. I felt like yelling at him, WHO AM I? Some silly Yank stuck out here on Never-Never island with an old black man!

As if feeling my frustration he said simply, "All the Voices of the Past."

Suddenly, beyond the low crackle of the fire, a loud squawking rose up from the mangrove scrub. The old man looked quickly in the direction of the noise and then back to me. His mouth spread into a wide grin. "I be goin' soon. But first I tell you the real reason I come here." The old man leaned toward me, speaking very carefully. "All behind you is Aboriginal land. You stay by the shore. Don't pass the line of mangrove trees."

I nodded, wondering if the road to the landing strip was within the boundary. Again Roper intercepted my thoughts. "After four sunrises walk with morning light down the track. You be safe. Find the iron wings."

The Aboriginal stood up to leave and now I feared his leaving. He had brought such a sense of ease and calmness. I didn't want to lose his company to the insoluble night.

"Roper," I said, trying to stop him, "can't we talk a bit longer? I'd like to learn more about—"

"You already know."

After saying this, the Aboriginal turned and walked away from me. Then Roper Jackson soundlessly disappeared into the black wall of mangrove trees.

In the nights that followed, I never heard any other human or animal sounds come from the bush. I did hear a deep rhythmic breathy sound coming from the direction of the trees. It sounded like wind being blown down a long tube, perhaps it was the sound of the didgeridoo. When I listened closely, it sounded like the earth breathing, as if everything around me was alive with a life of its own. I began to feel welcomed by the mystical land. No longer an outsider, I felt a strange sense of "home." Swinging in my hammock, underneath the pale ironbark tree, I listened to the earth's breathing and waited…

Chapter Thirty-Four

VOICES OF THE PAST

I huddled by the fire each night hoping Roper Jackson would reappear from the dark grove of trees. I thought I heard him coming out of the bush a few times, but as I stood up expectantly to greet him, I realized it was nothing more than a light evening breeze.

I slept little during those nights. On the trawler I had become accustomed to being awake at night. And so the nights became like an enchantress, casting a seductive spell as I lay in my hammock scanning the nocturnal sky, feeling an undefined energy pulling me into its celestial dome.

I contemplated Roper Jackson's words, trying to remember exactly what he had said, and trying to decipher their meaning. The words he had used were so simple. I wondered why I couldn't quite grasp what he was getting at. I tried remembering every detail about that evening outside the makeshift pub in Weipa. The only image that stood out strongly in my mind was the fragile black woman shaking inside my arms. I hadn't really done anything to stop the man from hitting her. I hadn't reached up and physically tried to stop him. I couldn't have. He was a strong man like Tugs. He could have crushed my skull with a single blow. What made him stop?

I dearly wished Roper would come back and sit by the fire with me. After two nights of solitude, I thought, perhaps, I had created Roper — a fatherly image to help me feel safe. But why would I conjure a prolonged conversation with an Aboriginal?

My thoughts wandered aimlessly. I saw the Madonna figure surrounded by her children out on the plains. Her image was so powerful. The old man at the fruit stand had talked about Dreamtime, but I didn't really understand what he was saying either. Bluey's visage came to mind. His wide smile was comforting, though his words of warning about the land still cautioned me.

Hour after hour I continued to stare into the night sky. It was so brilliantly alive. By drawing imaginary lines with my index finger, I tried connecting the various stars, recreating their constellations and their mythical stories.

The Southern Cross drifted along in the Milky Way. I wanted to admire it for what it was, but it reminded me of a crucifix — a beautifully polished crucifix gleaming in the night. The crucifix sparkled against the soft black cloth of the priest. I could feel the cloth drape over me, close in like the darkness, trying to suffocate me. I felt the shame — the shame buried deep within my soul — for not stopping the priest from molesting me. I knew Jamie's shame so well. She thought she was responsible for her mother's death because her mother had died when Jamie was born. I could see the tragedy in Jamie's misplaced guilt and yet I was unable to see my own. I felt responsible for not understanding that the priest — the man — was not a god. I had been obedient. I had done what I was told. I was twelve years old.

I dreamt about the snake and the crucifix again and again. I had not been saved. *Original Sin. Sinner.* I reached for the didgeridoo in my dreams, but I could not touch it. The black man's Magic couldn't save me. I didn't believe in it enough.

"DAMNIT, ROPER JACKSON," I yelled at the unrelenting darkness. "WHAT POWER? I DON'T HAVE ANY POWER."

I ran away. I'm a coward.

The darkness did not answer.

Roper Jackson had pointed to the Milky Way and called it the Dreamtime Cave. All the great mysteries of the Dreamtime, he had said, lived in the Cave. Encompassing the infinite night sky, the Cave embraced eternity. Roper had said the Dreamtime lived in everything.

I looked as hard as I could into the Dreamtime Cave. I saw the Magic, but I did not understand it. I tried to grasp it, but I couldn't. Daylight was little help. The heat-soaked days evoked different dreams, as if certain memories belonged only to day while others lived at night.

Rocking in my hammock, drenched in sweat and dodging sand flies, I swayed in a deep trance. Images floated airily around me — spirits from my past. Some floated by gently, quietly, touching me only for a moment; other memories lingered for a long time.

The makeshift sickroom at Penrhyn was one of the memories that seemed to linger. I remembered Tomai's voice whispering in my ear, urging me to wake up from my delirium. He had dripped cooling water on my forehead while waiting patiently for my fever to subside. More than a year had passed since then, yet I still heard Tomai's voice clearly — he had saved me from the shark and I was to be his wife.

Almost as clearly I heard William scoffing: "What the bloody hell did Tomai think he was doing, wanting you to be his wife?"

More persistent than William's jealousy was the threat of the Islanders' curse. William's words came back with a cool shiver:

"Those bloody Islanders even had the audacity to put a curse on us for taking you away…" Nothing short of death, William had said, would put an end to the curse.

I had certainly not forgotten the curse. Like the water-serpent Hydra waiting in the night sky, it had stayed with me throughout my journey. I remembered all the mysterious things that had happened along the way. Were they a result of a curse placed on me by the Penrhyn Islanders, or were they something else — something much more powerful?

As the stultifying heat of day increased, it became harder to think about anything. Drifting off, I'd follow a long-ago dream back to my childhood place, my family's summer home. High in the mountains of Pennsylvania, a cool breeze blew in off the lake. I'd dash down to the shore, listen to the inviting lapping of white-tipped waves and set off in my small sailing dinghy. With the breeze in my face — delicious, cool breeze — I was free. I was simply and wonderfully free. This sweet dream had pursued me across oceans, over continents — to find that one moment of longed-for innocence again, before the acid taste of anger and distrust had infiltrated my soul. I wanted that moment back again — the moment before the priest had touched me, taken my goodness and crushed it.

Swinging in my hammock, sedated by the tropical heat, I let go of the darker memories. In their place, I thought only of trying to touch the didgeridoo and Roper Jackson's words, "You already know."

What! What do I know?

The Aboriginal had told me that by touching the didgeridoo the bad spirits would go away. But would they?

"Don't be afraid of the power," he had said.

Why couldn't I touch it?

Chapter Thirty-Five

CHASING DREAMTIME

Leaving my campsite for the mosies and stinging nettles to occupy in peace, I started down the narrow dirt track just as Leah and Roper Jackson had directed me. At first I walked timidly, wondering if I was venturing onto sacred ground. As I walked I stared at the ground looking for any hint that I might be crossing some invisible line into the "Taboo." But I began to worry I might miss the plane, so I picked up my pace.

I heard a rustling somewhere in the low thicket of scrub. Spinning around, I looked in every direction. "Roper, is that you?" I called out. No one answered. I kept on, walking haltingly, so I could hear any sound, any footsteps in the brush.

Amid the stillness, there was the recurring humming sound I had become so familiar with while lying in my hammock. It was such an ethereal sound. It completely absorbed my attention until I heard the rustling in the bush a second time. Then I knew someone was close by. I thought about calling out again, but decided it was useless. Whoever was following me didn't want to be seen. I smiled, thinking about Roper Jackson. Real or imagined, he had become my guardian for the last part of my journey.

With the equatorial sun rising higher in the sky, it must have been late morning when I arrived at an open grassy field. Swatting the endless ambush of flies, I recognized the landing strip; it mirrored Roper's description perfectly.

My thoughts were interrupted by the tiny insect-buzzing of a small plane. As it grew louder, I looked in the direction of the trees. The metallic bird finally emerged, skimming the treetops as it descended onto the open field.

I was afraid it was going to plunge into the trees and cause a terrible disaster, but it landed safely. Mowing down the snarl of tall speargrass in its path, it turned around at the edge of the mangrove, before bumping and swerving back toward me. As it rattled and shimmied and shook its way over the sharp-daggered grass, I saw the plane as the Aboriginals might have seen it — a very poor imitation of a bird.

The engine noise slowly died as the props stopped spinning. A tall, rugged-looking man jumped down from the pilot's cabin. I waited for him to walk over to me.

"I guess you'd be the sheila off the Brafford boats, eh?" he said matter-of-factly.

It took awhile for the words to sink in. I'd been called so many things in the far north that I had forgotten I was still a "sheila."

"Things been a bit rough for ya, by the look of it," he added.

As the pilot looked me up and down, I was suddenly overwhelmed by a terrible self-consciousness. I hadn't seen a mirror for ages and had no idea what I looked like.

"How long ya been out 'ere?" he asked with concern.

I shrugged my shoulders, indifferent to the passage of time.

The pilot seemed concerned about my silence and softened his tone considerably. "Sorry, luv, m'name's Colin. Abo's give ya any trouble? Ya look a bit frightful."

"Ah no, I actually... no, I'm fine..." I stumbled along, realizing if I told him anything about my past couple of months in the Gulf, he might think I was completely mad.

"You caused quite a stir a while back in Weipa, I reckon."

I looked at Colin, my mouth falling open, absolutely stunned by his reference to the incident at Weipa.

"Quite a stir?" I choked.

Colin chuckled at my dumbfounded expression. "A little excitement goes a long way up 'ere, mate. After ya jumped into the middle of that brawl, all sorts of stories got goin'. Abo's call ya 'the brolga'. Well..." He hesitated, then smiled. "They got the bird part right anyway."

I started to giggle uncontrollably, telling Colin it wasn't the only time I'd been compared to the leggy crane. I continued to laugh, a bit madly, as my whole situation appeared ludicrous. Then Colin asked, "Did ya see anyone 'round while you were 'ere?"

I hesitated, wondering how crazy my story might sound, when Colin interjected, "There's an ol' fella, owe me life to 'im, really. He goes by Roper, Roper Jackson."

I nodded my head, hoping he would tell his story first and we could forget about mine. Colin started in, seemingly anxious to tell his story.

"Ah, mate, you wouldn't credit it, really. I was up on my regular mail run. I was just at the docks." Colin turned toward the direction of the long pier, swatting some flies with his hat. "It was hotter than the hinges, bloody awful, so I just scooped up a bit a sea water." He motioned with his hat. "And, bloody hell, a sea snake was right there... right there in front of me. Gave me a good snap on the wrist."

At the mention of "sea snake" I thought my legs were going to buckle under me. My mouth fell open again and the man must have thought I suffered from some strange affliction. He stopped his story and stared at me. "You right, there?"

"Yeah, I'm right... then what happened?" I asked him in a jittery voice. "Don't they kill ya, quick as that?" I snapped my fingers, mimicking what I had been told.

"Nobody I ever heard of survived a bite."

I was nearly breathless by the time he started up his story again.

"I don't remember much after that... only hearing some kind of humming sound and mumbling... When I finally opened me eyes, Struth! There was some blackfella starin' me straight in the eyes. I felt bloody awful, but I was alive. This blackfella called himself Roper Jackson, said he was the clan healer."

Colin suddenly stopped talking. He looked somewhat embarrassed about telling me the story. He swatted his hat at flies saying, "Don't know what got me started, really... just that I haven't seen the ol' fella since."

I had not made a move since Colin had begun his story. Having ended it, he seemed anxious to get going. I shook my head in amazement, but didn't offer any stories in return.

Colin turned toward the plane, still looking perplexed by something. "Well, I reckon we should get going, eh." We both started walking toward the plane.

After stepping clumsily into the low-bellied plane, Colin pointed toward a bucket seat stationed amid a pile of cargo and fuel drums. I slumped into the seat, feeling a strange resistance to leaving the island. I wondered if Colin felt it too.

Before turning on the engines, Colin tossed me a brown paper sack with two squished sandwiches in it. "I reckon you could use a bit of solid tucker, eh," he said with a wry grin. "I've seen dead birds with more flesh on 'em."

Because of the brown stain and spoiled gravy stink, I suspected they were Vegemite, but thanked him anyway as we prepared for take-off. It was an odd sensation, being in motion again. We hurtled down the grass runway, shimmying so badly my teeth banged together.

As we flew over Groote Island, I scanned the barren landscape, looking for any hint of an Aboriginal settlement. Squinting against the harsh midday light, I saw nothing but mangrove trees, low scrub, rock and red dust. The island appeared completely devoid of human habitation. I tried asking Colin about the Aboriginals and where they lived on the island, but it was impossible to talk over the deafening roar of the engines.

We rose into the sky, flying over the Gulf where I had been held captive for months on the prawn trawler. I looked down at the emerald green water in awe of its beauty, knowing the treachery that lay beneath it. I thought of Squids and the rest of the crew and the strange things I had learned from them. I had learned how to cook a meal for five different nationalities, half of whom had only a couple of teeth, and I'd learned about "prawnin'." After a time I had learned how to drive the winches, lowering the nets into the slate black sea. Many a night I had stood watch for Cap'n Bob, steering the boat through the bleak desolation of an uncivilized territory, while the Captain snored and puffed like a landed sea creature.

The sea was a strange place to live. Altogether we were an island of floating fugitives, where some were escaping the land; others, the law, or both. I was the only one trying to escape myself.

I couldn't think of the fishing boats without seeing the sea snake winding its way out of the net, his head arched toward my hand ready to sink his venomous jaws into me. Squids had said the snake had saved my life; it could have easily killed me.

In those mercurial waters I also saw the reflection of the ape-like Tugs, whose massive hands could have easily crushed the life out of me. As his hands reached for my neck, I heard Leah laughing at my bird-like leap to freedom.

The sunlight was so harsh, so unforgiving, it seemed to press down on the sea, forming and reforming it into weird contrasting shapes of light and darkness. The refracted light was so strong it was too painful to look into the sea. At times it appeared full of sea snakes slithering over its surface, where long, dark, squiggly wind lines cut across the wave crests. I shook. Perhaps it was just the effect of the vibration from the old propeller plane. Perhaps not.

Somewhere in the reflection of those waters, I saw my hands reach for the didgeridoo. I heard Roper Jackson's words again. "Dreaming is who you are. Don't be afraid of your power."

I reached for the didgeridoo with both hands, clutching the Rainbow Serpent's neck, shaking it with fear, anger and love. I held the painted wooden totem until the flood of pain stopped.

And then I saw it.

Flying over the Gulf waters, I saw all that had threatened me in the dark and murky depths of my soul had been covered by the sea. I saw that the memories of my past needn't hurt me anymore. I could let them go — the nuns and their small tortures; the deceitful parish priest whose dark desires lay hidden behind a well-polished crucifix; the ex-husband whose thinly veiled vow of love was an excuse to dominate, to greedily and violently satisfy himself. I had made them all into demons and the demons had chased me. I had let them crush my spirit and destroy my soul. And that's what I had gone in search of — something to fill the emptiness inside.

I thought of my father and how my love for him was overwhelmed by fear of his paralysis, and how readily I had let those fears paralyze my life. I knew it was time to let them all go.

As the gates to my prison cell flew open, I realized my constant agitation at having to outrun somebody or something was finally gone. A new view of the world was emerging. I marveled at the play of light glancing off the tips of waves exploding into radiant crystals. The crystals joined to form an unending pattern of blinding white light reaching toward the horizon. Roper Jackson had said there was a power, a Magic, in everything. I finally understood — it wasn't just something you could see, you had to experience it.

Roper's muffled voice emerged from the exquisite brilliance: *Don't be afraid. Touch the Didgeridoo.*

I touched the didgeridoo and was healed by the Rainbow Serpent. Finally, I had touched it, if only for a brief moment.

I touched Dreamtime.

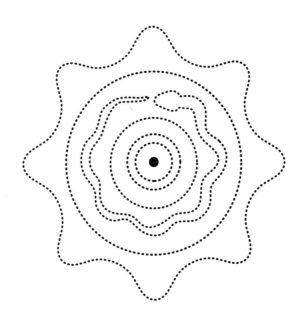

Shortly after the Groote Island mail plane landed on the mainland, Sullaway was taken into custody by Australia's Central Investigative Bureau. Having a number of large cash deposits (some nearly $4,000) at irregular intervals, her bank account had been flagged for unusual activity. Suspected of drug smuggling (again), Sullaway was detained and questioned for hours.

Her defense was weak. Although the payments were from fishing, she didn't have a work permit. Either way — illegal immigrant or drug dealer — she was guilty. Placed under house arrest, she suffered kidney failure from severe dehydration and was rushed to the hospital, thus missing her deportation flight.

Two weeks later Sullaway passed a large kidney stone and was released from the hospital to board a flight to Brisbane. Upon further interrogation there, she was able to convince an immigration official that she needed to finish working on a bicycling guidebook (which existed only in her imagination), and he extended her visa for another six months.

She traveled around other parts of the country, and ended up in a yacht club in Sydney talking sailing again. Within a year, she became the Australian Women's Sailboarding Champion. She lived and worked *legally* in Australia for the next four years defending the title and flying around the world several times to compete and report on sailing events.

It was a charmed life, but home beckoned. When Sullaway packed up and headed back to the States, her life had changed forever. She now lives in Southern California with her husband, who shares her love of the sea, and two children.

The author and crew of *Patience* were among the last yachties to see the reclusive Tom Neale alive. He died of stomach cancer in Rarotonga in 1977. Though he deleted all mention of it in his book, he had married once and had two children. The remaining crew of *Patience* disbanded in New Zealand in 1977. "William" settled in New Zealand with his wife and children. "Clari" married a farmer from rural Australia and they had one child. "Edward" took on another crew that same year and set up a modest trade route between Tahiti and Penrhyn. During one run to Penrhyn, the yacht sustained irreparable damage while passing through the narrow coral entrance, and sank. Edward lived in Australia for fourteen years in the 1980s and early 1990s, saving enough money for another boat. He set sail for the South Pacific with his new wife against Tom Neale's strong advice to "Never Get Married!" While attempting the dangerous passage on a return visit to Tom's island, the small yacht foundered on the reef and was lost. After four months shipwrecked on the island, the couple was taken aboard a motor yacht, owned by the nephew of King Faud of Saudi Arabia, to Rarotonga. Eventually, they returned to England.

When allegations of sexual abuse by clergy in the Catholic Church became widespread, other victims from Sullaway's home town of 25,000 came forward. As detailed in an article from the town's newspaper in 2002, eighty-five residents had come forth implicating three local priests in sexual abuse accusations over three decades. Investigations into the allegations continue...

Chapter Notes

Chapter 5

The Hiscocks were a renowned "cruising" couple who wrote many books about their sailing travels spanning forty years. "Edward" had met them in Spain where he risked his own life to save their yacht during a hurricane. Edward struck up a lifelong friendship with the famous English couple.

The *Hokule'a* was a replica of a Polynesian double-hulled sailing canoe which was built to sail roundtrip from Hawaii to Tahiti. Its purpose was to show that Polynesian craft were capable of sailing, not just drifting, from island to island. The traditional Polynesian methods of navigating were to be used (no instruments).

Chapter 6

The Suvarov atoll was discovered in 1814 by a Russian captain of the vessel *Suvarov*.

Chapter 19

The Never-Never refers to the sparsely populated desert regions which include almost two-thirds of Australia.

ALSO PUBLISHED BY

BROOKVIEW PRESS

STEEP PASSAGES:
A World-wide Eco-adventurer
Unlocks Nature's Spiritual Truths
by David Lee Drotar
(ISBN 0970764901)

About the Author

As a sea-going hitchhiker, Neva Sullaway lived the story of *Chasing Dreamtime* well before her twenty-fifth birthday. After settling in Sydney, she soon became the Australian Women's Sailboarding Champion, a title she successfully defended for four consecutive years. She built a career as a writer and photojournalist, covering sailboarding events in Australia, Europe and the U.S., and wrote *One with the Wind: A Guide to Sailboarding in Australia*. During this time she also created a magazine for sailors, *Freesail Australia*, which became Australia's top-selling sailboarding magazine.

Returning to the U.S., Sullaway studied filmmaking, receiving first place for her short film, *Woodcarver*, at the San Francisco International Film Festival. She wrote *Sailing in San Diego: A Pictorial History* for the 1992/1995 America's Cup. She continues to write, edit and do photography for maritime publications.

Sullaway lives with her husband and two children in San Diego, California.

CHASING DREAMTIME

"*Chasing Dreamtime* takes you on a gripping parallel journey sailing across the Pacific and through the emotional storms which cloud the writer's past. Neva Sullaway tells her story as she experienced it — through the eyes of a young woman exploring a new world with all the exotic locations, wild characters and death-defying circumstances that have faced less brave and more celebrated adventurers."

Kim McKay, former project executive
National Geographic Channel and Discovery Channel

"*Chasing Dreamtime* is the riveting saga of a young woman running away from demons unknown, into situations and characters unimagined. Neva Sullaway lived a life that most people would find an incredible adventure and we share that with her, along with the spirituality and peace she finds at the end of her story. This is a wonderful book and one to share with others."

Elizabeth Murphy Burns, President
Evening Telegram Company, Morgan Murphy
Stations, Queen B Radio and MEG Productions

"This is a remarkable story of personal discovery, a trip through the borderland where the tangible meets the mystical. Echoes of Florinda Donner and Carlos Castaneda! I couldn't put *Chasing Dreamtime* down; I read it in two sittings."